Back to Human Nature

Back to Human Nature

The Power of Emotion and Subjectivity in a Socially Fractured World

CHARLES B. OSBURN

McFarland & Company, Inc., Publishers
Jefferson, North Carolina

LIBRARY OF CONGRESS CATALOGUING-IN-PUBLICATION DATA

Names: Osburn, Charles B., author.
Title: Back to human nature : the power of emotion and subjectivity in a socially fractured world / Charles B. Osburn.
Description: Jefferson, North Carolina : McFarland & Company, Inc., Publishers, 2020 | Includes bibliographical references and index.
Identifiers: LCCN 2020025702 | ISBN 9781476681580 (print) ∞
ISBN 9781476640211 (ebook)
Subjects: LCSH: Emotions—Social aspects. | Human behavior. | Subjectivity. | Social interaction.
Classification: LCC BF531 .O83 2020 | DDC 128—dc23
LC record available at https://lccn.loc.gov/2020025702

BRITISH LIBRARY CATALOGUING DATA ARE AVAILABLE

ISBN (print) 978-1-4766-8158-0
ISBN (ebook) 978-1-4766-4021-1

© 2020 Charles B. Osburn. All rights reserved

No part of this book may be reproduced or transmitted in any form or by any means, electronic or mechanical, including photocopying or recording, or by any information storage and retrieval system, without permission in writing from the publisher.

Front cover image by Vladimir Sazonov (Shutterstock)

Printed in the United States of America

McFarland & Company, Inc., Publishers
Box 611, Jefferson, North Carolina 28640
www.mcfarlandpub.com

For my son Christopher,
who molded his own character to become
what generally is understood to be a good
human being, a "good man."

Acknowledgments

It is with the deepest gratitude that I acknowledge the support accorded me by the School of Library and Information Studies in The University of Alabama's College of Communication and Information Sciences. Administration, faculty and staff have provided the office space, equipment and positive academic environment necessary to my full engagement throughout the research and writing of this book and others. Though I am continuously and intensely conscious of time's rapid passage, its accumulated passage takes me by surprise.

Sharon Osburn, my considerably wiser and better half, may often have been pleased not to find me immediately underfoot during my retirement, but she more often has tolerated the kind of retirement that meant my extended absences—since 2001—from our home, while also serving as an objective critic of my work. There is no way I can adequately express my gratitude for the quality of life she has made possible for me.

Table of Contents

Acknowledgments vi
Preface 1

1. Being Human 5
2. Special Features of Mind 25
3. Knowledge and Industry in Evolution 42
4. Western Worldview 68
5. Tailoring Western Knowledge 90
6. Freedom, Motivation and Responsibility 109
7. The Western Ideological Environment 134
8. Human Stability and Balance 158
9. Invitation to a Stance 172

Chapter Notes 185
Bibliography 211
Index 223

Preface

> Our growing wisdom must be based soundly on an evolutionary view of man's past, present and future, and a knowledge of the ways in which the evolutionary process can be controlled.
> —*Bentley Glass, 1985*

Most of us have witnessed enough human behavior to make us ponder the future, and knowing that people behave on a scale of motivation ranging from rigidly controlled reason to total emotional abandon, we understand that anything is possible. On balance, my experience with others has been positive, suggesting that the majority of any large population comport themselves fairly well, far outnumbering those who do not. People of all backgrounds in all parts of the globe offer each other friendly recognition in expressions to which all have become well accustomed, and these expressions contribute toward the maintenance of cultural norms. My characterization of humanity usually has portrayed our species as evolving by stages that reflect a general kindness and a preference for making this world a good place and this life a good experience. Therefore, my casual analysis suggests that those who persistently display incivility and immorality—the steadfast hardcore offenders—account for approximately three percent of the total population, though they cause much more than half of the world's social problems.

Within the past several years, however, televised broadcasts from many points on the world map have focused on individuals and entire families trying desperately to escape their homeland's terror, chaos, and dim possibilities. They had undertaken these extremely painful journeys in hope of building their future in a more secure and nurturing environment, doing so with valid reason to believe in the probability of their success. But many nations responded with a hostility that crystalized a general deterioration in quality of life I had begun to perceive in the mid 1970s. Now demonstrated most prominently in the lowering standards of our discourse, this social conduct indicates a narrowing of mind and a threat to our quality of life. More than surprising, to me this spirit has been disheartening, as I had thought such conduct—even the atrocities of the Second World War—to be temporary anomalies in the normal human pattern, not representative of who we are fundamentally.

Our greetings and other learned acknowledgments may appear to be insignificant affectations or outworn routines but are deeply rooted courtesies, crafted through countless millennia to maintain the extraordinarily human sociality founded in emotion. They aid in controlling our complex social environment by reminding us of congeniality's significance to human life. Their pattern constitutes a barometer of our sociality, and now its negative signs have become too evident in their frequency to be ignored. If the downward turn of our discourse continues—and nothing on the horizon suggests it won't—what might it mean for us, and more so for those who follow? Are we not shooting ourselves in the foot, or worse? Do we understand why our long ancestry established, spread and strengthened these social gestures through continuous existential challenge? Have we really thought about it?

From an evolutionary perspective, this book explores emotion and its derivative feelings and morality, because subjective thought influences the quality of human life and so the direction of cultural evolution, which often and carelessly is labeled "social progress." It emphasizes that since the emergence of *Homo sapiens,* humanity's natural sociality has proved essential to the homeostasis required by any living organism. My contention, however, is that the specific industrial objectives of efficiency and profit have migrated to the general population, gradually invoking the diminishment or removal of some of our most distinctive human features from the cognitive challenge of decisions, which ultimately can influence evolution. Moreover, it is a commonly accepted conclusion that humanity's remarkably extensive and rapid change over the past few centuries has been made possible by rational thought and the human capacity to accumulate objective knowledge, leading me to contend that these capacities explain our extraordinary cultural evolution *only in combination with* genetically-transmitted subjective information. Supported primarily by the past three highly productive decades of research in neuroscience, cognitive psychology and evolutionary psychology, the essay applies their findings toward the advance of a more valid and meaningful public understanding of our current social environment and its longer-term significance. I find the current turn in the quality of our discourse an admonition we must heed, for it directly affects our worldview, the quality of our social life today, and the course in which humanity is likely to evolve, particularly as the Western culture and economy are globalizing. A dangerous situation is evident in the unnatural but spreading effort to exclude subjectivity from decisions, as it also is foundational to our capacity to collaborate, which in fact most directly explains the extensive social progress humanity has achieved thus far.

My intention in this essay is to stimulate public discussion by convincing the reader that, while we are quite complex and diverse as individuals, together we exhibit far more commonalities than differences and will fare much better by attending to our common ones. I ask the reader to contemplate how our social progress will feel to us not only as the sociality we do still experience diminishes, but also as its decline continues for our progeny. We have the capacities to undertake a successful change of direction if we start now, individually and collectively.

1

Being Human

> It is the dynamics between genes and environment that make a human being.
> —*Michael S. Gazzaniga, 2005*

Introduction

Science has extended humanity a considerably longer life potential than could reasonably have been expected only a half century ago, and technology has brought to many an unprecedented level of convenience and comfort. But today we also seem much less certain of our satisfaction with the general quality of our own individual life. How have we managed to develop an assessment of our quality of individual life so contrasting to these evident social benefits?

This book contends that the shadow over our self-assessment stems primarily from the modernist belief that our traditional model for social behavior—specifically its level of discourse and attention to morality—have become superannuated, no longer useful window-dressing, and even impediments to progress. Causing this problem, the essay claims, is our failure to understand the profound significance of our most human features, which emanate primarily from the subjective information provided by emotion, feelings and morality. My goal is to convince the reader that the cultural situation at issue bears much greater negative potential than lost window-dressing, yet the threat it poses falls well within the range of human correction. The essay's cohering theme is our natural penchant toward sociality, for it has proved fundamental to human cooperation as well as to the human sense of organic balance, and therefore to our ultimate quality of life. This chapter introduces the core of my contention about the role of emotion in the uniquely human capacities of our thought.

In the course of many millennia, our species has learned that we are most likely to manage our life securely, optimally and satisfactorily by living congenially with our conspecifics. The evolutionary perspective this essay applies to the current Western culture casts our sociality as fundamental and essential to human life. Our greetings, farewells and other stock social phrases and gestures are building blocks for the much larger complex of humanity's sociality that demonstrates the respect that is essential to our collaboration and societal well-being. Each of us is a complex system dependent on our capacity for reasoned thought, a system that combines objective knowledge with emotion and feelings in giving uniquely and eminently human direction and quality to our daily life. Relative to the complexity of most human projects intended to demonstrate progress, social interaction is a fairly pedestrian dimension of any individual's life, yet it is the most significant aspect of our well-being, our ancestors having experienced many millennia of trial-and-error in collaborating and optimizing communal life. Essential to both the long term and the quotidian is our maintenance and furthering of the dignity and mutual respect humanity has evolved on that very foundation: it is the essence of humanity.

Research of recent decades in cognitive science, cognitive psychology and evolutionary psychology demonstrates that emotion, feelings and morality are essential to the manifestation of human character and reveal the natural human proclivity to social interaction. This is most significant in decisions, as they can accumulate sufficiently to influence the course of our cultural evolution, which is stimulated primarily by knowledge. The concept of knowledge may be classifiable in various ways, but most frequently as either the objective knowledge we acquire by learning through life's experience, an example being the substance of academic disciplines and daily news, or the subjective information normal humans inherit genetically, reflecting our innermost thoughts and feelings. This essay surveys the significance of human subjectivity. It concludes that by merging our emotion, feelings and morality with objective knowledge in our species' best interest throughout *Homo sapiens'* evolution, they have been fundamental to the full realization of human potential. But the essay also contends that human efforts to diminish or exclude subjective information from the West's critical collective decisions have become quite evident in the current social environment.

Organic Stability

The most frequently accepted explanation of the West's extensive and rapid change during the past several centuries has been the production and accumulation of objective knowledge, guided by humanity's capacity for reason. Taking the longer evolutionary perspective, however, my primary contention is that objective knowledge and the faculty of reason explain *Homo sapiens'* remarkable material and intellectual advance *only in combination with human subjectivity*, the catalyst in our cultural formula. But our subjectivity often is stifled by industrial and governmental efficiency strategies to ensure the exclusive concentration of decisions on economic and technological issues. Consequences of these strategies include the degradation of discourse, the weakening or suppression of humanity in our thought, the distancing of humanity from nature, and the ultimate loss of quality in our life, individually and socially. The high level of sociality required by the civility, communication, cooperation, caring and dignity, which are prominent in distinguishing humans from all other beings, is situated in our emotion, feelings and morality.

Despite convincing statistical evidence of highly significant cultural change now witnessed within less than a lifetime, many scholars and social critics find the quality of our individual lives in decline, even as our remarkable technical capacities flourish as never before. Moreover, any comprehensive review of Western social history will reveal that the human evolutionary leaps of recent centuries are most clearly the consequences of cooperation (Black, 2014), a distinguishing *Homo sapiens* capacity made possible by our attention to subjective information (emotion, feelings and morality) and maintained by its expression in our quotidian discourse. As a flexibly cognitive and therefore rapidly evolving species, our subjective thought is fundamental to our continued cooperation, to optimizing our diverse individual potential for societal benefit, and to the continuation of our sense of organic stability, our homeostasis. As a social organism, therefore, the Western culture's stability, harmony and productivity continue to depend heavily upon a variable balance of objective and subjective knowledge. Normal human cognition comprises both objective knowledge and subjective information, their combination guided by the distinctively human capacity for rational thought (H. C. Barrett, 2015; M. Lieberman, 2013; L. Barrett, 2011; Gazzaniga, 2011; Damasio, 2010; Johnson-Laird, 2006). One logical conclusion is that subjectivity functions as the ultimate guardian of our species' well-being and the individual perception of life's quality. Until quite recently—in evolutionary time—the Western cultural course evidently has benefited from humanity's full cognitive range, which industrial expansion increasingly and purposefully has abridged throughout the past few centuries. The most evident model for social change during this period has been and continues to be the model industry projects.

Human Nature

For the concept of *human nature* to be useful, it must refer to the motivation of all normal humans anywhere, at any time. Observation suggests, however, that individuals are extraordinarily unpredictable, often straying from their usual behavior. As a species, we do tend to be patterned by our bodily requirements (Barrett, 2015), yet as individuals within that pattern we also know that each is psychologically unique and always changing.

Culture and Evolution

Our cultural trajectory is relatively stable, established through some 7 million years of evolution of which *Homo sapiens* has occupied only about 30,000 (Buss, 2004). Though the presence of numerous distinct cultural systems may cast some doubt on the concept of a human nature, anthropologist and neuroscientist Melvin Konner (1991, p. 103) observes that "there is, in each of the [cultural] systems in question, a core of features that do not vary," and in recent decades anthropologists, neuroscientists, and evolutionary psychologists have documented many universal traits of human motivation and behavior around the globe that are natural in the sense of constituting a human nature (Pinker, 2013). Moreover, cognitive psychologist Louise Barrett (2011, p. 176) reminds us that "the fact that all humans share a particular kind of embodiment can explain why, in general, we all see the world in our distinctively humanlike way." The broad spectrum of our connections with the physical environment constitutes a significant part of our identity as a species.

In quotidian social relations, our human nature is a condition on which most of our conspecifics first depend for an understanding of others and our expectation of their likely behavior, because this dependence is an essential part of how we make sense of our social world and discern its order. Psychologist Barry Schwartz (1986, p. 27) shares his insight into the place of human nature theory in contemporary social life:

> Resolution of moral debate depends on people's conceptions of human nature, on what they think it means to be a person. Where, then, do these conceptions of human nature come from? The answer is that they come from lots of different places. They come from our individual, everyday experience, from the so-called school of hard knocks. As people interact, they discover regularities in the way others react to certain situations. From these discoveries, they build up a picture of what a typical person wants, does, and expects them to do. This is so commonplace, and so inevitable, that it is hardly noticed.

We rely upon the idea of a human nature more than we are consciously aware, for we are sufficiently conditioned *to want* there to be a human nature to guide our understanding and expectations.[1] Anthropologist Adam Kuper (1994, p. 100) reports, "In virtually every culture there is a myth of origin, which defines a view of humankind." It marks a primitive step toward defining human nature.

Human culture is the product of many generations of interaction within any given group. The brain organizes our mind's reasoning, its neural sensitivities and deep memory. Humanity's extensive range of specialized social features is fertile ground for mutual understanding and the unparalleled communication capabilities that enhance thought and render it exchangeable. Consequently, humans exist not only as tool-making man (*Homo faber*), or economic man (*Homo economicus*), or artistic man (*Homo pictor*), or playing man (*Homo ludens*), or even knowing man (*Homo sapiens*), but also as a composite of these models and others, each rising to dominance in individuals according to changing situations and conditions (Kenrick and Griskevicius, 2013). Humanity has no pre-determined goal, only a broad horizon of possibilities arising from a versatile mind with imagination, values, genetically-inherited information about self, accumulated objective knowledge about the world, and the capacity for communicating complex thought, all making our species most diverse and dynamic. But psychologist Daniel Goleman (2006, p. 60) also indicates a common predisposition, writing, "Our brain has been preset for kindness," reflecting humanity's penchant for sociality, which becomes most noticeable when absent. These human features, unique among all animals by the degree of their influence, combine to provide an array of options and an ever-more complex basis for deciding among them. We humans also have the capacity to recognize the state of improvement or decline in the quality of the life we experience, individually and societally, the extent to which this capacity is employed constituting a uniquely human feature discussed in the next chapter.

Cultural change demonstrates that biology does not necessarily determine human destiny, for our life's trajectory is generated largely by our individual potential and our collective human will. As evolutionary psychologist Louise Barrett (2011, p. 222) observes, "The paradoxical conclusion that we come to, then, is that the difference between humans and other animals may lie in the extent to which we create and exploit the external structures of our world." Given the extraordinary diversity among us, therefore, it is quite possible that the explanation for the remarkable strength of human cultures resides in the fact of a human nature, sculpted through the ages by humanity's adaptation to and alteration of changing physical and social environments. Of particular significance to the strength of human culture and its relatively rapid evolution, developmental and comparative psychologist Michael Tomasello and developmental psychologist Hannes Radoczy observe (p. 142) that "humans identify with other persons in ways leading to an understanding of self-other equivalence ... leading to an appreciation of different social perspectives on things and ultimately to various kinds of derived normativity."[2]

Sociality and Relationships

The most obvious of human traits may be that we are foremost "social animals," a species extraordinarily interactive with conspecifics beyond the family, far exceeding the fundamental requirements of survival. Humans have many features in common with other animals, many of which strengthen our sociality to the extent that they surpass those evinced by any other primate (Høgh-Olesen, 2010). This single fact bears considerable significance for the worldview and behavior of both groups and other individuals, while also maintaining a balance with our strong sense of self. Sociality is the natural foundation of our species' coherence, even in its extraordinary individual diversity. A culture easily attracts and molds those who recognize the advantages sociality offers, as linguistic scientist James R. Hurford (2007, p. 249) explains:

> The addition of learning and culture to the picture constitutes a phase shift in the concept of "environment." The environment is no longer just the physical potentials and challenges, the food and the pitfalls. Surviving among foreigners is a totally different problem from surviving alone in the desert or the jungle. The trick is to learn not to be foreign.... Cultural environments can change very fast, much faster than typical physical environments, so an ability to learn whatever their characteristics are is the key to survival.

Genetically and culturally, humans are positively disposed to socialization. It is in our nature to depend upon and contribute to an active sociality because, writes neuroscientist Michael S. Gazzaniga (2008, p. 80), "we evolved with lots of other humans around, and developed brain capacity to monitor social behavior in large groups, so that we may assess the value of cooperation, the risk of noncooperation, and so on."[3] In combination with other aspects of human nature, our sociality explains the exceptional power of our cultures, which can structure cooperation according to the collective judgment of its individual constituents. Philosopher Mary Midgley (1978, p. 357) indicates this in her conclusion, where she writes, "A rational being is someone who sees himself as a unit among others, not as the core of the universe." And she continues (pp. 55 & 233) her strong assertion about the significance of individual decision to participate in society, despite the many challenges accompanying socialization:

> Immediately, a great many human traits and behavioral tendencies become plausible as being adaptive in the universe. Our desire to live in groups, our empathy, our feelings of love and grief—they all make sense. Virtue and evil both have a role to play, but the role of evil is changed from being hopelessly engraved in our genes to being amenable to amelioration by the changing of cultural beliefs and institutions.... The meaning of what I know, do, and am exists in relation to my social world. If I lose meaningful contact with others, I lose my sense of self. I become empty, dispirited, purposeless,

depressed. My identity, my conscious understanding of who and what I am, is a socially dependent self-image. It is formed by the ongoing sum of my experiences as they take on meaning in terms of the cultural narrative shared by those around me.

Such are the initial reasons for individuals to elect socialization over isolation. But once socially integrated, there are further attractions to joining with others in meeting new challenges and opportunities, the most evident being the strength of numbers in undertaking objectives too physically difficult or intellectually demanding to achieve alone. And humans also have established specific cultures related to the expanding variety of both occupations and leisure activities, for such groups facilitate a mixing of individuals within the general society, a mixture that otherwise might not occur let alone multiply, as their sparsity among other primates demonstrates (Richerson & Boyd, 2005). Beyond this consideration, research on the comparison of young humans with chimpanzees and orangutans—the primates closest to humans in cognitive ability—shows that humans have evolved an extraordinary set of special cognitive powers for collaboration. In summary, humans are uniquely equipped to optimize the benefits of both large-group socialization and individual. Moreover, sociality is sufficiently fundamental to humanity that it manifests benefits for our physical health, as Daniel Goleman (2006, p. 230) observes:

> The more we socialize, the less susceptible to colds we become. This idea seems counterintuitive: don't we *increase* the likelihood of being exposed to a cold virus the more people we interact with? Sure. But vibrant social connections boost our good moods and limit our negative ones, suppressing cortisol and enhancing immune function under stress. Relationships themselves seem to protect us from the risk of exposure to the very cold virus they pose.

The mixing of knowledge and skills, viewpoints and values, aspirations and fears, experience and belief, generates a comprehensive outlook for both individual and group, an outlook that most often leads toward a more fulfilling life through its revelation of further possibilities to contemplate and new decisions to determine, individually and societally. Neuroscientist Andrew Whiten (1999, pp. 184–185) perceives the centrality of this cultural phenomenon to the "evolution of the deep social mind."

> Learning from others enables faster, deeper penetration of the cognitive niche than an individual can manage by their own efforts in their lifetime. This is because with succeeding generations, the most profitable cognitive advances of the past can be accumulated—any one hominid does not merely exploit the cognitive niche by their own mental powers, but does so on the back of a string of progressive niche penetrations by their ancestors, as techniques such as those for hunting are progressively improved, refined and differentiated from those of competitor species.... To compound our metaphors, we can see that through what Tomasello *et al.* (1993) described as the "ratchet effect" of cultural transmission, the cognitive niche can become a progressively deep-

ening furrow. Cognitive achievements such as the acquisition of difficult-to-obtain knowledge and the solving of specific problems do not need to be repeated in each generation because they can be acquired socially, and each advance builds on the shoulders of the last.

Cultural evolution depends most heavily on the introduction of new ideas and perceptions about what could or should be accomplished within a society and the way for groups to proceed accordingly.[4] Initiated by a fresh perspective on the world and one's place in it, significant cultural change begins very often with new social relationships developed through communication, most efficiently and effectively through the exploitation of a common language.

Language

Not an animal system of communication, language is an exclusively human brain response that "guides itself" and "makes its awareness reflective," writes clinical psychologist Zoltan Torey (2014, pp. 10–11). By generating a secure bond between minds, a common language is central to human sociality, making possible an exchange of ideas according to individual logic, which linguistic communication aids in the organization of knowledge, values, emotion, feelings, imagination, and memory. Language establishes the logical sequence and emphasis of ideas, their clarity in communication governed by standardized and commonly understood guidelines for facilitating the exchange of thought. Of equal significance, language can abridge, elaborate, order or express a thought *process*, not solely the concluding fact toward which the process leads. As social scientist and philosopher J.T. Fraser (1999, p. 18) states it, "Language may well be the most versatile of all process descriptions of the mind." A human capacity of special value in thoroughly communicating complex thoughts, language facilitates the unraveling of tightly compacted complexities.

The point in human evolution when the vocalization of thought for communication first was uttered is the subject of much debate. Speech most likely emerged 50,000 to 150,000 years ago to facilitate social relationships. It was an early stage in *Homo sapiens*' evolution when, according to Michael Tomasello (2008, p. 2), pointing and pantomiming were "already embodying most of the uniquely human forms of social cognition and motivation required for the later creation of conventional languages." Regardless of exactly when it was introduced, speech quickly became the standard mode of human communication.[5] The act of speech, Tomasello (p. 231) says, built upon and expanded "some already meaningful action-based gestures—or at least some already meaningful collaborative actions." As is true for the cultural adoption of any new technology, the time had to be right for speech to evolve, because the given society had to have been well conditioned for any given change to be adopted, and in this case an advanced sociality surely prevailed for a very long time for speech to arise out of the common will. Furthermore, Tomasello (2009, pp. 98–99) emphasizes that humans had to have been cognitively equipped in ways other primates were not, and so were able to contemplate collaborative activities. "Specifically, humans came to engage in collaborative activities with a joint goal and distinct and generalized roles, with participants mutually aware that they were dependent on one another for success."

Language provides a more significant basis than physical gestures for sharing information, experiences, feelings, perceptions, desires, aspirations, fears, new possibilities, understandings and expectations, and can distinguish between what was and is from what will, should, or could be than previously were available. Language is dynamic, expandable and modifiable in meeting the changing demands of clarification, whether as sender or receiver of the linguistic exchange, and it can express any emotion or feeling necessary to its intention. Moreover, sender and receiver can collaborate in designing just the right manner required to advance common understanding or, depending upon circumstances, they can practice deception. And language has self-regenerating properties, as computational linguist Simon Kirby (2007, p. 677) explains:

> In other words, language can be reliably acquired purely through the observation of instances of its use. In a very real sense, language not only transmits semantic information, but also *information about its own construction*. This process of information transmission has been termed *iterated learning* to reflect the fact that linguistic behavior is learned through observation of that behavior in others who themselves learned that behavior using the same mechanism. Language is therefore repeatedly transformed from external linguistic behavior to internal linguistic representation to external linguistic behavior and so on.

Speech injected into human communication the power of phonetic symbolism. By agreement, carefully articulated sounds could represent specific thoughts and distinguish among their nuances. Thought and language skill are shared, developed and refined by carefully selecting and articulating sounds to convey meaning in speech, and eventually with new technologies, providing for deeper and more critical contemplation in its recorded state. The introduction of language into communication, therefore, greatly accelerated cultural evolution, the combination of language, thought and memory being a most potent cultural tool. Language is now sufficiently fundamental to humanity that the freedom of speech is recognized increasingly and protected legally as a right around the globe. "Symbols, especially languages, have the double function of expanding both individual thought and the sharing of thoughts among a whole group," writes Mary E. Clark

(2002, p. 161). They are, she adds, "what permitted our individual brains to become loosely linked into a 'group mind,' giving rise to coordinated group behaviors of increasing complexity." Although a person's emotion and feelings sometimes can be difficult to articulate and therefore to convey adequately to others, language meshes with the mind's flexible capacities to achieve finer distinction in dialogue, as words and sentences contain ideas capable of the most appropriate, precise expression of further thought and intention. Because all normal humans possess similar cognitive features, the introduction of a linguistic capacity would have caused a dramatic elevation in the sophistication at which the earliest humans were capable of cognition, communication and cooperation. Humans can transmit thought to another's mind and the minds of many others, or alter it.

With increased usage, speech gained in precision and contributed to the durability and spread of thought by technical advances made in writing, printing, telecommunications and mass digital communication in flexible formats. Although the unveiling of these major developments required countless generations, Michael Tomasello (2008, p. 317) proffers the reminder, "Even at the very latest stages of the process of language evolution, the fundamental skills and motives of shared intentionality with which humans began down the road of cooperative communication are still at the heart of the process." Manifestations of sociality pivot on shared intentions and goals, and cooperative efforts tend to enhance them, helping to refine and expedite cultural change just as the evolving culture advances language development with useful modifications. But we are quite aware that language potential is not limited to the advancement of a society's formal communication, as cultural anthropologist Christopher Boehm (2012, p. 245) emphasizes:

> I've mentioned, in passing, gossip's staying power as society modernizes. This appears to involve more than the purely habitual perseveration of a hunter-gatherer cultural habit. Indeed, it's likely, after at least 45,000 years of individuals gaining fitness by whispering back and forth about other people's behavior behind their backs, that discreet and intimate socially evaluative "talking" is part of our evolved capacity to behave morally—just as the internalization of rules surely is. Thus, gossiping serves us today as it served our ancestors in the past.

Scholars and scientists agree that language did not evolve primarily to aid in solving complex intellectual problems, as the primary place of gossip in the emergence of speech is well supported (Dessalles, 2007; Hurford, 2007). In this view, language contributes immensely to the culture's coherence, which is essential to a self-regulating society. Language, mind and sociality are mutually strengthening and enhancing human features that help us to cause change as well as to cope with it.

Cultural Diversity

Humans have extraordinarily flexible minds, a feature neuroscience often refers to as the brain's plasticity, and we also possess a disproportionally large cranial capacity. These physical characteristics mix with individual psychologies within their normalizing cultures to constitute an aspect of the human condition about which evolutionary biologist Peter J. Richerson and anthropologist Robert Boyd (2005, p. 57) warn, "Any theory that hopes to explain the behavior of contemporary humans must tell us what it is that causes humans to be so much more variable than any other species and why this peculiar capacity for variation was favored by natural selection." Their response (p. 91) is that "culture is a complex mixture of structures. Some cultural variants are linked into coherent wholes, while others float promiscuously from culture to culture." Humans thrive in nearly all corners of the globe most evidently because, by conditioning to collaborate within our cultures, we also have the capacity to adapt to radically different environments varying by weather, availability of natural resources, and nutritional support. Richerson & Boyd (2005, p. 243) place this human accommodation to the physical environment in its evolutionary context:

> Much of the diversity of human behavior in time and space results from adaptive microevolutionary processes shaping complexes of technology and social organization that suit us to live in most of the terrestrial and littoral habitats on earth. Other organisms must speciate in order to occupy novel environments, whereas humans rely mostly upon culture. Modern humans apparently have spread out of Africa to the rest of the world in the last one hundred thousand years, relying on their ability to generate complex cultural adaptations suited to virtually every habitat on earth.

Although diversity harbors an obvious potential for the conflict that can hinder societal cooperation, diversity's advantages throughout human evolution greatly overshadow its potential as a logistical impediment. Within diverse cultural influences leavened by language and the flow of new perspectives, the recognition of individual human uniqueness stimulates a positive inclination in values, attitude, expression, mixed perceptions, and new decisions. The inherent cognitive power of sociality resides in human diversity and explains why our peculiarly human capacity for variation has been favored in natural selection.

The extent to which our collaboration is successful indicates another clear distinction between humans and other animals, writes Hurford (2007, p. 254): "From the viewpoint of Darwinian theory, which emphasizes selection of traits benefiting individuals, it is a prima facie puzzle why any creature should help another, unless the helping is also to its own benefit, which often it is not." Our cultures are generally receptive to the concept of cooperation, so more is expected from it than can be expected from the individual working alone. Much like a successful technology, successful collaboration not only gets the job done but also inspires analogous applications and variations. Even among groups of varied background in nature and nurture, humanity undertakes organized effort extraordinarily well, and this abundantly evident fact indicates another distinguishing feature of humans among all mammals. Richerson & Boyd (2005, p. 195) describe it in their finding that "the symbiosis between genes and culture in the human species has led to an analogous major transition in the history of life—the evolution of complex cooperative human societies that radically transformed almost all the world's habitats over the last ten thousand years." Evidence abounds that language has been fundamental to the successful evolution of human cooperation, which in turn has been the engine behind the more obvious stages of cultural evolution, the direct consequences of facile communication.

Human communication occurs when one individual understands that another is conveying meaning. This action requires a shared context with a conditioned receiver, the communication itself indicating that the sender knows enough about the receiver to anticipate a successful effort. Such conditions exemplify the "mindreading" features (discussed in Chapter 2) supporting humanity's relatively high degree of sociality and dependence on shared assumptions (Corballis, 2011). Humans converse according to their presumed understanding of another's thought. This capacity is mostly unconscious in normal conversation because, according to cognitive psychologist Michael C. Corballis (2011, p. 154), "in normal conversation we hardly ever spell out exactly what we mean." He also notes (p. 133) that normal conversation "is recursive in the sense that it involves the insertion of what you believe to be someone else's state of mind into your own." We do not have to begin our communication as though from a blank slate, because we can presume the receiver of our message has achieved a certain level of readiness for our common understanding.

Cooperation

Michael Tomasello (2008, pp. 237–238) views the capacity to surmise another's thoughts as essential to understanding the full significance of human cooperation. He explains that "the cooperative structure of human communication is not an accident or an isolated human characteristic, but rather one more manifestation of humans' extreme form of cooperativeness." In the right social setting, this human capacity has the potential to result in the joint attention and goals Tomasello (p. 321) finds necessary to the "common conceptual ground within which human communication most naturally occurs." This shared ground derives from a meeting of the minds whereby each understands the other with regard to the given issue, step-by-step and recursively, each warily trusting the other's motivation. Most clearly, writes Tomasello (p. 95), "such recursivity is absolutely required for norms of co-operation in which it is mutually expected by everyone (including oneself) that everyone will be a cooperative communicative partner." These cognitive capacities are foundational to successful decision-making. We have the ability to contemplate, reformulate and recast the thoughts of others, a capacity necessary to the extraordinary human adaptability to cooperation, and often its mastery. Archeologist Steven Mithen (1990, p. 13) summarizes the value of cooperation and the reason it functions so well among humans:

> Technology may serve to overcome certain human physical and cognitive constraints, as does art and ritual.... But of greater importance is the need to co-operate with other individuals in the solution of problems.... From the decision-making perspective, co-operation allows new solutions to problems to be recognized and achieved, and indeed for new realms of problems to be tackled. The emphasis is on the mutual benefits gained from reciprocal altruism. It is the biological foundation of human behaviour, leading to the weighing up of the costs and benefits of different courses of action that allows this type of interaction to become pervasive in human society.

Cooperation is but one dimension of a rich human sociality, yet it provides a broad basis for understanding social interactions and motivations generally. This is of special significance because cooperation is the core of most cultural change undertaken as a result of individually contributed knowledge, skill, effort and time—not limited to one's own individual interest. Because this exchange holds little or no expectation of exact reciprocity, however, it raises the question of how cooperation can so often function so smoothly and productively among humans. In this regard it may be useful to bear in mind that individual behavior derives from a combination of genetic and environmental forces, a very large and especially significant part of the total human environment being social. It is a mixture of the minds and means behind the symbolic communication employed by others, who can be quite numerous and diverse. Both directly and indirectly, most of our learning is gleaned from those others, as psychologist Thomas Suddendorf (1999, p 306–307) explains:

> Each individual human has certain limited abilities to manipulate the world and learn from the environment. But humans can work in a coordinated fashion and can build on the accomplishments of other humans, across both time and space. We can build tools and then use them to make other tools; we can learn about different domains and then bootstrap from this knowledge to new knowledge.... Humans have certain beliefs about the world, in part as the result of our perceptual mechanism. We can then draw inferences on the basis of these beliefs, and communicate them to others. If it turns out that some of these beliefs are true, and some of these inferences are truth-preserving, then this might enable the creative process that we are concerned with.

The brain is an organ influenced initially and strongly by genetics, but the culture exerts an imminent and sustained pressure on its development and application. Knowledge increasingly is recorded in one form or another and passed from one generation to another, freed from the confines of genes and brains (Distin, 2011). Each individual mind is comprised of brain, body and neural system, connecting sensorially with the physical and social environments (L. Barrett, 2011). Through psychological and emotional adjustment and physical action, meaning is both the product of these connections and the essence of adaptation. Referring specifically to cooperation, Michael Tomasello (2009, p. 120) observes that "we have altruistic social preferences that motivate us to *value* the benefits to the group. This allows us to align our interests with interests of the group and to contribute to activities that have group-beneficial outcomes." Pursued in Chapter 6, altruism also relates to routine personal sacrifice, simply because doing the right thing can be intrinsically rewarding (M. Lieberman, 2013).

The earliest human societies did not include, in most instances, a natural or universal basis of domestic social organization other than the family, according to Adam Kuper (1994, p. 229), noting that "the principle of reciprocity always had a greater or lesser role in regulating relationships; but ancient forms of social life were surely very various." Each culture has evolved from the natural, biological basis of its individual constituents, and each continues evolving according to the system of meanings the culture develops and spreads through the variety of communication systems it establishes along the way, from physical gestures to speaking, writing, printing and the internet.

Humanity: The Dignity and Rights

Human rights and human responsibilities refer to the intellectual and spiritual dimensions of *Homo sapiens*, for we are proud to think of ourselves as considerably more than a vast herd of bipedal mammals.[6] Concepts of humanity, human dignity and human rights derive from our feelings of pride in self and species, but ultimately from our capacity to reason about ourselves.

The concept of *humanity* relates to the cognitive and motivational aspects of our life within a world of people, for humanity transcends physicality. Such a depiction follows from the fact that we possess an unequaled individual and societal capacity to contemplate our own significance as humans in a world of many other beings much like ourselves, doing so from a much broader range of possibilities and options, most of which we create. This capacity also includes at least the strong potential for a sense of responsibility toward other individuals, our society and our planet, qualities we claim warrant special consideration. Respect, thoughtfulness, gentleness, helpfulness and kindness toward other people—and care about other species too—are important aspects of the concept of humanity, as is the notion of a human nature. Beauty, gracefulness, physical strength and speed may be the characteristics we identify with select other creatures, but individual character and the human potential for almost limitless achievement appear to be the major human features for which we exhibit a preference. The capacity to *create* conditions requiring decision, and knowing so, to *create* knowledge and beauty, and to plan activity while aware of one's place in the activity—and even to collaborate in realizing the plan—furnish the guidelines for defining humankind. "The uniqueness of man lies in his capacity, for self-consciousness and self-transcendence, to stand continually 'outside' himself and to judge himself," writes Daniel Bell (1975, p. 69). "This is the foundation of human freedom. It is this radical freedom which defines the glory and the plight of man." That we humans are well aware of our distinctions is itself a monumental distinction, and because of it we acknowledge the humanity of others in greetings, farewells, apologies, thanks, pardons, congratulations, condolences, best wishes, inquiries about others' health, and a variety of verbal and gestural exchanges that may seem superfluous but are, in fact, the routine quotidian forms for acknowledging our special category of being. "Certain situations demand certain speech acts, and if they are not given, group coherence is weakened," confirms James R. Hurford (2007, p. 176). But he adds that "Greeting, apologizing, thanking, and congratulating on appropriate occasions are expected and their performance strengthens social ties." These social acts signal our individual dignity and our respect for others, the common courtesies we extend to and expect from fellow humans. "Nature puts a premium on smooth communication among members of a given species, sculpting the brain for a better fit—sometimes on the spot," writes Daniel Goleman (2006, p. 54), who also observes (p. 10) that "the social brain represents the only biological system in our bodies that continually attunes us to, and in turn becomes influenced by, the internal state of people we're with." Dignity is our state of mind relative to the special value we hold for ourselves as humans and prefer that others perceive us accordingly, for demeaning or humiliating situations challenge our dignity directly. Specializing in international conflict, physician and psychologist Donna Hicks (2011, p. 6) observes, "We have an inborn desire to be treated well because we are psychologically programmed to believe that our lives are dependent on it. We cannot help but react to being mistreated."[7]

The Western understanding of humanity as more than just another species has a relatively long history, reaching well beyond Roman and Greek antiquity. Associated with two fundamental assumptions, according to historian Bruce Mazlish, the principles behind this self-conceptualization were revived during the Renaissance and given wider distribution in the context of scientific, scholarly and artistic development during the European Renaissance and later, particularly during the Enlightenment. Mazlish (2009, p. 32) defines them:

> One is that humans are rational, or rather capable of rationality, so that interests can be balanced by debate and discussion of common needs. It is for this reason that democracy as a form of government is viewed as most conformable to the desires and needs of Humanity. The other is that humans are equal in principle, that is, legally, and must be viewed as having equal rights rather than particular privileges. Thus the concept of Humanity carries with it ideals to be realized over time; it is an emergent reality.

Our strong notions of human rights are complemented by significant feelings and reasons for humanity's obligations solely *because* we were born human. Our statutory laws, internal code of behavior and rules of etiquette do acknowledge violators, but we tend to articulate our human rights more clearly, loudly and frequently than our human obligations. We do this more clearly because our focus is through an idealistic lens on beings of our own kind; more loudly because, though guided by reason they may be motivated by deep feelings; and more frequently because we more pragmatically defend our rights than our obligations, which the letter of the law recognizes only infrequently. Such obligations are among the deontic powers philosopher John R. Searle (2010, p. 164) cites as "rights, duties, obligations, authorizations, permissions, privileges, authority, and the like." They may not always function at the surface of our consciousness, remaining for the most part unlegislated and unwritten, but are integral in humanity, as Searle (p. 130) explains.

> The way that the system of deontic powers works, then, is by way of human rationality. This is disguised from us by the fact that in most habitual cases we don't have to think about the matter at all. We simply carry out our daily obligations without reflecting on the underlying logical structure. They become part of our Background dispositions, though they can always be brought into the foreground and reflected on.

Rationality, feelings, ideals and social obligations are the major reasons for the strong sense of dignity normal humans are inclined to feel for themselves and to protect for others.

Human Dignity

A judgment we have of our individual worth, as well as our species, is crystalized in the concept of human dignity, though it remains undefined in the United Nations' *Universal Declaration of Human Rights* (1948). The term's meaning has changed over time but today is equally applicable to all humans and includes the idea that, within the human cognitive system there is an inherent moral value warranting special consideration, respect and guarded independence. Sociologist Manfred Stanley (1978, pp. 69–70) posits a helpful explanation of this enigmatic concept:

> Human dignity is the respect-worthiness imputed to humankind by reason of its privileged ontological status as creator, maintainer, and destroyer of worlds. Each self shares in this essential dignity (i.e., is recognizable as a moral entity) insofar as it partakes (whether by conscious intention or not) in world building or world destroying actions. Thus, human dignity does not rest on intention, moral merit, or subjective definitions of self-interests. It rests on the fact that we are, in this fundamental way that is beyond our intention, human. We are moral agents.

Appearing some 50,000 to 100,000 years ago as symbols and drawings on cave walls and other stone surfaces, our earliest art forms displayed uniquely human expressions in a highly self-conscious manifestation of individual pride in distinction (Dicke, 2002). The ancient Greeks then began to express their notion of human dignity by suggesting associated rights and privileges that had influenced other Western and neighboring cultures for many centuries. Nonetheless, political scientist Klaus Dicke (2002, p. 112) also finds, "Although the concept of *dignitas hominis* was dealt with in philosophical essays and although it was a key term in Kant's philosophy of freedom, there was no systematic reference to human dignity in legal language until the 1940s." Dicke (p. 113) also comments on the "legal tradition of (mainly French and German) enlightenment and natural law philosophy, which hold that all human beings are endowed by nature with reason and therefore are to be recognized as equals." Prior to the middle of the eighteenth century in the West, dignity had belonged only to the select few at the pinnacle of their social hierarchy, as the English noun *dignitary* suggests. Throughout industrial development and the multitude of cultural changes it introduced, this closely held privilege increasingly was extended to others, sometimes through law and morality because (as discussed in Chapter 3) a growing proportion of the mass population was nurturing or developing or inheriting sufficient self-esteem to aspire to individual, personal ideals their venerable faculty of reason indicated they deserved and could hope to realize. To the extent that the ascription of dignity bears social significance it also indicates humanity's sense of responsibility, a dimension of the meaning that transcends its purely social dimension and applies to other beings and the universe. Concurrent with cultural forces having the potential to erode this ideal sense, human dignity maintains a high profile that grows stronger as the concept of human rights continues to gain legal ground in democratic nations.[8]

Human Rights

Human rights arose as a Western issue in the spirit of the times during the eighteenth-century, when revolutions in France and America aroused strong feelings about the proper governmental and social treatment of human beings.[9] Such rights were considered self-evident: they were based on a genetically-inherited and culturally-maintained morality, and they tended to reflect a sense of the distinction between right and wrong, good and bad. Human rights are entitlements perceived as natural, universal, and attributable to both individuals and societies, constituting a new cultural idea in the eighteenth century (Searle, 2010).

As the concept of human dignity had been sustained largely by religion, much of the thought associated with human rights and the language in which the concept has been conveyed reflect church history. Today it remains an ideal, sufficiently secure that humanity's dignity constitutes the foundation of international human rights law. Physician and educator Yechiel Michael Barilan (2012, p. 152) concludes, "The ethos of human dignity animates the instrument of human rights and serves as its unifying template for the interpretation and implementation of human rights." Barilan (p. 302) also summarizes their complementarity: "Whereas human dignity has numerous normative dimensions, human rights distill the notion of inviolability and the strongest moral status within an enforceable and regulative conceptual system. Many issues of human dignity, and some rights-related values, are beyond the scope of human rights. Much of morality is not enforceable." Humanity is entitled to certain rights because of the dignity being human entails, leaving the determination of specific rights to institutions, the state and international law, while the concept of humanity tends to be accorded a high priority among many other interests and values. The purpose of these rights is to grant and protect an individual's life because, as human, each life has special worth. Quite provocatively, however, political scientist Jack Donnelly (2013, p. 15) contends, "Human rights are less about the way people are than about what they might become. They are about moral rather than natural or juridical persons." Human rights clearly project an ideal for individuals and a vision for humanity, emphasizing in worldview the quality of life toward which humanity strives.[10] Human rights exemplify our uniquely human capacity to think about ourselves as both individuals and a species. It is above all the human capacity to create, accumulate, and share knowledge that supports human dignity.

Knowledge and Worldview

All animals possess knowledge of some kind in varying breadth and depth, but humans know what knowledge is and that everyone else does too, and even that some people have more than others and can use what they have to greater or lesser advantage; and we have some idea of where we fit in this scheme. We know that knowledge has value for our purposes, whatever they may be, and that we're usually better off with it than without it. But biological and cultural evolution are continuous forms of change, each altering worldview, and one of the distinctions between these two evolutionary paths is the fact that we have no conscious control over, or even awareness of, our *biological* evolution at any given point within a period of ten millennia, while cultural change now can occur quickly enough for us to witness it throughout our lifetime and be well aware of this fact.

We humans also are quite aware that our decisions have consequences. But we may be less aware of their cumulative effect, which eventually sets a society on its trajectory for further change, sometimes momentous change. Our mind is part physical and part spiritual, a condition Clifford Geertz (1973, pp. 58–59) portrays from his anthropologist perspective:

> "Mind" is a term denoting a class of skills, propensities, capacities, tendencies, habits; it refers in Dewey's phrase to an "active and eager background which lies in wait and engages whatever comes its way." And as such it is neither an action nor a thing, but an organized system of dispositions which finds its manifestation in some actions and some things.... But the point is that when we attribute mind to an organism, we are talking about neither the organism's actions nor its products per se, but about its capacity and its proneness, its disposition, to perform certain kinds of actions and produce certain kinds of products, a capacity and a proneness we of course infer from the fact that [one] does sometimes perform such acts and produce such products.

Decisions cause change, opening the door to other decisions with new implications. Mathematician and biologist Jacob Bronowski (2002, p. 17) writes that "my self is a process: the unending process by which I turn new experience into knowledge." Given the continuous change in individual knowledge and the effect it has on the priority of our values, it is hardly surprising that the accumulation of individual change in worldview can lead swiftly to cultural change, even when change may require the profoundly penetrating effort of human adaptation.[11]

The increasing barrage of decisions about relatively insignificant commodities and their imagined distinctions of lifestyle in the Consumer Society (discussed in Chapter 3) may be supplanting some of our deepest thought, our introspection. In this displacement, therefore, the significance of value withers, the result of a passing whim stimulated only by objective data rather than by the judgment that marshals a complex combination of objective knowledge and subjective information, which can produce human understanding rather than an automatic reaction to an automatic stimulus. Just as knowledge loses significance when separated from value, value is barely conceivable in the absence of knowledge. We tend to dismiss our emotion, feelings and morality as irrelevant, inefficient and weak, being *only* subjective and therefore not real in the same sense as, for example, money. We routinely exclude them from formal judgment because of their presumed inherent incalculability as values in this world, its spiritual foundation increasingly displaced by material substance.

Such a conclusion ignores the many millennia through which our rationality has successfully guided the rich blend of learned objective knowledge and inherited subjective information through our species' evolution. The next chapter concentrates on the mental features that distinguish humanity from other mammals, yet also contribute to our paradoxical situation.

2

Special Features of Mind

> Just as evolution is driven by processes of different types, so human behavior is caused by different types of ultimate motive.
> —Elliott Sober and David Sloan Wilson, 1998

Mind Over Matter

We determine most decisions with our reasoned assessment of options and understanding of their likely requirements and consequences. Understanding is an ideal, a mental state achieved by learning about a particular issue and its connective context. It requires a highly self-conscious effort heavily dependent on memory for its depth and the imagination of possible outcomes; memory, imagination and feelings constitute the core of the human self. Understanding is a highly subjective cognitive state with the potential for causing the deep social tensions now increasingly apparent in modern Western life.[1] This chapter surveys the mind's central features for coping with its demands.

Motivation

Motivated by neural sensitivities, supported by sociality and orchestrated by the brain, the mind has led humanity's apparently successful adaptation throughout our evolutionary journey to the present. Clinical psychologist Zoltan Torey (2014, p. 10) writes, "The mind is neither an ephemeral entity nor brain function writ large, but a sharply delineated neuronal system that is based on language in the conscious brain," a definition he (p. 150) expands:

> As for the human mind, it is a neural subsystem of the brain. Its tool is language, while its range and experience are defined by what language is able to access and handle. The mind is not a nonmaterial agency, but a physical entity, a subsystem that uses the circuitry and brain processes that perception uses in registering and dealing with the world.

Our mind constructs knowledge by assigning meaning and value to the socially conveyed knowledge constituting each individual's external reality. Since sociality is deeply rooted in the self, individual development links directly with cultural evolution, their linkage becoming catalytic when the mix of diverse individuals occurs within a culturally self-regulated society where they stimulate new perceptions, insights, and understandings to an extent incomparable among other animate beings. Daniel Goleman (2006, p. 152) explains this feature, writing, "The human brain is designed to change itself in response to accumulated experience."[2] Any culture includes a multitude of individual minds guided by reason, which for millennia has been considered the primary distinction between humans and other animate beings. But paleoanthropologist Ian Tattersall (1998, pp. 233–234) theorizes that the evolution of linguistic communication, which depends upon the capacity to function well with phonetic symbols, did not require a vast trial period:

> Rather, its acquisition was an emergent event that was probably rather minor in terms of physical or genetic innovation, that was comparatively sudden, and that came very late in our evolutionary history.... The mind is a complex thing, not in the sense that an engineered machine is, with many separate parts working smoothly together in pursuit of a single goal, but in the sense that it is a product of ancient reflexive and emotional components, overlain by a veneer of reason. The human mind is thus not an entirely rational entity, but rather one that is still conditioned by the long evolutionary history of the brain from which it emerges. Great though may be the leap we have made away from the rest of the living world in the acquisition of symbolic thought, we have not entirely emancipated ourselves from the brain structures that governed the behavior of some very remote ancestors indeed. And it is precisely this interaction of the ancient with the new that makes us not only unique in many very admirable ways, but also uniquely dangerous—as much to ourselves as to the rest of the living world.

Though a relatively large cranial capacity may often be considered the primary distinguishing feature of humans—the brain being the central organ governing all functions of mind and body—its ability to reorganize connections and establish new ones is at least as significant. Often referred to as human neuroplasticity, this feature has the capacity to follow the thought progression that stimulates adaptive brain circuitry because attention activates physical change in the brain, accounting for the brain's dynamism and adaptive capacity (Schwartz & Begley, 2002). Attention is a biological function requiring an extremely gradual evolution by natural selection, a process involving masses of individuals with similar psychological need. Psychologists John Tooby and Leda Cosmides and anthropologist and evolutionary psychologist H. Clark Barrett (2005, pp. 310, 313) describe the evolutionary context for this kind of mental change:

> In modern terms, mutations that cause neural machinery to reliably develop useful, world-reflecting mental contents (or organizing principles, categories, etc.) give their

possessors a propagative advantage over blank slate designs that must consider an unconstrained set of possibilities, and are limited to applying the same procedures to all contents. Natural selection constitutes a second route, independent of the specific characteristics of individual experience, by which the mind might become endowed with knowledge, and endowed with the Kantian conceptual tools that shape and make use of experience in an evolutionarily functional way.... [T]he human neurocomputational architecture contains a language acquisition device in the form of a set of procedures at least some of which are language specific and whose embodied inferential strategies reflect structural or statistical regularities in the set of languages humans spoke ancestrally (as well as the contexts of meaning within which utterances were made).

The biological evolution of animals occurs very gradually through the processes of natural selection, and relates to cultural evolution.[3] Humanity, however, continuously re-invents itself socially in a relatively rapid cultural evolution, and in the course of this ongoing phenomenon the various segments and levels of social dialectic challenge established worldview. They introduce new knowledge and perceptions so possibilities previously unimagined become imaginable, while also initiating change in the value system's priorities. Special cognitive capacities have enabled humanity to evolve complex yet quite strong cultures, explains evolutionary biologist David Sloan Wilson (2003, p. 26), because "our minds are also packed with specialized circuits that enable us to solve our own problems of survival and reproduction as naturally as celestial navigation in birds and dead reckoning in ants.... Even without knowing the details, this basic conclusion almost certainly applies to our ability as a species to form into functional groups unified by moral systems."[4]

Cultural evolution is complex because mental evolution requires a combination of psychology and worldview representative of many unique individuals in sufficient number and authority to influence societal change. "Not surprisingly," says psychologist Hubert J.M. Hermans (2013, p. 52), "identity confusion, and its implied uncertainty, increases the need for clarity, purpose and direction in life. As a protection or even defense against the multiplicity of voices on the global-local interface, people retreat to social groups or traditions that liberate them from the multiplicity of voices that may end up in a confusing cacophony." Both individual and society require purpose, so either may discover or invent it. But there can hardly be purpose without meaning, so continuous mind development mixes with the human penchant for sociality, the combination becoming a seemingly irresistible force of culture to produce meaning.

Countless generations have chosen to bend the world to human wish, their success commensurate with the development of intellectual capacities which, if not unprecedented among other beings, are at least unmatched by the degree of their functionality to human benefit. Evolutionary psychologist

Dennis L. Krebs (2011, p. 186) places this collective phenomenon in its evolutionary context:

> Evolutionarily ancient mechanisms give rise to primitive prosocial dispositions, but recently evolved mechanisms that endow humans with unique intellectual abilities, the ability to engage in symbolic communication, and the ability to create and refine culture endow them with the ability to create uniquely human societies and engage in the uniquely human types of prosocial behavior necessary to uphold them.

Among the mental capacities humans possess and use to advantage, including perception, perspective, meaning, insight, imagination and curiosity, two are of special significance in this context: consciousness and judgment.

Consciousness

Consciousness is a persistent state throughout our lifetime whether awake or asleep (when it is dimmed), for we are as Zoltan Torey (2014, p. 106) says, "inextricably a part of what we are conscious of." Owing to the human capacity for reflective thought, our attention is raised to a more acute awareness of ourselves, our total environment, our own thought, and its meaning for us.[5] Consciousness is the constantly flowing and ever-changing succession of perception, thought, ideas, sensations, emotion, feelings, values, attitudes, and judgments common to all normal people. It is who we are at any given point in our being, so it defines us as individuals among others. Ian Tattersall (1998, pp. 191–192) further illuminates the significance of our consciousness:

> One currently popular approach to the problem of understanding consciousness has been to view our brains as machines. For in one limited sense they must indeed be machines, at least to the extent that there is no reason to regard consciousness as anything other than the product of processes that take place within the physical brain. And it is, of course, the inherited mechanical similarities of our brains to each other that permit human beings to assume their consciousnesses are more or less the same and to deal with each other on that basis. The notion that all normal human beings have consciousnesses that are comparable to each other certainly works well enough in practice.... In theory, an artificial brain could be constructed to reproduce the functioning of the human brain, up to and including the experience of consciousness; but we really have no idea how this might be done in practice.

Consciousness consists in a tightening focus on the inner experience of the naturally subjective individual. It is the awareness of self as an entity capable of contemplating itself, a phenomenon described simply but most famously by René Descartes, in the seventeenth century: *cogito ergo sum* (I think therefore I am). These very few words have been repeated through the centuries so often and with such profound meaning that they have recast Western worldview. It is a prime characteristic of modernity philosopher Owen Barfield (1977, p. 181) refers to as "that long drama of individuation," which today is a motivator of the consumer society. Subtle but highly significant, consciousness is the vehicle for the human cognition discussed throughout this essay.

Judgment

The action following from our decisions enables us to evaluate the quality of our capacity for this cognitive act. Good judgment is fundamental to any individual's physical, social and psychological survival, and stems directly from a sound understanding of its total environment in relation to values and their priority order. The quality of good judgment, like poor judgment, depends upon the extent of context one believes pertinent to the cognitive effort. For the social system to work well and its benefits to be realized fully by the given society, differing values and their order of priority must be involved in a continuous process of review and assessment as an integrated system, a complex of ideals toward which the culture advances without ever fully attaining. This state relates to intelligence, the ability to learn and apply knowledge, which is a most complex human feature to fathom. But social psychologist Roy F. Baumeister (2010, p. 33) provides an evolutionary cultural perspective that describes the concept intended in this essay:

> [I]ntelligence increases only in step with its ability to bring palpably large payoffs. For most creatures, those prospects are limited. A larger brain might occasionally enable a creature to outwit a rival or predator, but the increase in daily cost for the larger brain's upkeep could produce a net disadvantage. All this changes with culture, however. Culture is based on information, and so there is more possibility for intelligence to come into play in acquiring, storing, and working with all this information....
> Another point about intelligence is that if it seems to have evolved to deal with specific sorts of problems, despite its reputations as an all-purpose reasoning machine.... As I said, economic exchange relationships are crucial to culture (and relatively unknown in other species), and so for people to be successful at them—individually and collectively—it is necessary to watch, avoid, and punish people who abuse the system.

Knowledge, learning, experience, and values are central contributors to judgment, whether individual or collective, but some values are quite personal, such as those accompanied by the experience of strong emotion and feelings. When not taken into account as part of the context, the quality of judgment eventually will fail to meet the desired standard, which calls for the best information available at the time, and the outcome can reveal oversights in the decision process. Determining the most appropriate course of action is a challenge in any situation, however, even though judging is so fundamental a human capacity that it vastly distinguishes humans from other beings. This is primarily because judgment is founded on reason, to which humans can apply a greater diversity of mental capacities. Repeated and expected demonstration of good judgment is a sign of wisdom, which is not absolute—if there really is such a state. It is in the self-consciousness of the human capacity to take appropriate action that the dominant ideas of both individual and society are most clearly understood to be founded on sound or unsound judgment. Either conclusion is attributable to the extent of context included in the decision.

Objectivity

The long trend toward quantification reflects the West's blanket acceptance of the objective stance, a distinctively human capacity most evident in its effect on decision and judgment. A particularly troublesome adherence to objectivity, which has been exercised increasingly through the modern era, is the current attempt to minimize the application of human judgment, if not to eliminate it. The effort to purge judgment has come about primarily because of its foundation in subjectivity, its humanity, its personal biases, hopes, opinions, beliefs, affinities and fears, as though uncontrollable. Upon initial consideration, and given its clear logic, such a goal may seem difficult to refute, but further reflection illuminates the validity of the more comprehensive assessment philosopher and intellectual historian Stephen Gaukroger (2012, p. 3) advances:

> A methodology that bypasses the assumptions, values, and beliefs that inevitably accompany the exercise of judgement thereby makes claims to neutrality and objectivity. Standardized decision-making procedures stand in for reflection on the nature of the problem for which the decision is sought in the first place. Wholly misconstruing the nature of objectivity, they employ pseudo-scientific means of bypassing understanding and evaluation in favour of something that is deemed to transcend bias and prejudgement.

Objectivity claims to exclude personal bias, so it wields considerable influence in most decisions, even when the outcome has implications for other people. But objectivity is not the problem. The problem develops when objectivity is extreme in its focus on the narrowed purpose of effacing select possible outcomes bearing the potential to hinder progress toward goals so specific that they exclude the fundamental human consideration of values and feelings.

An individual's worldview begins to form at birth when the immediate caregivers, usually the parents, objectively define the infant's surrounding world. And since neither the caregiver nor the infant were the creators of that world, it becomes the infant's de facto objective knowledge, his or her reality (Berger & Luckmann, 1966). This initial impression is re-enforced every day as social experiences unfold at many levels and amid changing environments. Sociality and language are mutually enhancing, and their processes expand the individual mind by converting experience into clusters of manageable thoughts to be visualized and stored in memory.[6] An objective stance has proved essential to the natural science epistemology, where its logic is quite apparent (see Chapter 4). Generalized in the West, attempts to apply strict objectivity in other academic disciplines and in other endeavors not only fails but also reveals a worse effect, for it can lead to conditions that may never have been considered. Gaukroger (2012, p. 86) provides a précis of such an exercise:

> In particular, while it might be appropriate to "stand back" from phenomena in the natural sciences to achieve objectivity, this is inappropriate in the case of the human sciences, where we are dealing not with an objectified realm, but with human beings who have intentional states, emotions, the ability to exercise judgement, and so on. These are attributes that they share with the investigator, and which the investigator is therefore in a position to interpret and of which he or she can make sense.... In other words, what is being argued is that the physical sciences have been taken to provide a model of objectivity *per se*, something that can simply be exported to any other area of study.

The objective approach has migrated with other industrial strategies, principles, and values into human life beyond the regimented workplace. What is damaging to humanity and therefore wrong, in this regard, is that the indiscriminate or thoughtless application of a rigid objectivity in human decision may not only be ineffectual but also may ignore or trivialize subjective considerations that may be central to the given issue, even though never part of the intentions embedded in the otherwise scrupulously designed technical function.

Although a step easily taken when objectivity is invoked under the cloak of perfect rationality, such action is a crucial step toward the general diminishment of distinctively human qualities from decisions. A studied avoidance of emotion and feelings in decisions requires a concentration on objectivity that is forced and awkward, because it is an abnormal human thought pattern.[7] The laboratory in which principles and ideals of natural science are valued may be removed to a satisfactory distance from the general population and, therefore, may not be socially influential. But the preference for objectivity is brought closer to home in the ideology and ubiquity of technology where it is nearly synonymous with rationality, as Daniel Bell (1975, p.189) observed decades ago:

> Technology has created a new definition of rationality, a new mode of thought, which emphasizes functional relations and the quantitative. Its criteria of performance are those of efficiency and least effort. This new definition of functional rationality has its carryover in new modes of education, in which the quantitative techniques of engineering and economics now jostle the older modes of speculation, tradition, and reason.

Subsequent decades of experience in these matters support his conclusion. The more we immerse ourselves in a material ambience the more materialistic we become, and now technologies may be trusted more than people (Turkle, 2011), who are thought only to be trustworthily selfish. Relevant scientific research cited in this essay shows that *all* of us are subjective and *some* are selfish, not the reverse.

Through their collaborative provision of formal guidance, social institutions have evolved considerable power in supporting the culture's normalizing strength. Each institution is "a complex of positions, roles, norms, and values lodged in patterns of human activity with respect to fundamental problems in producing life-sustaining viable societal structures within a given environment," according to sociologist Jonathan Turner (1997, p. 6). And because social institutions such as families, collaborative groups and cultures existed prior to *Homo sapiens* they are part of our objective reality. Thus, the cognitive function of reification is a quite common phenomenon.[8] Individual humans are surrounded by a physical environment and a human social environment that comprises many collectives and countless other individual minds. Each of these individual others, however, also incorporates a strong, subjectively-oriented being.

Subjectivity

Subjective knowledge is inherited genetically to contribute to our species' ultimate balance as a living social organism. Moreover, we are aware that our conspecifics are similarly equipped, this awareness making emotion and feelings a sound basis for mutual human understanding. By contrast, objective knowledge is individual, acquired through effort, discovery or creation in the experience of complementing and supplementing other specific objective knowledge extant individually, and it pertains specifically to time and place. "Modern natural knowledge, both scientific and technical, is information and as such culturally disembedded, which means: differentiated from encompassing moral values, social concerns, and political goals," writes political sociologist Wolfgang van den Daele (2004, p. 34). Yet the separation of these two spheres of knowledge in an artificial structuring of the knowledge foundation for decisions not only raises concern, it also interferes with normal human cognition and destabilizes the social organism.

Subjectivity is each individual's domain of meaning. When the brain receives a message from the senses, that percept registers a meaning. Information triggers the knowledge process of connecting to select extant information with the purpose of assessing the new information's meaning, its effect on accumulated information and the reverse. This knowledge includes values, meanings, beliefs, emotions, feelings, desires, tastes, the continuous updating of technical knowledge, and all aspects of consciousness, along with thought derived through reason, curiosity, and imagination. Anthropologist, social scientist and linguist Gregory Bateson's (2002, p. 28) insistence that "all experience is subjective" paints a thought-provoking perspective on subjectivity's significance. Subjectivity is a defining factor of humanity, for no being would be truly *human* without it, and since it also functions in conjunction with other mental capacities for understanding some aspects of another's frame of mind, subjectivity occupies a central position in sound judgment, but it does clearly add a complicating dimension to any decision. Therefore, judgments rendered solely on the basis of objective information quite likely can be accomplished much more expeditiously, clearly, and unequivocally by computers than by humans. But subjectivity resides at the core of being human, directly connecting knowledge, values, and human experience in a physical, social, spiritual, and intellectual environment. Barry Schwartz (2004, p. 88) finds, "What becomes clear about 'satisfaction' or 'preferences' as they are experienced in real life is that they are subjective, not objective."

Thought drives the continuously evolving self, the nucleus of individual identity and subjectivity. The self is spiritual, formed within each individual by information received from external sources of many kinds that include socially-held information about the external world, which enters the individual mind as perception. But the self is constituted as well by information received from internal sources: inherited genes. The resultant rich and complex combination is an important dimension in our social construction of knowledge and a significant part of paleontologists Rob DeSalle and Ian Tattersall's (2012, p. 304) conclusion that, "our brains are splendidly jury-rigged affairs that no engineer would ever have designed. Indeed, to a large degree it is because the human brain has *not* been optimized for single purpose that it is the hugely creative and simultaneously both logical and irrational, organ that it is." New ideas are the fuel of cultural evolution and therefore are of incomparable significance to humanity. Language renders them easily communicated and essential to decisions when founded on a solid body of relevant knowledge. Because of the self's nature, individual minds are sufficiently flexible to assume a new course by adjusting to new ideas and information and considering alternative perspectives, which history demonstrates are boundless.

Differing perspectives are part of the reality in which all of us live, part of the subjectivity that stimulates further thought and reconsideration either by reaffirming our worldview or challenging it, and they often demand a rethinking. Such a portrayal projects the image of a factory for new ideas, new possibilities, new answers to old questions, new problems to be solved, and new opportunities to be tested. It depicts human thoughts, most or all of which each individual has reasoned, not just as an individual but also as one among others. The subjective human perspective is revealed for others so they will have the option of applying a similar, yet not identical, process in determining where they stand on a given issue, or whether they have any interest at all in it. For the current Western culture, this amounts to a grand tableau of new decisions to make and for which plans of action can then be established. The tableau presents a social world from which individual identity is carved, and in which emotion, feelings and the sense of social responsibility occupy a prominent position. Political scientist Ty Solomon (2015, p. 206) finds that, "what becomes 'common sense' is obtained through the fantasy of subjectivity that the discourse projects." Common sense is a result of the social dialectic.

"Emotion runs the mind," writes computer scientist David Gelernter (2016, p. 70), but the literature describing impressive human strides from generation to generation and century to century now concentrates principally if not solely on knowledge related to the industrial, scientific, and technological advances reflected in the economy and the general standard of living: our objective knowledge. In technical matters such as science, technology and economics, scholars tend toward a careful and self-conscious avoidance of subjectivity and its related potential for violation of the guiding and more socially acceptable objectivity principle. Public health administrator and consultant Daniel M. Fox (1967, p. 176) claims, for example, "Most economists avoid the issues of abundance because the concept involves a degree of subjectivity which threatens their efforts to create a 'value-free' science, such as physics." This is because emotion and feelings have a long history of discounting by scientists and philosophers, some of whom consider them mere remnants of our less sophisticated ancestry and their closer connection with other animals: vestigial, reactive impulses serving only to cloud modern rational thought.

As they commonly are understood, emotion, and feelings have little or no connection with the concept of progress, a situation Gelernter (2016, p. 116) summarizes: "Civilized bias in modern times runs strongly for the rational, against the emotional. In normal talk, rational is clean, well lit, tastefully decorated. Virtuous. Emotional is sticky and weak." Feelings and emotion may even be considered deterrents to social progress, if not blatant obstacles, a valid assessment, however, only when efficiency truly is the sole *ultimate* goal. But what purpose can human progress have if it fails to instill a sense of satisfaction, comfort or general well-being, which are primarily subjective? Emotion, which includes interpersonal relationships, and feelings, which include morality, are cognitive functions the normal human organism generates and communicates continuously. Their function is to inform, so they convey information about their first concern, the human self, which reflects thoughts and feelings shared among normal human beings. Philosopher Michael S. Brady (2013, p. 28) emphasizes that "emotions alert us to the import of objects and events, and in so doing seem to involve an appraisal or evaluation of such objects and events."[9] They prepare individuals to cope with matters of particular human significance more effectively and in a procedure that psychologist and neuroscientist Philip N. Johnson-Laird (2006, pp. 74–75) sketches:

> Emotions are a meeting place of mind, body, and behavior. In a complete emotion, we have a subjective feeling, we're aware of its cause, we experience bodily changes as a consequence of our autonomic nervous system, and we may make various expressions, gestures, and actions. The signals that communicate emotions are innate, and hence universal to all human cultures: facial expressions of emotion are the same the world over.

Subjectivity conveys humanity's part of the thought process leading to any decision whose likely outcome involves fellow humans. Social emotions "are central to human social decision making," writes biological and experimental psychologist Keith Jensen (2012, p. 302). They are central, pivotal features of human experience and thought, offering direct insight into the full value of human subjectivity. Emotion and feelings are active, continuously performing as the individual being's inner reflection of human sociality, not solely of the individual self, and they "involve long-term desires, fantasies and wishes," writes psychologist Harry Smit (2014, p. 111). Precisely because they are subjective, these cognitive processes render the experiences of others widely intelligible in the course of decision-making, our most evolutionarily critical act.

Balancing Subjectivity and Objectivity

Neither objectivity nor subjectivity is right or wrong, good or bad, but simply common and fluctuating human states of mind, two mutually dependent dimensions of a wondrous organism, and like any other category of knowledge, their value depends upon the use to which they are put. "Objectivity is not merely an intellectual virtue," concludes Stephen Gaukroger (2012, p. 104). "Rather, it is something that we learn how to achieve, and because it is context-dependent, we learn how to achieve it in context-dependent ways. It is not a one-size-fits-all notion." But in our acquiescence to a misleading path to decision we have devised special means for separating the highly significant subjective dimension of our knowledge from our normal, continuous thought, a practice that makes little sense in all but some select and near-unique instances where objectivity may be of absolute and overriding significance. Whereas subjectivity is a normal human *state of being*, objectivity is a uniquely human *strategy*—an ideal to be tempered in the light of human purpose and context. Neither objectivity nor subjectivity replaces the other. Humans have evolved cognitive capacities for strengthening judgment in situations requiring collaboration, and in conjunction with these capacities an attitude that distinguishes humanity from all other mammals and from technologies.[10]

Objectivity is the distinguishing human capacity to maintain thought without personal bias, a stance of primary significance of principle in natural science and strategic utility in other aspects of life, most often in decisions and judgment, having migrated to the general public more directly from industrial strategy than from scientific principle. The rigidly objective stance against subjectivity—even when human circumstances and conditions are affected—has become an influence on most other cultural change and steadily has diminished "the importance men attach to the search for permanent values as a basis for their decisions," according to philosopher and economic historian John Nef (1964, p. 354). When science initially entered the public sphere of interest via industry's adoption of the natural science attitude, it also tightened the linkage between culture and the economy, which until then had not captured the prominence it apparently holds today in the mind of most citizens. Filtered through industrial enterprise, the scientific approach had demonstrated that major change could be planned, managed and tested entirely on the basis of objective knowledge, so it soon became evident that knowledge discovered and proved scientifically could be applied to any task, making quite manageable those which otherwise would be impossibly difficult, complex, time-consuming, and even unimaginable. Science historian Margaret C. Jacob (1997, p. 11) succinctly recounts the hegemony of science two and a half centuries earlier in her conclusion that "the transition from seventeenth-century science to late eighteenth-century industrialization changed the values and perspectives of Westerners forever." Given this environment, technology could be perceived—could literally be viewed—as the model for all system elements in the accomplishment of complex and extensive undertakings. Moreover, technology was understood to be quite manageable because, unlike people, it is comprised of parts interrelated according to a plan that anyone could read. But people are not nearly as understandable, manageable, or predictable as machinery, for people are complex and quickly changeable. More comprehensibly, technologies are highly predictable since their moving parts depend upon neither values nor knowledge beyond the confines of their own functionality with other technologies. Application of other considerations is extraneous, rendering the given task unduly complex, frustrating, time-consuming, and expensive: inefficient. Determination of the best balance of subjectivity and objectivity requires the kind of thought for which humans possess the broadest yet most profound capacity, which is introspection.

Introspection

The conscious internal deliberation of concentrated thought is the uniquely human experience of introspection (or self-reflection), a form of deep solitary thought critical in determining one's own understanding. Sociologist Margaret S. Archer (2007, p. 4) defines the process quite simply as "the regular exercise of the mental ability, shared by all normal people, to consider themselves in relation to their (social) contexts and vice versa."[11] Philosopher, paleontologist and Jesuit priest Pierre Teilhard de Chardin (1959, p. 165) elaborates on this function:

> From our experimental point of view, reflection is, as the word indicates, the power acquired by a consciousness to turn in upon itself, to take possession of itself *as of an object* endowed with its own particular consistence and value: no longer merely to know, but to know oneself; no longer merely to know, but to know that one knows. By this individualization of himself in the depths of himself, the living element, which heretofore had been spread out and divided over a diffuse circle of perceptions and activities, was constituted for the first time as a *centre* in the form of a point at which all the impressions and experience knit themselves together and fuse into a unity that is conscious of its own organization. Now the consequences of such a transformation are immense, visible as clearly in nature as any of the facts recorded by physics or astronomy. The being who is the object of his own reflection, in consequence of that very doubling back upon himself, becomes in a flash able to raise himself into a new sphere.

Only through introspection can a solitary individual conduct a debate-like assessment of any issue by assuming different voices, adopting multiple perspectives, and taking opposed sides of an argument without suffering the slings and arrows of bystanders or the ignominy of making a premature commitment to one side or another. Linguist James R. Hurford (2012, p. 170) situates the origins of this uniquely evolved human capacity:

> It seems very likely that the impressive human problem-solving abilities are due to having learned a language, containing a repertoire of public tokens for complex concepts, accumulated over many previous generations. These meaning-form connections were communicated to us. The private thought function of language could not exist to the impressive degree that it does without this communicative function.

A substantial proportion of this internal debate focuses on morality (examined more closely in Chapter 6), which can apply the force of law without constituting the law. Closely related to morality are values, which in deep reflection are conducive to the personal struggle over priorities.

Western cultural evolution has accelerated remarkably since industry's birth in the fifteenth century, but with extraordinarily noticeable speed in the late twentieth and early twenty-first, when industrial development and technological innovation generated change so rapidly, their concurrency having made daily life far more complex. In this context, the concept of alienation describes individual and social reactions to the now common phenomenon of incessant change and its tendency toward complexity. It is perfectly logical to expect many individuals to withdraw for further internal conversation in an effort to make sense of the situation and determine its meaning for oneself, as well as the most generally advantageous attitude and course of action to adopt. Introspection has been increasingly valuable as a means of coping with the world and maintaining a healthy mind and outlook, much as sociologist John H. Gagnon (1992, p. 239) portrays the individual's position:

> In this construal, the self is the sum of an individual's changing internal conversations, the forecastings, the recollections and the wishes, the voices that make up our intrapsychic life.... The domain of the private has ineluctably grown as cultures have become more complex and the intrapsychic, that is, the domain of the self has become the crucial mediator in a world in which the collective connections between meaning and action, meaning and meaning, and action and action have grown less compelled and hence less compelling. As concealment and the necessity for playing with roles has increased, so has the problem of intrapsychic "negotiation." In this way, the boundary between self and other, between public and private, has grown more permeable throughout the life course.

Introspection has become the most dependable way to synchronize self understanding with an understanding of the external world. But it requires an influx of new information and a malleable perspective for coping with a world in change, an internal global positioning system to provide the individual a choice of roles to project or a changed perspective on the more objectified globe, and thus to make it one's own. Only the act of reading can provide a similar but more externally-guided function.[12]

Deep introspection replays recent past events in the manner of a video news report. It can immediately recast selected events, freeze-frame them and insert supporting or dissenting documentation in voices and images drawn from sources both internal and external, all stored in memory and mixed with imagination and speculation. The enriched recasting of events and sensations can be analyzed, repeated, altered and studied at one's own rate of speed in making connections that may have been overlooked during the original scenario, while assessing the surmised reactions, feelings, and intentions of others involved in the experience. The purpose in employing this internal activity is to develop an understanding of the total experience, its implications and meanings, in preparation for establishing a validated and self-confident personal response that makes sense. When accomplished, the entire extended experience has been internalized and integrated into the individual who, having thoroughly considered the external and internal context of the process, better understands it and oneself. Archer (2007) frequently refers to introspection as "the internal conversation," and specifically (p. 150) as "the dialectic of context and concern." Introspection is a summarizing and clarifying growth experience that draws deeply on one's consciousness. Collapsing a broad span of scholarship on the relevance of modernity to reflection, Archer (2007, p. 317) concludes, "Whether the key transformation was conceptualized in terms of the transition from segmented to cooperative social organization, from feudalism to capitalism, or from pre-reformation to post-reformation, the common denominator was 'contextual discontinuity,' represented by new forms of dissimilarity, alienation, aloneness and uncertainty."[13]

It is logical that most of the knowledge generated this way is about the self and may be the ultimate vehicle for optimizing any knowledge. Whether aware of it or not, most of us function on the basis of assumptions, as behavioral psychologists Frank C. Richardson and Robert L. Woolfolk (2013, p. 11) observe: "Our thoughts, emotions, decisions, and behavior presuppose deep assumptions or coordinates, however inconsistent, whether we are aware of or can articulate them or not, about what is truly good or worthwhile." This capacity applies to identifying for ourselves our personal requirements for clarifying new information, a feat we accomplish through the self-interrogation basic to our sense of well-being and our social success. Introspection is primarily the contemplation of our own thought, so it is an ever-present way to adjust our self-assessment. Within the culture, comprised as it is of unique individuals, each inevitably possesses a strong psychology always at work in assembling knowledge and values to accommodate certain individual desires, to calm fears, or to justify a belief or a contemplated action. Over the span of a lifetime, each individual may be a microcosm of humanity. Benefits accruing to the self are discoverable through introspection, the kind of thought in which Teilhard de Chardin (1959, p. 300) finds an "irresistible deepening" quality. It is at once a manifestation of curiosity and a drive to connect the cognitive dots. But introspection is subjective and does consume time.

Theory of Mind

Theory of Mind (ToM) is another particularly valuable mental mechanism incorporated in human introspection. It is a form of mindreading, a cognitive capacity that relates not only to the way one generally understands a situation from the perspective of self, but also to the way humans understand each other's intentions.[14] Cognitive psychologist Thomas Suddendorf (1999, p. 218) adds that it "seems to depend on mental computations that gradually develop over the first four years of life and… have evolved over the last five million years of human evolution." He (p. 219) expands his explanation:

> The mind can be regarded as a representational system. Understanding mind might develop in the same fashion as understanding other representational systems such

as televisions. For example, with primary representation one simply perceives other's actions. With secondary representations these actions can be interpreted in terms of what the person wants, intends, or pretends. Only with metarepresentation, however, can one appreciate that these mental states are *just* representations. One can simultaneously entertain somebody else's beliefs and evaluate them as true or false, and wonder whether the other wants to deceive or how one could change his or her mind.

Extending the self-conscious ability to contemplate our own mind's activity to the contemplation of another's, including their emotional state, is a result of interactions between human nature and the culture's strong traction (Jensen, 2012). Both are aided by the guidance of a complex and nimble mind, exercised largely through linguistic activity and stimulated by humanity's high degree of sociality. The advantages of this capacity in gauging the thought of others are numerous, foremost among them the reasoned predictability of their behavior by inferring their emotion, feelings and intentions.

These mindreading capacities are fundamental in determining the trustworthiness of others, and when supported by prior experience they contribute to the high degree of human sociality that is essential to both successful cooperation and our shared morality. Moreover, the combination of Theory of Mind capacities and our concept of human nature adds considerable support to the idea of a "social mind." With the commencement of a societal sense of modernity, which the eighteenth-century Western culture introduced, social change became quite noticeable, even well within the parameters of a single lifetime, only to speed by ever more quickly as the decades rolled on. In very recent times, nearly all aspects of our social environment have been evolving with such apparent velocity that the world has become almost a foreign place for many, thereby stimulating a still more intense self-consciousness and, perhaps, anger. It is hardly surprising, then, that the natural response is to withdraw into oneself with the purpose of reconnoitering and reassessing through careful contemplation of others' viewpoints, desires, fears and intentions to better understand our own. Theory of Mind, and similar capacities not yet fully verified, may account for our underlying attention to the species' well-being (Gazzaniga, 2005), for it is foundational to human cooperation in decision-making. Self-understanding is the basis for understanding others, so if we hold certain beliefs, understandings, intentions, questions, emotions and feelings, we also know that others most likely do too, just as we know they can similarly think about us. The capacity to understand others' intentions without exchanging a word or gesture holds advantages for complex cooperation and for simply getting along civilly, if not congenially, in an increasingly complicated society. In this regard, James R. Hurford (2007, p. 8) observes another human distinction, "Humans can no doubt introspectively distinguish between a great variety of mental states which bear on situations in the world. For non-humans, there is only evidence of a relatively crudely carved-up space of possible intentional mental states, and these can perhaps be classified along a very small number of dimensions." The full range of reflection, rationality, emotion, feelings, and morality—in short, subjectivity—constitutes the distinctiveness that uniquely enables humanity to enhance and extend potential, as both individuals and societies. Yet, as significant as they may be, subjectivity and the introspection that reveals its value consume time in a culture that has evolved to prefer immediate compensation of some kind for its expenditure of that ever-more rare commodity, time—or to stifle it when possible.

Human subjectivity is a highly significant dimension of the knowledge foundation for decisions because it is, foremost, significantly human. David Gelernter (2016, p. 9) emphasizes, that "Mental life *is* irreducibly subjective." *Homo sapiens*' strong subjectivity long ago set humanity on an evolutionary course different from that of any other known species, a course so productive of options that it is impossible to imagine how, in its absence, we could ever have become so different from other mammals. The next chapter explores the industrial environment's influence on the human mental capacities just discussed, and this mixture's influence on our evolution.

3

Knowledge and Industry in Evolution

> Knowledge *is* instrumental: it puts us into a different relationship with the world.
> —*Louis Menand, 2010*
>
> One cannot defend production as satisfying wants if that production creates the wants.
> —*John Kenneth Galbraith, 1978*

Industry: The West's Cultural Model

A half millennium ago, Western industry introduced to the world a new kind of employment, structured by regular work hours and compensated by predictable income. Concurrent with its early development were related signs of astounding scientific and technological progress, and as both phenomena are absolutely dependent upon knowledge, they also projected a high social profile. The industrial approach to life's general condition of scarcity soon produced a greater abundance of commodities and other products than preceding generations had experienced or could have imagined, so industry revealed opportunities for a new kind of life. In this liberated social environment, money quickly became the predominant facilitator of material exchange and cultural change, elevating its status among all other means of cultural identification. Money eventually rendered commodification applicable to more than just inanimate physical objects, for it complemented the near limitless potential industry increasingly was perceived to wield. A new reality bolstered the modern spirit sufficiently to create a consumer society, discussed below in this chapter.

The Cultural Context

To the extent that a society is self-aware it fosters the norms constituting its identity, which is its culture. But because cultural change depends on

3. Knowledge and Industry in Evolution

the introduction of novelty into the scheme of social life, the prime position among the forces for Western cultural evolution since industry's beginning has been occupied by the innovation, development, and expansion that most exemplify change. Historian Jeremy Black (2014, pp. 115–116) succinctly states the Western connections among religion, science and industry creditable for generating the new environment:

> The belief that man could come to understand much about himself, the world and God through his own reason and empirical investigation played a major role in the Scientific Revolution.... The greater understanding of physical laws was to be important in a manufacturing system that benefited from enhanced ways of using objects, notably by pushing, lifting or rotating them. Innovation was revealed as possible and controllable.

Where manufacturing was established, factories employed increasing numbers of individuals from diverse ethnic, cultural, and linguistic backgrounds, and in this relatively sudden and newly-imposed human mix, individuals had to determine how to get along together, at least while at work. Often encouraged by common condition and circumstance, many shared their knowledge, values, perspectives, feelings and reasoning.

It may be anachronistic today to refer to a middle economic class since it is more likely that four or more classes exist in the West, but owing to industry's expanded mass production and society's rapidly-mounting mass consumption, a true middle class began to emerge and flourish for several centuries. In eighteenth-century England, for example, much debate centered on theories of class consumption (Gilboy, 1967), the lower classes no longer lamenting their bleak and static position in society, and factory workers able to rise to managerial and ownership levels. The traditional distinctions of royalty, aristocracy, and peasantry were beginning to fade, and toward the close of that century, the introduction of new enterprises and the expansion of former ones had grown sufficiently numerous and rapidly-developing that social and economic conditions began to destabilize. Driving the population's consumption was the need to individuate culturally in a liberal range of almost every sort of material entity, but above all, anything commodifiable. By creating demand via its increasingly important marketing dimension, industry had begun to establish a symbiosis of production and consumption to ensure its future expansion; in this essay it is referred to as the production/consumption system.

A consequence of industry's development, which was astonishing in its speed and means, the general population could create its life as individuals according to a new worldview that indicated a major social change philosopher Michael Ruse and biologist Edward O. Wilson (2009, p. 370) explain:

> In a phrase, societies feel their way across the fields of culture with a rough biological map. Enduring codes are not created whole from absolute premises but inductively, in

the manner of common law, with the aid of repeated experience, by emotion and consensus, through an expansion of knowledge and experience guided by the epigenetic rules of mental development, during which peoples sift the options and come to agree upon and to legitimate certain norms and directions.

Industry had brought to the West a level of economic stability previously unknown on such a large scale, while also providing the general population a new way to perceive its world through a new epistemology founded on reason and proof, rather than religious faith or deference to aristocracy. Owing to this new fact of life and its trust in the value of theory derived from rigorous observation and logical thought, the planning of one's future became a pragmatic and productive effort rather than the idle dreaming it long had been. One could reasonably engage in strategic personal planning by acquiring appropriate knowledge, and sometimes by creating it. In virtually all occupations of their day, people began to work more frequently with technologies, whose power and efficiency also had been little known before, and to work in situations where enthusiasm for the application of new techniques and principles could spread beyond the workplace to otherwise unrelated settings. The West was becoming a world of knowledge in action.

Knowledge

The discovery, creation and transmission of knowledge dominate cultural evolution, for knowledge is the basis of meaning. The concept of knowledge includes information, specifically discussed below. Knowledge can be either objective, which we learn from experience and others, so it varies considerably among random individuals, or subjective, which is generated internally and includes primarily information inherited genetically as feelings, experienced by all normal people. Modernity means possessing and employing modern knowledge. Knowledge is subjective because it operates within a human mind, where it remains indefinitely while undergoing processes of refinement and combination with new objective information. Since it would be unrealistically impractical, and most likely impossible, for any individual to validate the detail of all the information encountered every day, we ordinarily proceed by tentatively accepting the assessment of trusted associates. This simple and common epistemology exemplifies the theory that knowledge is socially constructed (Berger & Luckmann, 1966), and it is, as discussed later, a crude adaptation of the much more carefully controlled epistemology developed in the natural sciences. Despite human skepticism and curiosity, therefore, we necessarily tend to accept information as valid if it seems well-founded, is logical and makes sense in the context of our extant knowledge. We do this *necessarily* because it is the only practical way to proceed through life, for by acting otherwise we would soon lose the self-confidence to attempt any decision at all. Thus, we most often are motivated to accept knowledge on a variable level of faith in humanity as our epistemology.[1] Throughout modernity, sources of information became ever easier to generate, and eventually so abundant, accessible and manipulable, that its image now commonly embraces the entire continuum of the knowledge concept, which can generate confusion. Jeremy Black (2014, p. 408), for example, finds "The idea that biology itself is an information system with genes as key players, not least because they encode past information, most notably as the relationship between organism and environment, is a potent instance of the range of application of the use of the term and concept information, and the related porosity of other disciplines." But when information leading directly to action began to overshadow the significance of human understanding, the value of our human context diminished in the public mind, subjective qualities were more easily ignored, and the human effort of thought was devalued. The public at large seemed to value information more than knowledge; we were trading away our most fundamentally human values.

Cultural Evolution

The discovery and social communication of knowledge dominate culture's evolution because knowledge is the basis of meaning, the premise of communication, and the fuel for further thought in valuation and speculation. Although usually portrayed as a positive phenomenon in and of itself, knowledge can be used for good or evil, while its absence leaves a gulf of ambiguity and, by definition, ignorance.[2] No consciously intended social action occurs in the absence of knowledge, which tends toward greater complexity as it expands, for new knowledge alters extant knowledge whether by adding to it, detracting from it, or suggesting a new perspective on it or insight into it. The first and probably most enduring influence on human knowledge is conveyed biologically in the form of information transferred genetically prior to birth, primarily as emotion and feelings (M. Lieberman, 2013; Gazzaniga, 2011; de Waal, 1996), but it is eclipsed rapidly by the ongoing flurry of increasingly required objective knowledge.

Extending from data and information to understanding, the knowledge continuum has the capacity for both analysis and synthesis, while knowledge is at once product and producer of sociality and social change (Berger & Luckmann, 1966). Knowledge is the product of learning, the process of new knowledge making connections with extant knowledge in a cognitive advance toward the uniquely human ideal of understanding. This scenario can be conceptualized as a continuum whose extent is indefinite because knowledge always is subject to enhancement, correction, and rejection. Essential to individual human development and cultural evolution, developmental and cultural psychologist Lev S. Vigotsky (1962, p. 125) describes the connection between new and extant knowledge:

> [P]arcels of knowledge derive from experience of one kind or another, and because they are but constituents of greater knowledge, knowledge is always incomplete, so it is also expandable as it incorporates more of the phenomena to which it is connected. What humanity does is perceive and discover the connections. Completeness, wholeness, and oneness are the ideals of the knowledge toward which humanity strives.

Information

Information is the elemental aspect of the knowledge continuum.[3] It flows from our social and physical environments through the body's senses and nervous system to the brain, which orchestrates many connections with our extant knowledge and often requires the greater concentration of memory and imagination found in introspection. Though evolved from medieval Latin to English, the word "information" gained extraordinary popularity in the last three or four decades of the twentieth century because of its importance to industrial and commercial interests. Frequent and ubiquitous usage of the word *information* is itself a noteworthy phenomenon, competing with the word *knowledge* in quotidian usage during the twentieth century's final decades, nearly replacing it, the relevant literature having grown remarkably. Furthermore, in reference to the current abundance of knowledge and information sources, social anthropologist Thomas Hylland Eriksen (2001, p. 149) agrees with many others in his theory that proposes, "When there is a surplus, and no scarcity, of information, the degree of comprehension falls in proportion with the growth in amount of information." His theory suggests that at some point, information's growth (knowledge as product) may *hinder* thought (knowledge as process) more than stimulate it. One indication of this complicating perception is the much greater accumulation of the technologically-generated information product, whose ubiquity and therefore requisite management draw attention to information's importance, even when it may otherwise lack significance. But the present culture reflects more than a greater public awareness of information, as this awareness leads to a deeper transformation in the societal conceptualization of knowledge. Testifying to this perception is the unprecedented variety of commodities and commodifiables delivered since the Second World War by innovative production technologies, prompting the West's refocus of admiration away from the intellectual potential of knowledge (human capital) and toward our increasingly materialist culture's technological potential, a change that distances humanity from nature.

3. Knowledge and Industry in Evolution

The Price of Progress

In orchestrating this dynamic economy, industry also began designing an equally dynamic and complex culture, identifiable pre-eminently as diverse but concentrated on the then newly popular idea of social progress. Technological and economic capacity expanded quite noticeably in this transition, while moral considerations and self-control slipped from view. Similar negative effects continue today, even damaging personal human health in the latter twentieth century and early twenty-first, as evolutionary biologist Brandon Hidaka (2012, pp. 210–211) describes:

> Accumulating evidence indicates that the social environment in modern-industrialized countries, especially in the United States, has become increasingly competitive, threatening, and socially isolating.... By appealing to evolutionary proclivities, like a desire for energy-dense food and status competition, the economic and marketing forces of modern society have engineered an environment promoting decisions that maximize consumption at the long-term cost of well-being. In effect, humans have dragged a body with a long hominid history into an overfed, malnourished, sedentary, sunlight-deficient, sleep-deprived, competitive, inequitable, and socially-isolating environment with dire consequences.

Not that most of the Western population is isolated. But as the urban populations grew denser and communication technologies became ubiquitous, a common feature of contemporary life soon was its sense of loneliness, which also bears implications for physical health. Daniel Goleman (2006, p. 239) reports, for example, that "the lonelier a person feels, the poorer immune and cardiovascular function tends to be." Human beings do constitute a highly social species.

Moreover, although industry has infused into Western society an astonishing array of commodity options, the economy it has fashioned in concert with an expanding democratic polity now incurs social costs that exceed money's potential for solution by ignoring human values and dismissing the very meaning of humanity. Political economist Robert Reich (2007, p. 163) at least partially explains this situation in his observation that,

> Our voices as citizens—as opposed to our voices as consumers and investors—are being drowned out. We may even be losing confidence that what we have to say as citizens is important. This is not because big corporations have conspired to drown out or marginalize our citizen voices but chiefly because corporations are engaged in escalating competition for political outcomes that advantage them over their rivals.

In matters of industrial health, of course, the vote of an average CEO or board chairman greatly outweighs the votes of a multitude of putative average or ordinary citizens.

Modernized Knowledge

The industrial revolution had been well under way in the eighteenth century, when commodification began to influence the spirituality and intellectuality previously not believed amenable to it. But as market expansion depends upon greater demand, industry also was stimulating consumer desire and activity. Greater profit could be gained and the market itself expanded, by selling in higher quantities at lower unit prices (Shammas, 1990), which contributed to a new-found sense of security and thus a new kind of societal happiness. Such is the logic of the contemporary "consumer society," sketched below in this chapter.

Except for times of war, natural disaster or major technological change, the established pattern of human knowledge growth in the West had reflected a consistent, gradual accumulation until the twentieth century, when historian Carl L. Becker discerned an innovative turn. Becker (1936, p. 93) saw that a major change was intended by "a new class of learned men ... whose function is to increase rather than to preserve knowledge, to undermine rather than to stabilize custom and social authority." In this vision, new knowledge no longer simply contributed to its accumulation in the continuous refinement and clarification for advance toward better understanding. Instead, knowledge accumulation was achieving greater value in its support of theory. As the utilization of new knowledge increasingly was intended to contribute to discovering new means of social power and control, as well as new uses for existing technology, knowledge became a tool for accelerating any immediately useful production process. Several decades later, sociologist Daniel Bell (1973 p. 20) clarified the nature of this change:

> Now, knowledge has of course been necessary in the functioning of any society. What is distinctive about the post-industrial society is the change in the character of knowledge itself. What has become decisive for the organization of decisions and the direction of change is the centrality of *theoretical* knowledge—the primacy of theory over empiricism and the codification of knowledge into abstract systems of symbols that... can be used to illuminate many different and varied areas of experience. Every modern society now lives by innovation and the social control of change, and tries to anticipate the future in order to plan it.[4]

Effects of Modernized Knowledge

With industry's division of labor came the systemic development of a knowledge cadre recognized as the technical experts in all fields. Their ranks swelled at the end of the twentieth century in a wave of digital communication and information technology experts quickly populating virtually all industries. Accordingly, political scientist Frank Fischer (2009, p. 297) observes, "In the 'knowledge society,' where professional experts move to the center of the policymaking processes, the political role of expert discourses becomes increasingly evident." Depending on need, they are largely experts in the technical aspects of economics or technology. But they are at least equally expert in the mounting of an irrefutably rational and compelling case, which they do when industry or government engages their services to meet with the public in finalizing a decision or plan that eventually touches many human lives. This procedure is regimented in the circumscribed terms of the economic and/or technological system whose representatives staunchly refrain from addressing considerations other than the material ones. Concerns for the quality of life relative to its increasingly altered technical functions are destined to hold little or no sway in the project's decisions, for corporate interests are focused on confirming functionality and fiscal implication. Industry and culture are collaborators up to the point of industry's continued capacity to produce, sell and expand, and the culture's continued capacity to satisfy its own psychological needs, nothing else warranting space on the industrial agenda. Economist Friedrich A. von Hayek's (1979, p. 166) interpretation of the concept of tradition suggests his perspective on this eventuality:

> It is not society with a given structure that creates the rules appropriate to it, but the rules which have been practised by a few and then imitated by many which created a social order of a particular kind. Tradition is not something constant but the product of a process of selection guided not by reason but by success. It changes but can rarely be deliberately changed. Cultural selection is not a rational process; it is not guided by but it creates reason.

Monetary gain—like nothing else—justifies whatever steps need be taken to ensure full realization of the corporate or state agenda. For the Western culture of the past few centuries, therefore, material and technical terms have defined both rationality and success: proof of both are recognizable in technological development, industrial expansion, economic growth, and specific goal achievement. The close relationship between economy and culture in the kind of evolutionary process Hayek outlines is not difficult to comprehend.

To maintain its competitive edge, capitalist industry must forever change, which it does by expanding its share of the market and moving into new populations to increase the market's size and economic potential, while also managing to achieve efficiencies and profit primarily through continuous technological innovation. Reflecting this industrial strategy, the current culture is motivated increasingly to find novelty by distinguishing itself, individually and collectively, but above all by remaining *au courant*, as illustrated in the early decades of the twenty-first century by the universal popularity of mobile communication and information technologies. Through the mental transformation of ideas and people into physical objects and their treatment as such, commodification leads to market expansion and cultural diversification. These signs of large-scale change are accompanied predictably by considerable public attention, which has long been a key industrial incentive. But Daniel Bell (1975, p. 54) describes another generalized cultural change affecting the economy more directly:

> What men now want begins to affect the levels of production and to dictate the different kinds of items to be produced. It is this change from supply to demand which, in the intellectual sphere, that creates modern economics. In the social world, it creates an entirely new attitude towards the world, wealth, and happiness; the three become defined by the sharp rise in the standard of living of the masses of men in the world.

These developments have managed to position industry at the foreground of Western cultural evolution, its evident influence flowing from industry's early association with science. Constituting a new synergy, this association demonstrates the potential of knowledge discovery and creation by "ordinary" people who choose to make the effort and seize the opportunity. The insight has proved powerful and widely popular, and means that epistemic authority can reside within those who belong to neither the aristocracy nor the church, that all paths to epistemic authority have become accessible and that anyone has the potential to lay claim to knowledge. Consequently, inventions and other manifestations of this newly-understood authority status have grown more numerous and are scattered more broadly. Noteworthy is the conditioning for social acceptance of a new environment with greater complexity, which requires an evolved psychology (Richerson & Boyd, 2005), for individual psychology changes worldview when a new desire or fear dominates the majority population's daily thought. The economy became a new focus of common social attention, a humanly designed and constructed entity wielding unprecedented influence over human life.

The new value assigned to knowledge signals an aberration from its established connotation. The social phenomenon we now call "industry" was new on planet Earth and just beginning to reveal its unrivaled potential, for such a powerful and coordinated human influence never before had been witnessed, its leadership managing to effect change more sweeping and profound than any monarch or religious leader of earlier times could possibly have achieved. Occupying influential positions situated primarily throughout the West, a relatively small number of individuals determined to advance their economic interests and social influence via industrial success and control. Jeremy Black (2014, p. 263) is more specific about the influence of theory in the nineteenth century, writing, "The prestige of science, and the conviction that research should, could and would yield valuable insights, encouraged professionalism, the development of academic structures and culture, and the belief that science should receive special support and respect. Prestige was linked to the supporting interaction of experimentation and theory." Clearly, this marked a cultural turn because it changed the way we think.

The Economy: Everybody's Business

By providing the ambience for a culturally transforming merger of consumption and technological development, the nascent industrial revolution has been the most significant, visible, and dramatic motivator in spreading the West's acute awareness of modern times. Furthermore, accompanying the early wave of scientific discovery during the fifteenth and sixteenth centuries was a mathematical revolution that expedited technological development and solidified the foundation for modern science. "The essential role mathematics has played in causing scientific knowledge to separate from experience and culture is one and the same as that which transformed technological knowledge," writes mechanical engineer Willem H. Vanderburg (2005, p. 202). Accompanied by the influence of other social and cultural changes in the making, this objective stance has achieved authority over longer-term alterations of the Western conceptualization of knowledge and its use. Vanderburg (p. 204) explains, "Mathematics helps to create a scientific and technological approach to the world that separates itself from experience, thereby making it possible for modern science and technology to become universal." Unlike most if not all other material things, the value of money is sufficiently simple to convey meaning numerically; we certainly trust it. In a formal way, the removal of human qualities from the phenomenon of knowledge initiated the general sweeping trend toward quantification, discussed in Chapter 5.

While the system of monetary value and exchange became the organizing agent for the material dimension of social life, the economy began to represent the relative state of health among discrete and large populations, such as nations. The system includes activities ranging from corporate investment and share value, production, and marketing to shopping and cultural display, its growth or decline following recognizable patterns that add historical dimension to those belonging. Social philosopher E.M. Adams (1997, p. 129) concludes that the economy "became the engine of the society and, in time, the values and logic of the new economic system became the controlling values and modes of rationality of the whole social order." Industry, government and the general population established the economy, which first had become an entity to be modeled for study and theorization in late eighteenth-century England, particularly in association with economic theorists Adam Smith and David Ricardo.

Free Market, Commodification and Abundance

The free market concept may suggest varied meanings within the general population, but for the many non-economists among them the freedom of cultural choice is primary. By means of commodification, a mass societal diversity can accommodate tremendous possibility in its infinite range of cultural combinations, transient psychological needs, and the culture's continuous search for novelty. No longer does the concept of utility apply solely to physical materiality but also conveys a social statement with varied meanings: belonging to any culturally distinctive group is good in the consumer society, but better if it is highly exclusive, for one can individuate quite securely within a group bearing similar yet not identical characteristics differing from those of the mass, which can be accomplished most easily and certainly by material means. Precisely because humans are eminently complex social creatures, many if not most need to project an individual persona, a distinction the diversity of abundance in mass production facilitates. Much of the Western hemisphere governs itself by democratic means in a quasi regulated economic environment characterized as a free market. The market is an idea, a conceptualization of values and a portal to economic investment and exchange, all based on money. Its activity is dynamic throughout the current Western culture, which ascribes extraordinary significance to materiality and choice, and these cultural forces are globalizing.

Unceasing cultural stimulation fills each day with a material meaning realized most easily, quickly, rationally, and visibly in the purchase of commodities, as they are quantifiable and readily exchangeable on an objective monetary basis unaccountable for subjective human motivations. Mass production at affordable prices has made possible the liberal commodifiability of nonmaterial desiderata in a world of previously unknown abundance, a dazzling array of choice for the individual shopper who assigns the meaning necessary to the projection of individual or collective distinction. These decisions are related to social status and they dominate much of the Western mind, leaving little space, time, or energy for the contemplation of more universal and timeless matters. The complex social phenomenon known today simply as *the economy* is itself an amorphous and often mysterious entity designed to capture and hold public attention as it never could have prior to industrial development. Except during times of war, the mass population had not been such an active and significant part of national-level change (Shammas, 1990), which had been the business only of royalty and aristocracy. The economy is widely understood to be the key indicator of present and likely future outcomes for the quality of individual and societal life because news headlines, which are conveyed via any of the ubiquitous mass communications media at any moment of any day, unfailingly remind the general population of its responsibility as part of this amorphous juggernaut. Particularly in the West but increasingly elsewhere, most citizens know something about the economy or has some perception of it as a dynamic dimension of modern life commanding close attention, so the Western mind allots precious little opportunity to stray for very long. From an evolutionary perspective, Manfred Stanley (1978, p. 32) summarizes this cultural absorption:

> In the ideology of the market principle, the multigenerational "society" of shared authoritative and continuous traditions is replaced by an "economy" based on calculations of contemporary self-interest. Liberal freedom, at its root, stands for the principle of a fresh start for every individual. It promises liberation from the fate of the fathers and in this sense annihilates social time. In its place is substituted the breathless freedom of an eternal now.

A general knowledge of the economy is a continuous reminder of the citizen's own critical role in the system, for it is founded on a high level of production expansion expected to be matched by consumption. Each consumer is duly inspired to purchase more, just as the number of consumers also is expected to increase and its topography to expand. In this culture, experience is of little value to prediction, as the variables are so many and their relations still so little known, for they undergo continuous change. The economy can be gentle, friendly, and helpful at times but threatening and fiercely destructive at others, the latter behavior leaving a residue of deeply-felt devastation that flows into the culture's legends to mar the social image. For better or worse, everyone is part of the economy, each aware and wary of it, each possibly feeling some degree of credit or guilt, victory or victimization, according to the turns it takes.

An outstanding feature of the West's economy is its heavy dependence on cultural choice, for in industrialized societies it is largely through the often overwhelming presence of material things that the culture becomes more complex and aggressively competitive in its continuous prodding of industrial expansion. Cultural choice accounts for an unknowable but surely very substantial part of daily decision-making. Thus, the economy is a spiritual participant in all aspects of contemporary life in industrialized societies, where cultural evolution proceeds at an ever-faster pace because the economy is founded on industrial and technological development, whose *purpose* is to foster the change demanded by the culture. But Richard Sennett recalls the proverbial lesson that the act of thinking about economic matters supposedly saps the energy normally directed toward the government's activities, a lesson Sennett (2006, pp. 137–138) observes was revived in the industrial era by Marxist thought:

> Now, it was argued, the physical deprivations and soul-destroying rigors of factory labor focused workers simply on survival, leaving no mental room to re-imagine a different form of collective life. A revolutionary vanguard would have to do that thinking for them. The political imagination, that is, requires a certain measure of protection from economic experience. Today this classic, negative proposition has taken another turn, one that more concerns everyday life than theory, due to the meaning of consumption itself.... Today's economy strengthens this kind of self-consuming passion, both in shopping malls and in politics.

The present culture is a demanding dimension of the economy, while the economy more tightly weaves together the general culture's multivarious fabrics into a new kind of society, one that appears wholly dedicated to commodity consumption.

Significance of the Economy

A host society constructs and maintains the free market economy, but there can be little doubt that industry is the economy's principal navigator. Therefore, political scientist and historian Ellen Meiksins Wood (2003, p. 9) concludes that the economy has become "a fundamental condition of existence." As developed throughout the past half millennium, the current economy is a behemoth in its influence over virtually every aspect of human life, closely interlocking with the culture so that economic change usually requires deep cultural change. Comprising industry and its entire workforce, but also embracing the multitudes who now closely follow technological development as a cultural avocation, the economy satisfies some of the human needs formerly found in religion. It is a source of belief and hope, awe and fear for the population at large, whose common ground for communication is the market, which provides "the only media in which dialogue on a public scale can take place: no idea can reach or change moderns unless it can be marketed and sold to them," as political scientist and philosopher Marshall Berman (1999, p. 135) characterizes the economy. Commodities, therefore, often replace friendships, family, and communal activity (Leiss, 1976), and the market maintains a persuasive and well amplified voice in the industrial advertising that saturates mass commercial media and social media via the internet. In this market-driven democratic culture of widespread abundance and choice, the competition for attention and time has forced out those values whose connection with materiality may be negligible. It is a cultural feature that results in the disconnection among individuals and groups and the general decline of socialization, a cultural turn that creates time/space for more technical (work-associated) knowledge.[5]

Modernity evolves erratically but according to the social environment's vicissitudes. Modernity is the preferred Western state of being, and the only way to achieve it is through cultural change, of paramount significance to industry's advance because change stimulates demand for the production of innovative commodities and styles and the provision of new services, demand being essential to the economics of continued industrial expansion. Both individually and socially, choice is craved but also afforded by a very large and growing segment of a society whose need for more of almost anything grows stronger, the most desirable being the latest version of whatever may be on the market. A superflow of change realizes individual and societal motivation and constitutes a conscious opposition to the concept of durability, once a critical consideration but today associated most often with tradition, and therefore is connoted negatively. Social change is the perfect complement to industrial motivation, while novelty is the consequential foundation for this cultural mélange, novelty alone offering a sufficiently broad scope to accommodate the qualifying distinctions among individuals and groups. The idea of social change became a favored topic of discussion in the early days of modernity. "Thus, the understanding and analysis of public opinion were to be linked to information about social structure," says Jeremy Black (2014, p. 302), "with the latter treated as dynamic, which entailed additional requirements for information, namely about the extent, rate and causes of change." With an increasingly rapid transience of interests, commodities and cultural events, it is not surprising that the whole society experiences life's acceleration both individually and collectively, for it disjoins the population from associates whose differences may not be generational but are distinguishable on other cultural bases. A frantic psychology dominates most individuals who do not necessarily perceive themselves this way, as the combined sense of speed and complexity is beyond their understanding and control. Referring to this seemingly regimented industrial setting, sociologist and philosopher Gilles Lipovetsky (2005, p. 50) finds further consequences of the direct connection between industry and the general population. He writes, "There are ever more demands for short-term results, and an insistence on doing more in the shortest possible time and acting without delay: the race for profits leads to the urgent being prioritized over the important, immediate action over reflection, the accessory over the essential." Change is the one reliable constant of modern Western life, new decisions at once the most reliable product of change and its initiator.

Technology for a Change

A fascination with technology and an almost unwavering belief in its magical powers are among the most evident characteristics of contemporary Western culture, which just within the past four or five decades has evolved from the merger of rampant capitalist industry and technological systems development to become the economic and cultural platform for a new wave of globalization. The rapidity with which this social phenomenon has occupied center stage is owed to human decisions, of course, but these actions could not have been successful without the drive of technological development at each step along the way. Daniel Bell (1975, pp. 235–236) summarizes the basic facts behind the widespread Western dependence upon technology, writing, "The crowd, which always worships success, is quite naturally enthusiastic about those spheres of thought where our greatest achievements have been won, the more so as they are so easy of appreciation." But technology's social influence has penetrated much deeper than this single statement suggests because, in its realization of the ideal of human action, technology has become the first impulse in response to virtually any problem, challenge, or opportunity. Change is what this culture seeks, and technology's purpose is to set it in motion. "[N]ew technology and techniques transformed culture and society across the world, and created an understanding of the modern based on an expectation of the new," writes Jeremy Black (2014, p. 339). "Appreciating the new thus became an important aspect of information, as well as a key way by which it was presented for purposes of affirming national and sectional success, whether in totalitarian or democratic regimes."

No single cause has led to the various directions chosen by Western culture, its present status often referred to generally as the "consumer society." But the technology bias since modern industry's inception has played a major role most obviously since the strategic joining of commercial and engineering forces. As management and engineering have become a joint profession spread through enterprises of all sorts (Burnham, 1941), engineering authorities make decisions directly affecting millions of lives, which they are expected to do, but with greater frequency and closer alignment to technical values than human values. Moreover, like many other industrial features, it is the overpowering desire for money—unlike anything else—that now dominates the general culture.

Technology's Influence

The mutual dependence of technology and industry is straightforward: advances in science and technological development are expensive and their financing often unpredictable, so they are dependent on industrial development for adequate funding. Conversely, industry is highly dependent on science and technology for the creation of its new products and the implementation of their more efficient production and timely delivery. The economy's fate hangs logically and largely on industry's health, so when industry first became linked inextricably to capitalist strategy and spirit, technological development elevated the modern Western economy to the daunting prominence it maintains today. Technology creates change and change generates decisions, in turn stimulating industry, the culture and further technological development, which evidently is as boundless as the human imagination. Cognitive scientist Philip Lieberman (2013, p. 152) emphasizes the close connections of technological and cultural evolution, writing, "Imitation complements innovation, pushing forward the pace of human culture and technology. It is always the case that some few are creative innovators—the vast majority imitate, whether it is a matter of jeans or a different view of the nature of the universe, or a better way of gathering food. Neanderthals seemed to be nonimitators." Technology continuously enables us to perceive, utilize and evaluate time differently, opening our horizons to a modified and often completely different worldview. And in this accelerating process we become more acutely aware of technological development and internalize it, experiencing it as it occurs because technology alters our established patterns and very quickly can be used as a basis for cultural competition. We no longer need to consult history to discover that the world and all of us have changed, since the difference unfolds before our eyes. In retrospect, for example, although the past five centuries of Western industrial and economic activity exhibit a pattern of technological development leading to the economic systems development that continues today, accelerated, it also exhibits one remarkable difference: whereas centuries used to pass before major societal change could become widely evident, in recent decades that effect is witnessed as an actuality. In today's economy, the flow of innovative digital information technologies and networks supports industry's globalization within a general movement toward corporate merger. These mergers greatly facilitate the establishment of new and relatively unregulated markets with accumulated capital, which also gives them the capacity to mix their transmission of business information and marketing tools with cultural products. But their single most significant collective product is consumer choice, recognizable as modernity.

Evidence that many artifacts are invented as tools with the purpose of accomplishing tasks faster and easier is perceptible among other primates, as well as the earliest *Homo sapiens* (Boyd, Richerson & Henrich, 2005), so it is no surprise that technology, a cultural artifact that enhances and extends human capacity, exerts considerable influence over our worldview and aspirations, individually and societally. Its diminishing size, weight, and energy requirement greatly belies the power, capacity, and dense complexity of the digitization most technologies now conceal, and their design reflects sufficient ingenuity to capture the imagination, which is triggered by a broad range of perspectives that ultimately encourage cultural evolution. By the middle of the eighteenth century—the generally-acknowledged awakening of the modern period—it had become evident to contemporary observers that the rapid introduction of innovative technologies was bordering on revolution, no longer just evolution. The fact that in the final two decades of the eighteenth century more patents were issued in Great Britain than had been in all the rest of that century (Adas, 1989) proved what people felt. Technology's prominence in Western culture is among modernity's most outstanding indicators, and as technology both results from and stimulates further innovation, the fast pace of technological innovation leading to broader cultural change has continued unabated in the past two centuries (Chandler & Cortada, 2000), exhibiting further extraordinary acceleration in the current digital era. The more profound consequence of our human fascination with technology, which has been evident since *Homo sapiens* first appeared, is that technology's exponential growth commensurately matches resource depletion and population growth (Dilworth, 2010). Formulated in just the right proportions, the mixture of economy, industry, technology and psychology has produced the current Western culture.

When industry began infusing consistently more powerful and complex technologies into the lives of the ever-increasing number of workers, these mass segments of the working population had to be conditioned to perceive and accept them as part of their new order and integral to the larger, enveloping social norms; this was and is a conscious decision. Thus, professional management had become another new dimension of the work protocol when introducing new strategies, principles, and values to the workers, who then repeatedly witnessed their (usually) successful applications. They were socialized to begin understanding that their purpose in life was simply to work, and that life's guiding principle is accomplishment. This meant the exclusion of emotion, feelings, and morality from the industrial setting, where sentiment was held in low esteem as a distraction from accomplishment and therefore discounted from significant decisions. Lives also began to change outside the workplace, which had become the source of new perceptions and ways to act, so they were disseminated through the varied layers of social circles, eventually to a degree that profoundly altered the culture. Social change for the sake of change had become the demanding cultural goal.

Capitalism: The West's Spirit

In eighteenth-century England, renowned codifier of capitalism and founder of modern economics Adam Smith (1723–1790) reasoned that financial stability could best be achieved in a market protected against state intervention. Referring to modern Western humanity as "economic man," such a population would make rational, informed economic decisions derived from self-interest, their decisions eventually accumulating to benefit the whole society as though managed by an "invisible hand." Thus, in a competitive environment, and with the passage of sufficient time, human nature would regulate these decisions and cause the market to result in a positive outcome for the entire society. So far, however, history provides a dearth of examples of occasions when everyone managed to emerge a winner in the mass free market, as well as a plethora of instances when the public suffered quite serious financial difficulties, with many families losing their homes and some large industrial enterprises closing in bankruptcy. Market and economic stability simply are not similar to human stability.

Subject to emotion, feelings and other forces beyond the control of this otherwise perfect system, we humans are not always rational about our decisions in the market, or anywhere else (Kenrick and Griskevicius, 2013; Gazzaniga, 2011; Johnson-Laird, 2006). When we do prove to be rational, however, we are culturally drawn to employ the extremely narrowed version of reason conforming to industrial values and principles, which often are taken as the models of rationality to be followed in the critical human acts of decision. Nonetheless, there remains in the West an even louder and clearer voice for the capitalist free market, as it spreads its seductive message through the synergized economic and cultural globalization.[6] Industry quite necessarily is managed to achieve specific objectives, society is not. Moreover, unlike networks of earlier capitalist eras, today's networks around the globe are extraordinarily powerful and flexible, joined in their increasing capacity to accommodate versatile, culturally-oriented genres of communication while also exploiting their potential to extend reach in defiance of the more conventional confines of space and time.

Strategy and Spirit

Capitalism's strategy and spirit manage the present Western economy, for it is the commanding force in virtually all aspects of life (Hochschild, 2003; E.M. Wood, 2003), and has been especially successful in establishing a much more significant linkage between production and consumption than could ever before have existed. E.M. Adams observes (1997, p. 127) that "the capitalist system is the embodiment of modern materialism." Through both a tightening of production processes, which persistently are made more efficiently effective, and the strategic innovation of marketing prowess, the capitalist strategy and spirit broaden industry's scope in targeting the population's growing mass rather than its wealthiest segment alone. Industry generates sufficient profit to stimulate flexibility in the market as a means of accommodating the expansion needed to maximize market share, even as it expands the market itself. Economic historian R.M. Hartwell (1967, p. 30) finds that the Industrial Revolution was triggered in eighteenth-century England when supply no longer could meet demand without a "technological breakthrough." By fanning the fires of consumption, industrial advertising and related marketing programs are able to instill and maintain a constant pressure on modernity's cultural competition via the tremendous variety of communications media saturating the social environment. These efforts have converted the consumer mass to its willing partnership in the total economic/cultural enterprise, but sociologists Robert R. Alford and Roger Friedland (1985, p. 427) take a slightly different perspective on this conclusion:

> The population was symbolically integrated by the emerging rights of citizenship, which established a form of universal equality—the adult franchise—as a substitute for the economic equality denied by capitalism.... Autonomy allowed interest groups to capture particular pieces of public authority and others to compete with them. Both state and capital were therefore insulated from the full impact of mass democratic participation.

Since a great proportion of the consuming population is employed in production and service industries, the public supposedly has the income for seriously considering cultural choice among the products for sale and availing themselves of the services, but only if the retailer remains competitive and continues to expand. Though not often discussed publicly, this set of mutual dependencies has become a necessary and carefully orchestrated symbiosis of production and consumption in which everyone can win, at least theoretically.

The mass consumption of commodities and anything judged commodifiable provides capitalism's sustenance, and the consumer psychology constitutes a special kind of power for both individual and society. Functioning at the pivotal point of social relations in this dynamic material world, commodities dominate life in the West and constitute the material aspect of a culture that vividly reflects the continuous change through which individual and society concurrently experience and witness life. The world of things never disappears but always expands to suggest new comparisons, perspectives, interpretations, uses, and understandings. And because the process is pragmatic, the material view predominates as the perfectly rational springboard for action. Western culture and economy have readily united, segmenting the market less by traditional classes and more by age and personal interest, so the symbiotic connectedness of industry and culture presents the perfect rationalization for materiality. Economic historian Elizabeth Waterman Gilboy (1967, p. 137) observes, "Whereas in the early stages of the Industrial Revolution demand was, if anything, in the van of production, today the reverse is true. Over-expanded industries resort to high-pressure salesmanship of the most farfetched nature in order to increase a demand already existent, or to arouse it where there is none." It is the standard operating procedure, and having grown thoroughly accustomed to this arrangement, the West now depends upon it. Much as a forest fire thrives on its consumption of contingent combustibles and then must rage into new territory, so does the relationship between industry and its consuming society. Called globalization, the strategy has a long reach but is not infinite.

The Consumer Society

The consumer society is a product of capitalist strategy and spirit. It can be portrayed as a materialist outlook assumed and acted upon by nearly the entire culture, and although it may appear superficial, the consumer society's impression on an individual's underlying worldview is profound.[7] "The success of the free-market system," writes E.M. Adams (1997, p. 131), "depends on converting human beings into economic beings—individual rational self-interest maximizers who try to get the most for the least." In the Western hemisphere of the twentieth- and twenty-first century, material motivation is rewarded by production in abundance. Therefore, production conveys a tenaciously pragmatic worldview that ensures the inclination to make full use of the culture in fashioning one's goal of individuation, whether personally or in association with a distinctive group. This is the rational attitude. One could well refer to Western society from the last quarter of the twentieth century to the present as the age of abundance and access, its condition for human life the opposite of scarcity and limitation, which has been the reality of life for many societies and remains the subject of study and social criticism in its long history as an example of conditions to be avoided. Social theorist Daniel M. Fox (1967, p. 44) further observes that,

> As industrialization increased the rate of economic growth of Europe and the United States in the nineteenth century, economists shifted their attention from the problems of production to those of the distribution and consumption of wealth. Although this changing emphasis in economic thought reflected the changing environment of Western man, most economists clung to the assumption that scarcity was the normal condition of life.

Finding this attitude prevalent through the middle of the twentieth century, Fox (p. 171) writes that "it seemed clear by the early 1950's that most men professionally concerned with social change were content to work within the existing order to make more efficient the social theorist distribution of the goods with which an age of abundance had begun to be established." In the production/consumption society of unprecedented abundance and access, advertising via a growing variety of media became a social branch of industry in its own right. It focuses on current events and provides the principal means for industry to gain control over the public, doing so increasingly by appealing more to base instincts than to elevated human ideals. Thus, the consumer society's evolving ethos is at once broader and deeper than it may at first glance appear.[8]

There can be little doubt that commodity consumption, practiced in the present as an ongoing open-house festival, offers the preponderance of the population a strong competition with organized religion. Attesting to this notion are the inadequately-concealed graveyards of no-longer-wanted vehicles, appliances, gadgets, their wrappings and containers and other destroyed or superannuated objects that symbolize the commonly-held negative attitude toward tradition, including not very old architectural structures, such as the vast shopping malls that formerly housed the commodity bazaars.

Mass Consumption

The term "mass consumption" has been in use since the early twentieth century, although "consumer society" appeared toward that century's close (Trentmann, 2006), and consumption's social noteworthiness first attracted attention in the second half of the nineteenth century. By the early twentieth, the commodity trash piles and junkyards were considered blights on the landscape (Mumford, 1950). But that was barely the beginning of what would become today's challenge, for very many among us routinely recycle only when there is money to be saved or earned immediately for doing so; ostentation sometimes can be secondary to pragmatism. Mass consumption has become the new tradition because this high level of buying is the absolute necessity for both industry and culture, and thus for the economy. Sociologist and social philosopher Edward Shils (1981, p. 287) explains these phenomena in terms of the cultural need of dynamism:

> One of the reasons why modern societies, especially in the West, have been damaging to substantive traditionality is that they have cultivated, in many forms, ideals which are, explicitly or implicitly, directly or indirectly, injurious to substantive tradition and which have become traditions in their turn. These ideals have been urged on rulers and in public opinion. Most of the ideals which have been held up as worthy of pursuit have been "dynamic" ideals. They are ideals which require active and deliberate movement away from substantive traditional patterns of belief and action. The dynamic ideals are not ideals of heroism; they are ideals which entail rationality in the application of abstract principles, and the thoroughgoing utilization of empirical knowledge for the attainment of ends still unrealized thus far in departures from traditional ways of seeing and doing things.

Industry designed and built the present Western culture to finance the expansion capitalist strategy and spirit require, but industrial expansion also is the undeniable result of a long, developing sequence in the care and feeding of individual and social decisions. In both cases, a new culture has emerged—as though spontaneously—from the carefully construed mixture of industrial strategies and principles, so its values soon spread throughout Western society and now are eastward bound.

Mass consumption is the sustenance of a capitalist society. It is enacted in shopping and buying things mass-produced to sustain a high level of production of the things most readily divested. Shopping arguably has become more significant in defining the culture than hunting and gathering had been prior to agriculture, some twelve thousand years ago, although now surely with much deeper, or at least more complex, psychological implications. Its complexity can be exhausting and frustrating. Aided by government privilege for industry, mass production and its requisite mass-consumption counterpart have transformed the Western culture, so consumer spending can proceed at a continued high level toward a future reward that most seem to believe is not forever beyond actual reach. It is our de facto ideal. Moreover, according to philosopher and communication scientist William Leiss and colleagues (2005, p. 295), "The profusion of media and commodity signs are understood to have become dominant structuring agents in society, and consumption an elaborate game of culture where the materiality and usefulness of goods has become secondary to their communicational aspects." In a world of abundance and access, cultural choice distinguishes one individual or group from others, often in the most subtle ways, with social status the driving force. Among nations, the annual economic report is the basis for comparison. Commodities are not intended to satisfy basic needs in the same sense as would have applied to our primitive forebears, but rather to satisfy— if only momentarily—the cultural and psychological desires of a more complex society comprising more complex individuals.

In this culture, the West finds its general abundance to be a different and more acceptable way to replace the former class structure, which had been controlled very little or not at all by the general population. But since the institution of industry, the West has breathed new life into its mass society, bolstering its underlying freedom with a sense of authority that may be unwarranted. Lifestyle has become an engaging feature of distinction, as the mass commitment to it indicates not only a sweeping acceptance of social change but as well a demand for it, accompanied by a commitment to personal change in values. Made possible by technologically-inspired production strategies and capitalist principles and spirit, a new importance has attached itself to materiality since early in modernity's evolution, eventually altering worldview, according to sociologist Leslie Sklair (1991, p. 41). He finds, "The culture-ideology of consumerism proclaims, literally, that the meaning of life is to be found in the things that we possess. To consume, therefore, is to be fully alive, and to remain fully alive we must continuously consume." Commodity consumption is essential to modern life because people make choices to identify their status as human beings (Kenrick & Griskevicius,

2013). Different in the present time is the magnitude and nature of the many minds dedicated to what can be considered cultural change, because the word "mass" in "mass consumption" includes those who actively engage in the dominant culture plus those who would like to but cannot afford to, as well as those who only follow the activity from a safe distance (Lury, 2011) but with a silent, obsessive fascination.

Mass consumption is the nearly unanimous cultural choice for this society. Also new within the long modern period is a developing societal desire to consume not just well beyond mere survival, but also beyond the former bounds of rationality. Through the public's compulsion for novelty it is co-opted to consume, which is an urge industry and its multifaceted ancillary forces have instilled with the intention of expanding the capitalist system forever, somehow, a plan they expect the consumer to continue implementing, somehow. And the consumer obliges not simply by following a narrowed gauge of reason, but also by inventing its reasons. Essential to consumer capacity in this regard is the phenomenon of commodification, writes cultural theorist John Frow (1997, p. 134), who justly contends, "The history of the capitalist mode of production is a history of the progressive extension of the commodity form to new spheres." Mass consumption means that virtually all members of a given society constitute the market, which is tied to mass production, each of its functions continuously stimulating the other, but in a kind of balance that so far has defied definition because it is understood to be boundless. The production/consumption system has jolted Western life out of balance, because by its nature, decision-making is stressful, while abundance transforms the culturally significant concept of choice "from a blessing into a burden," as Barry Schwartz (2004, p. 48) writes.

Cognition and Sociality

Let us take but a moment to ponder the significance of the preceding sketch of the Consumer Society as it may or may not accommodate the classic picture of humanity. Rational cognition is the mental effort often acclaimed the most distinguishing of human capacities and surely, no progress toward understanding is achievable without it. Whether or not other creatures possess all the cognitive features known to privilege humanity remains to be proved, but it is fairly evident that no other creatures either control or benefit from them to the same degree as humans (M. Lieberman, 2013; Kenrick & Griskevicius, 2013; Gazzaniga, 2008). The human mind is extraordinarily complex, networked, and orchestrated with considerable plasticity by the brain, which neuroscientist Michael S. Gazzaniga (2011, p. 61) explains is organized into "multiple dynamic mental systems."[9]

The human environment both stimulates cognition and is molded by it, our body being the point of contact with its environment. Louise Barrett (2011, p. 219), concludes about humans and all animals that "there is a true sense in which the real 'problem-solving machine' is not the brain alone, but the brain, the body, and the environmental structures that we use to augment, enhance and support internal cognitive processes." Observing that our perceptual system involves the entire nervous system, Barrett (p. 108) further notes that

> Perception is not "in" us and it doesn't happen "to" us; it is something in which we actively participate.... Transforming the optical array so as to perceive invariants is also the strongest way to make the case that perception is a function of the mutual organism-environment relationship and can't be considered as something internal to the organism: whatever 'cognition' is taking place, it is taking place not solely in the animal's head, but out in the world: action in the world can, justifiably, be considered to be just as "cognitive" as things that happen inside an animal's head.[10]

She concludes (p. 85), "The main thing a brain does, then—particularly a large one—is give an animal a degree of independence from circumstance: it allows the animal to operate in a manner that, while constrained by selection, cannot be traced in any direct way either to genes or to development." Tradition and learning assist in this process, and for reasons discussed throughout the rest of this essay, sociality is the vital ingredient in the creation, discovery and utility of human thought: the knowledge process. Again, knowledge fuels cultural evolution.

In conjunction with objective knowledge, the subjective information furnished by emotion, feelings, and morality are always involved in normal human thought processes. Thus, our purposeful diminishment of these social insights is hardly rational, foremost in decisions of high human impact. To be fully self-realizing among others, we humans require unqualified acknowledgment of our human mental context and capacity. "You cannot even be rude or unconventional unless you know what you are doing, and that means knowing what things count as," claims moral philosopher Mary Midgley (1978, p. 296), that is, understanding their context, meaning and value, and it is only through thought that we can hope to understand. Cognitive scientist Paul Thagard (2010, p. 94) is more specific, writing that "without emotion there would be no sense of what matters, and hence no wisdom."

Words, emotions and feelings are manifestations of information whose influence varies with the mixture. Words are the expressed elements of meaning, so information is articulated by human beings for the purpose of communication, modified to suit our relatively static physical environment and our dynamic social environment. Emotion and feelings constitute information humanity has inherited genetically from primordial ancestors through countless generations of testing and refinement; they are active elements of the meaning generated within humans to aid in regulating attitude and behavior in our struggle to achieve goals, whatever they may be. The ultimate and most significant contributions emotion and feelings make to humanity are in sociality and judgment, which unequivocally are fundamental to the maintenance of our species' stability.[11] Other animals also experience emotions and feelings but we humans complement our subjective motivations with reason, a process that is common among all normal individuals. Given the great significance we accord our social environment, all our knowledge participates in the thought motivating human behavior because social circumspection is essential to success; but it tends to be lost in the effort to be strictly objective.

Knowledge and information constitute the substance of our cognition and communication, but influenced by industry's obvious success, the Consumer Society seems determined to diminish the knowledge foundation for decision-making. We are encouraged to suppress subjectivity throughout our social environment and under certain identifiable influences: the industrial requirement of efficiency and effectiveness; the market's competition and values; the innovative technologies infused into life to extend our physical and intellectual capacities. The natural science epistemology strengthens these influences. Indicating the depth and complexity of the thought that combines objectivity and subjectivity, anthropologist and developmental psychologist Emily Wyman and developmental and comparative psychologist Michael Tomasello (2007, p. 235) conclude, "To explain human cognition and social life, one needs both the biology of shared intentionality and the psychology of cultural-historical interaction." Rationality may enable people to think like a well-programmed computers, which seem to be our preferred models, but when joined with our subjective features it accommodates much more: it accommodates our sociality, which enables us to think like human beings, so this rare mixture also has made possible the evolution of incomparably strong cultures, even as our individual diversity is infinite. "The message is clear: our brain is profoundly social, with some of the oldest social wiring dating back more than 100 million years," writes Matthew D. Lieberman (2013, p. 241). Subjectivity is foundational to our humanity.

The basis of human sociality is our continuously experienced, demonstrated, and long-nurtured individual sensitivity to other beings recognized as human, a sensitivity that is universal among normal people (M. Lieberman, 2013; Krebs, 2011; Pinker, 2011; Damasio, 2010; R. Joyce, 2006; Nichols, 2004). Commonly referred to as information, this essay treats emotion, feelings, and morality as knowledge, for they maintain a strong and continuous presence in our cognition and their meaning is readily understood precisely because of their genetic inherence. "Emotions are not an alternative to or an enemy of thought. They arise and are perfected in thought-like reflections," writes sociologist Jack Katz (2012, p. 28). And like all other considerations applied to the critical act of decision, the human information conveyed in emotion, feelings, and morality also incorporates a variable value that makes them meaningful when conjoined with objective knowledge. Most of our knowledge is acquired in the course of some form of socialization, where it moves cultural evolution toward the realization of individual and societal potential. Michael S. Gazzaniga (2008, p. 83) summarizes the explanation of sociality's prominence in our evolution, writing, "We now think about others all the time because that is how we are built. Without all those others, without our alliances and coalitions, we die. It was true ... for early humans. It is still true for us.... Our big brains are there primarily to deal with social matters." Much of the knowledge humans need is acquired socially, so in a diverse and dynamic society living in the midst of general abundance, the many options require an extraordinarily protracted maturation to prepare us for life. Learning through socialization, therefore, begins for humans immediately upon birth and continues with the guidance of those who assume responsibility for the young throughout a much longer time for humans than for any other beings.[12]

We are endowed with three special features that have evolved humanity to dominance in the living world: a proportionally large and unusually flexible brain with many special connections for managing the mind; the capacity for language, which constitutes a uniquely labile and expansive symbolique apparatus for speech communication; and an extraordinary penchant toward sociality, which is the foundation for physical and intellectual collaboration. From his perspective, economic historian Joseph J. Spengler (1961, p. 6) describes the continuing socialization process in its most general function as the coalescence that forms the knowledge base (the reality) for people as they advance through life:

> The manner in which men respond to what is for them largely an environment of constraints is affected both directly and indirectly by the contents of their minds. It is upon the contents of a decision-maker's mind that depend both his manner of sizing up his environment and his subsequent response thereto. He does not respond to an environment as such. Instead he responds to his image of that environment, to an image that is conditioned by his map of the somewhat larger and more inclusive but seemingly relevant world.

In this scenario, the individual's relationship with others constitutes both goal and method. Mind and culture develop concurrently and dialectically, just as mind and language evolve in mutual influence through a process that can be fully conscious, unconscious, or simply so casual that it can pass unnoticed, yet registered. For the past half millennium, the combination of knowledge and near-unique human features have evolved individual and societal worldview quickly enough to warrant the adverb "radically," which is the next chapter's subject.

4

Western Worldview

> One can imagine a future environment that adequately provides the material basis for human life but is psychologically and socially intolerable.
> —Rosalind Williams, 1990

Founding the Modern Society

Modern society is founded primarily on knowledge and increasingly on its creation. Knowledge of the physical world is established by natural science, the methodically controlled observation, theorization, testing and communication of their results; it reveals proved fact for further questioning and testing in the context of related knowledge continuously coming to light. Natural science is the epistemology that most fundamentally has altered Western worldview, paving the way for continued exploitation of the world's resources by means ever-more powerful. The industrial blending of science and technology with commerce has contributed substantially to the West's evolution, doing so at speeds unknown prior to the fifteenth century and ever-accelerating. Their combined cultural influence is the subject of this chapter.

Science, Industry and Society

Industrial advance meshes tightly with scientific and technological development, for industry has a continuous need of the expansion and competitive advantage that earn the financial support necessary to industrial development. Guided by a triumvirate of science, technology and industry, the impact of natural science epistemology on Western culture has been profound, rapidly replacing the earlier unquestioning belief in and deference to the authority of religion and aristocracy with a more solid grounding in skepticism and proof. But technology's impact is more readily understood and widely appreciated by the public at large than that of science, technology being much more visible and familiar than science in both industrial and domestic settings, and it immediately alters the way tasks are accomplished, stimulating insight into further applicability.

Natural science is a social phenomenon because it assigns human communication the supreme position in its highly principled rationality. But communication within this framework is controlled by its limitation to an international coterie of those with the demonstrated competence to evaluate pertinent tests, findings and related issues prior to their public unveiling as new knowledge. By means of experimentation with theory through trial and error, science multiplies human potential, its abiding value situated in the accumulated knowledge that points the way toward further exploration. Not trained to judge the particularities of scientific investigation, the public can accept or reject new knowledge but places a new faith in natural science, whose record of success is long, pragmatic, and convincing. Nonetheless, to the public the activity and ethos of science constitute a mystery.[1] By the seventeenth century, intellectual curiosity had been liberated sufficiently in the secularization of thought that the scientific attitude attracted a dedicated core audience from which public discussion arose. Science became a distinct intellectual entity accountable to itself on the basis of its own principles, leaving the work of significant discovery relatively unencumbered by external scrutiny, and this set of conditions has made possible its establishment as a distinct culture, an international community within the larger Western society and the world.

A key feature of these conditions is a skeptical approach to knowledge by way of testable theory, an explanation following the natural science principle of falsifiability: for a theory to be truly scientific there must be a way to disprove it, so if tested and not disproved, the theory is validated and accepted as knowledge—although forever subject to a trial that may eventually disprove it because it *is* disprovable. European historian Alan G.R. Smith (1972, p. 26) outlines the influence of the scientific perspective on western Europe's rapid intellectual evolution:

> The mistaken "scientific" ideas of 1500 were shared by virtually all sections of society. There was no significant difference between the general assumptions of the highly educated "scientists" of the universities on the one hand and the illiterate ploughmen of the fields on the other.... Two centuries later these common assumptions no longer existed. By 1700 many members of the educated elites of western Europe had, in the broadest sense, absorbed the implications of the scientific discoveries of the sixteenth and seventeenth centuries. The peasants had not.[2]

By the eighteenth century, industrial production, communication, and transportation sponsored this mode of inquiry in the course of solving problems and planning future endeavors, while the public was adopting a relative freedom of thought and a higher level of confidence in individual potential.

When founded in experimentation, the rational explanation more than countered the theological explanation founded in belief, so the social transition that had begun with the secularization of thought in the seventeenth century, was realized more fully as a "great intellectual change from a providential to a scientific world," in the words of historian J.H. Plumb (1982, p. 333).

What most aroused the public imagination about science was and still is the sense of power it instills in the average citizen, for it promotes a sense of cultural security in its association with the progress that technology is much more likely than science to render visible and understandable. Science historian Herbert Butterfield (1957, p. 197) observes that toward the end of the seventeenth century in Europe, "The passion to extend the scientific method to every branch of thought was at least equalled by the passion to make science serve the cause of industry and agriculture, and it was accompanied by a sort of technological fervor." The West generally adopted new perspectives as increasing segments of the population formed a more accurate image of its history, especially its medieval period, which by the nineteenth century had become a rich field for interpretation in the Romantic spirit by historians and prolific writers of non-fiction. More than any single discovery or invention, it was likely the spirit generated by this activity's intensification that enabled science to penetrate society so deeply, the idea of its unknown but apparently unlimited possibilities having become more integrated into quotidian thought. Science provided a frame through which to view the world and an attitude conducive to contemplation and dreams that no longer were impracticable. Scientific knowledge and attitude increasingly shaped industrial decisions about the means for accomplishing tasks other than scientifically on a large scale, but in doing so began to surpass common-sense understanding. Select portions of the strategies, principles, and values science introduced began to filter from the laboratory and workbench to industry, and from there to the home. Only a relatively brief period was required for the Western culture to adopt the natural science epistemology as a generalized model, albeit loosely, but cloaked in an ambience of success that seemed to work magically in society's favor more often than not. Given no clear alternative, natural science also is the model constituting the one clearly pragmatic course to follow. This acceptance of or acquiescence to science constitutes a collective decision that places faith in humanity, as long as there is a justifiable reaacquiescence, and its rationality eventually was utilized to justify many kinds of Western decision, as subsequent chapters will demonstrate.

Technology, Industry and Society

Technological applications and their consequences are more visible, understandable and debatable when the science underpinning them is accepted.

Modern society demands change and experiences it more rapidly as the culture structures life and finds its quality in the rhythm of technological systems development, for it is an industrial value that has migrated to the general culture. The combination of system function with the growing expectation of ultimate and undeniably positive outcomes explains the phenomenon of technological momentum, so the more experience any society has with technology the more accustomed that society is to change, and to anticipate, accept, and welcome it as the normal course of life, much like the adjustment to seasonal weather. Sometimes subtly and sometimes obtrusively, the adoption of each technological advance, regardless of its magnitude, is repeated many times throughout any modern society, eventually causing further abrupt and well-defined cultural change. And because the primary purpose of technological innovation is to alter both the effort's functionality and its results, a re-examination of purpose and potential interrelations with other functions also accompanies this kind of change, which then promotes a greater understanding of process while paving the way for new social relationships not previously associated with the original technological function. Technology is the near-perfect example of knowledge utility, as its evolutionary path outlines the various stages of cultural evolution. DeSalle & Tattersall (2012, pp. 273–274) find that the fabrication of stone tools was "perhaps the most fateful behavioral innovation ever made in hominid history.... Once stone tools were on the scene, the lives of the hominids, and their way of looking at the world around them, had changed forever."

Technology is a by-product of the problem-solving that ferments most quickly in social settings, the larger and more diverse the richer the product. According to Boyd, Richerson, and evolutionary psychologist Joseph Henrich (2005, p. 272), technological development depends upon a high degree of sociality within a large group. Maintenance of "an equilibrium toolkit as complex as those of late Pleistocene [12.5 million years ago to 12,000 years ago] hunter-gatherers likely required a rather large population of people who interacted fairly freely so that rare, highly skilled performances, spread by selective imitation, could compensate for the routine loss of skills due to imperfect inference." This interpretation suggests that since our emergence, *Homo sapiens* has assigned a commonly-shared high value to technology. Neil Postman (1992, p. 11) also finds that, "in cultures that have a democratic ethos, relatively weak traditions, and a high receptivity to new technologies, everyone is inclined to be enthusiastic about technological change, believing that its benefits will eventually spread evenly among the entire population." The West has been thoroughly conditioned to value technological development.

But it is especially in technological innovation's close interlocking with industrial development of just the past several centuries that it has made possible a reshaping of the economy's image as an integral social concern, elevating its profile in both individual and social mind. Technological development has been the driving force behind industry of the past several hundred years, as well as the decisive ingredient in the history of capitalist strategy and spirit. Technological development has contributed at the forefront of making the economy the most influential feature of a globalizing culture. Expanding on a similar judgment more than half a century ago, sociologist Robert MacIver (1937, pp. 456–457) reasoned, "Social evolution is, in short, the process through which our social systems reflect technological advance." It can hardly be overemphasized that technology is the clearest representation of knowledge in action, a conclusion that makes instrumental knowledge essential to modern success, at least as success is defined most commonly.[3] Technology is the bridge connecting science with society and the model for both, science now favoring application at least equally with discovery and understanding, and society now having chosen material ease, comfort, and a sense of power over most other values.

Underlying much cultural change throughout modernity is the epistemology founded by natural science and adopted subsequently by other disciplines, sufficiently to influence the general public's knowledge foundation for decisions. Natural science has demonstrated that reality can, by and large, be constructed according to an individual's potential and will, and that human life and nature itself are explainable, not unfathomable mysteries. But applications of the model epistemology beyond the realm of natural science now tend to misdirect the purpose, methodology and evaluation of activity in other knowledge spheres, and can be disadvantageous to scholar and layman alike. Such applications, of course, tend to be tailored closely to the advantage of industrial and economic interests.

Ideology

As the significance of technology's power and presence grew more apparent to social leadership and general public alike an ideology began to develop, its ubiquity forcibly raising the question of whether each individual would actively partake of technology's apparently inevitable social pressure to change or, more passively, be bumped along by it. Perceived almost as an organismic phenomenon upon which the quality of life depends, technology stimulates much public attention. Following the Second World War, science became more applied than basic, as its applications—particularly in health care—were by their nature more accessible to the public and more understandable in relation to each individual's life, and this general condition was amenable to the more decisive hand of mass-media advertising.[4] Owed primarily to the public's greater familiarity with technology, applied science is considerably more commercially-oriented than basic science, pharmaceuticals being an example. Moreover, industry has instilled in and attuned the public consciousness to a firm belief in competitive production which, however, translates into an actively competitive culture, so the slogan "survival of the fittest" was misunderstood in its misapplication to humanity's social environment. Similarly, industry also has filtered a more scientific attitude throughout the general public, along with other strategies, principles and values favoring its own quite remarkable development. These include the scientific ideal of objectivity, the concentration on time as an economic value, the necessity to exclude from functional design any consideration believed irrelevant to the technical (economic or technological) system, and the planning of human integration into these systems, which too easily can be imagined as wholly mechanistic. But the more significant aspects of social change have to be sufficiently comprehensible for people to perceive order rather than confusion in life, because one's own sense of order is prerequisite to determining the value of change and the perception of individual fit within the society.

In many instances, technology has become so complex, its functioning parts so far removed from public view and its capacities understood only in a gross way by the vast majority of onlookers, that the Western population has lost its sense of order in the midst of fairly radical yet associated societal change. Inferred from daily experience and hearsay is its prevailing meaning for individuals, which is that things are done neither *by* them nor *for* them but *to* them. A genuine sense of societal and individual decision is lost even in technology, no longer solely in natural science. Realized in technology and any applied science, humanity's extended powers appear more often to have been turned against humanity itself: "The gross efforts to remove nature as an obstacle to human determination, and even to render nature useful, have made the environment in which most people live almost entirely a reflection of human will," writes sociologist Chandra Mukerji (1983, p. 260). But it also reflects individual collective decisions. Mukerji's thought on this topic presents a curious paradox, one at least partially explainable by the prevalent ideology that spreads commensurately with technological development.

The concept of ideology must be at least as old as language, but the word "ideology" was introduced in France by social theorist Destutt de Tracy as the label for a science of ideas he proposed in 1796, a moment in Western history when the mixture of thought about acceptable social life and appropriate governmental motivation was extraordinarily rich and intense on both sides of the Atlantic. Ideology is a coherent and pragmatic composition of theory, concept, belief, myth, vision, fear and aspiration, all capable of rendering life explainable to the public, for whom it also provides guidance. The concept suggests competition among worldviews, so sociologist John B. Thompson's (1984, p. 73) explanation, proposing, "The study of ideology may be conceived as the study of the ways in which meaning (signification) serves to sustain relations of domination," places it in an intellectual and social context that is foremost pragmatic. A solid foundation had already been laid for the development of a more popular ideology prior to the latter part of the nineteenth century, when generous support for science as a positive influence had been developing incrementally for several centuries. For a long time, according to social philosopher Jürgen Habermas (1971, p. 4), science could be perceived, in fact, as "the heir of the theory of knowledge." As such, he adds, the social attitude was "the conviction that we can no longer understand science as one form of possible knowledge, but rather must identify knowledge with science." Indeed, natural science had become the epistemology to follow, even if sometimes thoughtlessly. Technology has always depended on science for its knowledge base, and science increasingly has depended upon technology for experimentation and validation; the West depends quite heavily upon both.

But the ideology surrounding technology eventuated into something much more elaborate than that of natural science, for technology had always affected the general public more directly than science. Individually and consistently, most people are kept aware of technology because of their hands-on or eye-witness experience. And technology's wonders are a much more common product than those of science, for they occur daily; furthermore, the frequent reporting of technological development is a narrative more adaptable to the flow of ideology, and a common cause of ideology is technology's proximity to the general public, person-by-person, stemming from individual cultural choice in the market. Technological development evinces a kind of trajectory that suggests a likely next stage. By contrast, there is precious little popular understanding of what science may yet discover, so public decisions in the science domain present themselves quite rarely; but when they do, they tend to be related more to institutions than individuals. Technology is primarily about change, the kind of change made readily visible to the onlooker. But change also means new decisions, which can be accompanied by loss.[5] By the close of the nineteenth century—and most certainly by the end of the First World War—individual purchasing decisions clearly were becoming the popular hallmark of democratic culture, with individual power and convenience its most enhancing features and those most likely to attract public attention, which was the connection to satisfaction (White, 2008; Williams, 2002; Heilbroner, 1972; Ayres, 1944).

Great expectations for technology have developed in virtually every aspect of Western life. By the twentieth century it already had become abundantly clear that technology is essential to military strategy, and by the end of the Second World War, thought had turned to maintaining world peace on that very basis: a Cold War threatening accidental action or mindless decision provided the intellectual frame for much Western government policy into the twenty-first century. It was a dubious peace. The strategy has worked so far, but in the process has prolonged and deepened the concern of anyone with a roughly valid conceptualization of the technology's potential. Again, the conclusion is that technology, like knowledge, like language and like science, can be used for purposes both positive and negative, and that human goals can be reversed or silenced by technological imperatives and simply by technology's presence, because there remains a latent and disquieting human notion that if technology *can* accomplish a particular task that task *will be* accomplished. The combination of institutional and technological powers can quickly and easily achieve joint purposes, whatever they may be.

Because much human activity can be conceived as mechanical, technology is perceived almost instinctively as the solution to virtually any problem. For more than a century and a half, published accounts of technological wonder have referred casually, if not glibly, to its raw power and its symbolism of human progress, most often Western progress. A more valid portrayal would be mixed, but would cast progress in a more negative or at least obscurant light. Science writer Robert Pool (1997, p. 281) posits a more pragmatic explanation of how technology can generally affect the problem-solving aspect of planning:

> Technological problems generally demand technological solutions, of which the technical fix is just one component. Sometimes what appears to be a likely engineering solution is not practical for reasons that have nothing to do with its technical merits. But then again, sometimes an issue that seems to be all about politics and personalities can be resolved only with a technical breakthrough. The trick lies in seeing the technical in the context of the technological and working from there.

The deeply penetrating and broadly disseminated applications of science, but more so of technology, have assisted and guided the West in its creation of new ways to live in a world that is, as a result, in perpetual change. As the once new routines become the standard operating procedure and therefore the one way to understand any situation or condition, so technology structures much of our life. Because of this acceptance, technologies are felt more a part of the social structure and less an added feature; it becomes all but impossible to imagine life without benefit of these structuring, enabling, and physically comforting Western qualities. When new challenges and opportunities arise, either the next generation of the current technology will be the automatic response to whatever new problems eventuate, or there will be a yet-unknown but "cutting-edge" technology available. The most certain possibility, however, is that technology will be the solution to the problem, the sole solution given any serious attention. Other options would pose too many deep, possibly divisive but definitely inefficient challenges stemming from their human implications, any one of which would amount to an insufferable loss of time. Thus, technology is restrained primarily by the aura of its legendary power, prompting political theorist Langdon Winner (1986, p. 174) to introduce an associated social irony:

> In our society's enthusiasm to rationalize, standardize, and modernize, it has often thoughtlessly discarded qualities that it might, on more careful reflection, have wanted to preserve. Our institutions have engaged in a continuing process of reverse adaptation, in which things are reshaped to suit the technical means available…. If there is a distinctive path that modern technological change has followed, it is that *technology goes where it has never been*. Technological development proceeds steadily from what it has already transformed and used up toward that which is still untouched.

A new technology is adopted readily because nontechnological options are unthinkable. Historians Will Durant and Ariel Durant (1968, p. 95) remind us that we "repeatedly enlarge our instrumentalities without improving our purposes," which may be the principal source of our many current difficulties.

A different worldview also begins to emerge among the individuals directly participating in these technological advances and eventually also among those on the periphery, the activity occurring at a much faster rate in the digital environment than ever before. There is no question that in many ways, social and individual reliance on technology has brought considerably more order to life, a regimented order in many if not most instances. Yet there are those who, like automobile industrialist Aurelio Peccei (1977, p. 18), find the opposite: "Technology has turned out to be an anarchical factor." And while this conclusion may not fully reflect the physical world surrounding us, there is a general uneasiness about contemporary life that begs further thought: how can both assessments of so tightly integrated a dimension of modern life as technology yield a valid depiction?

Capitalist Industry and Market

Western industry developed from a small number of loosely scattered factory sites. It then began spreading around the globe in conglomerations of innumerable factories and services, employing millions who influence their many more millions of associates, some of whom may not be industrially employed, but eventually generating the predominant drive behind both the economy and the culture. Almost from industry's beginning in this environment, writes historian E.P. Thompson (1963, p. 191) "The physical instruments of production were seen as giving rise in a direct and more-or-less compulsive way to new social relationships, institutions, and cultural modes." Theorizing more broadly he adds (p. 204) another chapter to the story: "The process of industrialisation must, in any conceivable social context, entail suffering and the destruction of older and valued ways of life." Industry had taken science from laboratory theory and testing and applied it to the production of goods in its factories, and by applying scientific principles to its commodity production and subsequently its services, industry demonstrated for all to see on an unprecedented scale, that human capacities can be extended technologically and collaboratively in ways never before attempted, generating an image that nourished individual ideas about one's own potential in the world. Several centuries ago, industry began creating a by-product, a new forum for socialization and diverse cultural exchange; it fused capitalist strategies and spirit with its commercial goals and technological development. It created what was to become the economy, which rather quickly assumed major cultural significance.

The Capitalist Spirit

Since the middle of the nineteenth century, the application of Charles Darwin's theory of biological evolution by means of natural selection often, but erroneously, has been associated with economic aspects of human social life in a pseudo scientific justification for management decisions that otherwise would be interpreted as mean and ruthless human behavior. Introduced by engineer and evolutionary philosopher Herbert Spencer (1820–1903), the theory was utilized to rationalize an explanation of the linkage between social progress and the elevated value of monetary power, which proved helpful in attracting the attention of wealthy and influential industrialists (Daniels, 1971). Science was employed to lend a rose tint to industry's graying image. Thus, the somewhat unflattering interpretation of humans as innately and primarily selfish animals held sway for many decades, raising "the 'pitiless' struggle for personal advantages to the height of a biological principle," as Darwinian Petr Kropotkin (1842–1921) wrote in an early attempt to counter their claims (1955, p. 4 [1890–96]).[6] This radical (social Darwinist) but more dramatic interpretation of Darwin's evolutionary theory doubtless was influential in biasing the Western culture toward materiality while justifying the spread of select industrial strategies, principles and values, and it supported development of the market economy by weakening any sense of industry's social responsibility.

Monetary exchange is the market's chief activity in fostering the unification of capitalist production and public consumption more cogently and symbiotically now than previously was possible. It has the advantage that, depending upon the goods and services of interest to a limited social segment, the market is a system that can be modeled in pictures, mathematics, words, or other symbols. Whereas the market formerly had been the place to acquire goods the customer was unable to produce, it soon became the junction of exchange and capitalism and the sole place to acquire anything (Fulcher, 2004). Capitalism's sustenance is situated in the mass consumption of commodities and anything judged commodifiable, so when the synergy of consumption and capitalism had become sufficiently dependable, commodification began to affect social phenomena not previously considered amenable to it. In this new economic environment, the West's cultural profile was elevated considerably and advertising could shift its strategies to address the emotional dimension of its target audience rather than its intellectuality, thereby further uniting culture and commerce; the market could then expand to be less segmented by traditional classes and more by age and personal interest. This spread of ideas and images constitutes the sowing of social change that economic historian and philosopher Karl Polanyi (1944, p. 75), surrounded by Second World War military action at the time, described with stark brevity: "All along the line, human society had become an accessory of the economic system." The Western culture and economy merged in their common reliance on money, which indisputably ranks among the very highest of current Western values. The economic system has proved to be both a concerted effort to maintain societal stability and an unequaled instrument for maintaining its cultural dynamism. But it is a mixture that contributes to human stress, because the vast system's objective is narrowed specifically to the maintenance of industrial health not human health—without which, of course, the whole system would crash.

Systems Theory

Considering the extent of its influence on management, systems theory occupies a remarkable position in forming societal worldview. It perceives most complex entities as arrangements of many integrated parts, each with a different function but collaborating to accomplish one larger task, for the system is greater than the sum of all its individual parts. Systems theory's purpose is to aid in understanding a complex entity as a whole in the context of its associated socio-economic phenomena, and to provide a holistic view easily manipulated while also suggesting seamless and rational connectability with other systems. The systems concept presumes a continuous flow of the organism's energy and processes, all parts functioning together in a common, directed motion, and systems also evince a strong tendency toward expansion as they increase in complexity. Systems theory is applicable in virtually all fields of organized activity because it lends itself especially well to an improved understanding of the functions and relationships of individual parts, as well as to prediction and the planning of change in the total system. It is a powerful tool for dealing with complexity and change because it facilitates modeling. Frank Fischer (1990, p. 204) describes the system's internal control, which is a particularly noteworthy feature of this management theory.

One of systems theory's most basic propositions is the idea that, as a system evolves, one of its parts invariably emerges as a central and controlling agent for the system as a whole. The unit's function, in brief, is that of central guidance of the system's development. Empirical evidence for the ubiquity of this phenomenon is said to be found everywhere, from embryonic development to telephone networks and national defense systems.

A tool used widely for planning and control in management throughout government and industry, systems theory tends to raise problematic issues from the perspective of goals, primarily in connection with the industrial principles of efficiency, rationality, and objectivity.

Capitalist Reason and Worldview

Among the mental faculties most critical to the West's social evolution is the capacity for reasoned thought, which the success of science, technology, and industry well illustrates historically, for their development consistently has been guided by an overall rationality leading to specific action.[7] Integral in the systems approach to functionality, reason has been the underlying principle in strategic industrial thinking from the start, and since then has become influential throughout the general Western population. But when honed to keenest edge and applied to non-technical aspects of human life, reason can easily slip into rationalism, the conviction that reason is the sole valid basis of knowledge and a more valid basis for planning than experience, tainted as it is by subjectivity and therefore irrelevant. The rationalization of plans to achieve specific goals and objectives by a more selective application of knowledge and values has been the intellectual foundation of capitalism, at least since the seventeenth century, by which time science and technology had given life to the idea that new knowledge could be created by anyone and put to the proof for general acceptance or rejection. This approach was understandable and challengeable at the time, but most significantly it encouraged "the development of a rational bourgeois life," standing "at the cradle of the modern economic man," as sociologist and philosopher Max Weber (1930, p. 174) observes, a style of life that constitutes the core of mass production and consumption. The past cannot be controlled but the future sometimes can, so when joined by pertinent considerations, a rationality causing the future to overshadow the past's importance was widely adopted by much of the Western social mind (Bell, 1976).

The capitalist spirit encourages a way of perceiving and thinking by means of its logical support for a materialist orientation, and in a world guided largely by material goals, principles and values, the faculty of reason proves highly practical. A versatile form of rationality has replaced the kind of reason formerly given direction by the cultural norms following traditionally from individual desire and tending toward mutability in association with morality: behavior right or wrong, good or bad, and a sense of social responsibility. Reason is even supported by the phenomenon of speech, the articulation of fine phonetic distinctions to convey meaning according to its special rules rather than uncontrolled emotion (DeSalle & Tattersall, 2012). In decision-making, however, attention to these aspects of knowledge and value simply requires too much precious time for thought, rendering it inefficient and relatively ineffective for determining strictly technical decisions, for contemplation easily strays into the more peripheral issues of context. This reaction against sociality's spiritual and intellectual dimension laid the foundation for a kind of engagement in social action that bears perceptible kinship with technological function; that is, achieving the desired efficiency and effectiveness through the more direct linkage between the mind's clarity of thought and its executive functions. It is a highly pragmatic approach, and in a pragmatic society action supersedes contemplation (Arendt, 1958), whereas worldview and action are not independent of each other but are mutually influential: we act on the basis of our worldview, then our action changes the world and consequently our view of it. This process alone accounts for a considerable part of our cultural evolution, which reflects multiple, individual changes of mind and the reworking of old material more than the creation of new. Thus, modern historian Lynn Avery Hunt (2007, p. 34) quite justifiably insists that "any account of historical change must in the end account for the alteration of individual minds." The human faculty of reason is a leit motif of this essay.

Values

Values constitute a set of standards for decisions about individual priority.[8] Depending on experience, some values are fixed very early in life and therefore can be a rather profound and durable part of each adult, but more values are added as more is learned, and priorities are altered as conditions and circumstances change. Specific values may be relatively stable but their priority is subject to quite frequent change. Change in absolute or long-term values usually is quite slow, although external pressures can interrupt their stability (Kluckhohn, 1961). Values can be strengthened by their repeated invocation but can dissipate in strength with the passage of time, or as perspective changes, or the competition of other priorities. Formed on a base of knowledge and related feelings, one's value system ultimately defines the character of the individual much as the culture defines that of the society, and because values are ascribable to every recognized material and spiritual entity, they figure in some way in all societal challenges and successes. A hierarchical system, the priority order of values can be altered in the process of adjustment to the evolving cultural system, which also accommodates new values. Individual and collective decisions to act reveal much about values and worldview, which are closely related, and it can safely be assumed that differing values among people constitute a prime source for both individual and social conflict; this is true especially when values express individual or societal beliefs, aspirations, or ideals. Cognitive scientist Keith E. Stanovich (2010, p. 145) interweaves aspects of cooperation and altruism in the place of values in individual cultural choice:

> Most people take a stance toward the choices they make and the goals that they pursue. Both the choices and the goals are often evaluated by external criteria. The choices are evaluated in terms of the meaning they convey to the person making the choice and the goals are evaluated in terms of whether they are consistent with the values the person holds…. People may be fully aware that performing a particular act is characteristic of a certain type of person but does not contribute causally to their becoming that type of person. But in symbolizing the model of such a person, performing the act might enable the individual to maintain an image of him—or herself.

In short, a critical part of change in any social system is its frame of reference for values within the vicissitudes of environmental conditions, because whether learned in childhood, altered in the priority ranking or displaced by a different understanding, values are of critical significance in decisions and the assessment of other people. Values are highly significant in defining the character of both individual and society.

Materialism

Materialism is a cultural system of values in which human motivation is aroused at least equally by life's physicality as by its intellectuality and spirituality, for it is "a cultural system in which material interests are not made subservient to other social goals," as Chandra Mukerji (1983, p. 8) states it. Just as an artifact is a human creation connecting people, objects, knowledge, value, and purpose in a social system, the human-made material world demonstrates that a society can design its image even to the detail of individual taste. This path to value is a culturally complicating factor, as material culture accumulates simply *because* of its physicality, and therefore is durable. Moreover, other entities, for example any random thought, can readily be commodified and treated as a physically durable object, but are even more easily cast aside when no longer needed. Introduced in Chapter 3, commodification is the assignment of monetary value to an entity; it applies most evidently to material things, but often and increasingly also to intellectual and spiritual entities. Social anthropologist Michael Thompson (1979, p. 77) describes commodification:

> The basic idea is that physical objects have certain important properties imposed on them as a result of the processes of human social life, and, conversely, that if these properties were not conferred upon them then human social life itself would not be possible. Since people are physical objects, they too are subject to the same process. Nor does it stop here. Ideas, since they must always be generated and communicated in a social context, are also constrained so as to become, to a somewhat variable extent, thing-like.

Not limited to physical objects, materiality is motivated by a strong modern attraction to change through innovation for at least these two reasons: change introduces novelty, and an artifact or an ides is a human creation connecting humanity with materiality in a cultural system change that is easily accelerated.[9]

Prior to the modern era, Western life was characterized by the general condition of scarcity. But as an ever-broadening base of human consumption nourished mass production, such a characterization consistently was eroded by a confirmed faith in the abundant flow of new commodities. Thus, the pressure behind mass consumption emanates not as much from the technologies employed by industry as from the possibilities suggested by minds conditioned to acquire commodities routinely in one form or another. Such people reason that materiality is more valid than intellectuality or any other mode of self expression. And by serving as a toolkit in the renewal of social motivation and organization, a material world is essential to the evolutionary processes of modern culture, for it is a world of accumulation leaving visible and tangible evidence of what once was, not only of what is and can be, thereby inviting comparison. Materiality leaves a huge, unmistakable imprint of change that makes its significance decidedly more apparent than spiritual or intellectual representations. Objects have become the most common instruments of cultural change, and owing to commodification, are consciously controllable in the aggregate. Furthermore, as representations of ideals and desires, objects have been assigned value far beyond their physical utility and are bought and sold in exchange for such values.

Modern materialism came into vogue with the dramatically increased availability of commodities and the equally wide-spread accessibility to a dependable income for their acquisition to apply toward goals practical and cultural, the resulting mélange presciently concocted by industry and commerce to condition and mold the culture most likely to complement industrial aspiration. Historian and social critic Stuart Ewen (1976, p. 214) summarizes the evolution of materialist motivation in a society of mass consumption and its general influence on Western culture, writing, "More than a vehicle for the good life, self-definition by commodities pointed the way to a safe life." Commodities are judged safe because the pertinent rules are established socially within the mass. Furthermore, materiality is much more self-evident than other means of projecting one's station in life, being what the senses reliably communicate and requiring little explanation and perhaps no convincing. The natural, physical environment has always limited humanity (yet has provided many advantages), but the difference in modernity is the much greater extent to which the material environment has become the source of present-day motivation. This distinction is significant: it can easily be perceived as the contemporary manifestation of declining interest in existential and other concerns that demand deeper and sometimes more unsettling thought, but without also providing a venue toward quick, corrective action. What materiality most certainly provides for longer term consideration is a vast collection of remnants: residue of the time, thought, and experience invested in their acquisition.

Industrial Influence on Western Culture

Industry could scarcely have developed to its present magnitude and influence without the dazzling world of things, for it is doubtful that the consumer society would otherwise find material desire so useful a human condition. But capitalist industry made the fostering of this desire one of its strategies, since even hopes and dreams can be manufactured to guide rational behavior, and more readily so if motivated materially. Never quite disappearing, the world of things always suggests new understandings, interpretations and perspectives, as well as another new worldview, another new opportunity or idea, just around the market's next corner.

Several other cultural features have combined to stimulate the gradual evolution of a society once rigidly delineated and stratified by ancestral circumstance into a new order founded on self-determination, self-individuation, and self-absorption. They are states of mind fostered by several psychological and cultural conditions: the importance of materiality, as symbolized by money; the ability to earn and accumulate money; the time-consciousness reason requires in an industrial setting; a more versatile commodification; and the democratization of knowledge, made possible by the spread of natural science epistemology. Western society has transformed itself from a culture of tradition previously obscured in the shadow of its political history (royal, aristocratic and church), into a vibrant, dynamic, and popular culture of high profile that crosses all social classifications. Motivated more by innovation in life's potential than by survival in the status quo, this self-conscious and self-renovating society grew to favor the manipulability of material entities and the power of material innovation over spirituality and intellectuality. Very broad and widely-shared affinities for actuality have gained influence but without completely replacing traditional order. Thus, cautions Gilles Lipovetsky (2005, p. 43), "Our inability to imagine the future increases, but it goes in tandem with a super-powerful science and technology more than able radically to transform the coming age: feverish short-termism is merely one of the faces of the future hypermodern civilization." A central feature of this consequence is the fixation on efficiency.

Efficiency

Throughout the course of this cultural transformation, capitalist industry's equation of time and money has stirred a consciousness of time related to purpose, a feature of consciousness that has encouraged the societal adoption of an exclusive and stringent rationality for both the general perception and the preferred path to new knowledge. Meanwhile, industrial development continues to accelerate, clarifying its distinctions between work time and leisure but always adhering to work's operational requirements. But the efficiencies demanded by industry's time-consciousness (discussed in Chapter 7) and systems planning gradually drifted into the domain of daily life, accompanying the general migration of industrial strategies, principles, and values. Together, they introduced a refashioned rationality.

Reason

For present purposes, reason is the logical and therefore rational progression of thought toward an endpoint. The societal propensity to accommodate industrial influence eventuated into a barely noticeable cultural pattern, creating an environment in which reason's utility was and continues to be narrowed to its least tolerance. But the pattern surely was purposeful. Efficiency and reason became mutually supporting concepts, even to the extent that efficiency arguably has been made an end in itself, and the change in culture proceeded through a continuous diminishment of the knowledge foundation for the evolutionarily critical human acts of individual and collective decisions and their elimination from any remaining and well-preserved vestiges of human subjectivity. Specifically, this means the subjective information embedded in emotion, feelings and morality, these sensitivities incorporating a steadfast attention to responsibility for others.[10] For industrial purposes, such considerations *do not add* anything to the knowledge foundation for decisions but *do detract* considerably from system efficiency. Nonetheless, for human purposes they are a central focus of cognition, introduced in Chapter 3 and examined in subsequent chapters, and they do this quite naturally because, inherited genetically, such sensitivities are embedded participants in the thought of all normal people. But this conclusion leaves only an unnaturally narrow focus, which easily reverses the order of means and end when applied to non-industrial purposes, and arguably to some industrial purposes, so for several centuries the tendency to prejudice subjectivity in decisions has been conveyed from industry to home. The ultimate consequence of this diminishment in the knowledge foundation for decisions is its disregard of the way lives are experienced beyond the stark materiality of an extremely fluid social milieu. Because human systems are deeply multi-dimensional and highly unpredictable, they are quite unlike technological and economic systems. Daniel M. Fox (1967, p. 46) observes that even in the nineteenth century, "Too many economists confused the laws which governed machines with those which ought to govern men." He later (p. 165) adds that for at least the first two thirds of the twentieth century, the only obstacles to rapid industrial development "were short-sighted men who did not perceive that the organization of society had not kept pace with the inventive momentum of science and engineering." In this view, quotidian life best fits the underlying strategic pattern for economics, the capitalist spirit, and science, leaving technology as the sole technical dimension of Western life with which the general population maintains some degree of hands-on experience. Indeed, the West is so deeply immersed in technology every day in every way that the necessity of its presence can be taken for granted, on faith, and without question.[11]

Stimulated by the intensity of public infatuation with technology, analogies between technological function and the human mind emerged, as had occurred at points in industry's earlier history when the similarities of biological and mechanical functions first attracted attention. An unusually clear example of this phenomenon had arisen in the seventeenth century when theoretical scientific work was beginning to attract followers and the belief was circulating that sensations are atomic, existing in the form of data. But science historian and philosopher Carolyn Merchant (1980, p. 233) observes that the public took this analogy still further in the development of a supposed path leading from sensation to reason. She writes, "The adding machine, the precursor of the modern computer, was a model for Hobbes' concept of the human brain: to reason was only to add and subtract or to calculate, 'For reason ... is nothing but reckoning, that is adding and subtracting.'" Lacking any reference to emotion, feelings or morality, this line of thought spread quickly to become popular in identifying evident patterns in nature that might well be analogous with human mental functions (Tooby & Cosmides, 1992). This was the cultural foundation for the equation of mind and machine which, with the advent of digitized computing, became a staple for exercising the imagination. The public's alternating attraction to and fear of technology is much like the human fascination with the coiled, standing cobra literary theorist Kenneth Burke (1954, p. 44) refers to it as "a technological psychosis ... at the center of our glories and our distress."

When industry developed its service dimension by subsuming the "culture industry," which may dominate today's media advertising, its targets were individual character and societal culture. Experiencing a raised profile following the Second World War, this relatively new industry now tests the financial capacity of individuals of all ages and economic strata as well as both genders, remarkably accelerating its market command early in the twenty-first century. Sociologists Scott Lash and Celia Lury (2007, pp. 3–5) observe that "globalization has given culture industry a fundamentally different mode of operation," and they explain:

> Culture has taken on another, different logic with the transition from the culture industry to global culture industry; our point is that in 1945 and in 1975 culture was still fundamentally a superstructure.... Cultural entities were still exceptional.... But in 2005 cultural objects are everywhere: as information, as communication, as branded products, as financial services, as media products, as transport and leisure services, cultural entities are no longer the exception: they are the rule. Culture is so ubiquitous that it, as it were, seeps out of the superstructure and comes to infiltrate, and then take over the infrastructure itself. It comes to dominate both the economy and experience in everyday life.... In global culture industry, production and consumption are processes of the construction of *difference*.

The differences that can separate individuals and groups from others have become more culturally instrumental—even weaponized—and thus are more significant than the similarities that can join them, leaving for the political stage only a conflicted and decidedly negative cast.

If Western economy and culture are not fused today, they are at least highly symbiotic, insofar as the culture feeds the economy via its reflection of industry's production and maintains the continuous flow of money on a global scale. The balance of expanding production and its necessary consumption—both derived from decisions rendered by a culture that demands no less than that—determines the economy's health, and most certainly the Western hemisphere's health. In a host of clever strategies that saturate the media, two aspects of advertising in pursuit of this balance are particularly noteworthy: the multifarious variety of commodities or services themselves, and modernity's ideals, which align most comfortably with those of democracy. As a result, Western society is characterized simply and perhaps most accurately as the "consumer society," introduced in Chapter 3. Long in the making, it evolved neither by chance nor formally agreed societal design but by repeated individual and collective decisions made in adapting to environmental challenges and opportunities, having altered the social environment. The streamlining of our knowledge process was intended to tailor the knowledge foundation required for decisions *of almost any kind*, and is a social phenomenon of great proportion. It recalls the warning issued many decades ago by sociologist Talcott Parsons (1935, p. 231), writing, "Where action becomes a direct expression of ultimate value attitudes outside the sphere of practical techniques, the means is no longer intrinsically related to a tangible end but becomes a symbol."

Rigid rationality began to dominate situations and conditions well beyond the technological sphere. They increasingly gained influence as the standard protocol for decisions, because this view fit well with the material environment the Western world had been constructing. Progress could most readily be displayed, witnessed, and understood in material development, which made individual and societal change the passport to modernity, while the principal obstacle in the path toward progress was perceived to be tradition, in any manifestation. As these cultural features evolved, they nurtured industrial development, which in turn whetted the public appetite for more change and choice in the course of cultural self-realization. Attitude and action can be determined more efficiently, unequivocally, and visibly to the extent that it relates to materiality, so the decision-making processes following from cultural choice are standardized and lubricated for smooth meshing by the multifaceted powers of money to resolve the potential of obstacles or problems; money is the most flexible of all technologies. The economy and the culture were rationalized to merge in the production/consumption system. Diminished in its linking of knowledge and values with decision and action, however, was the function of thought, which in normal people includes emotion, feelings, and morality. Thought—at least critical thought—was no longer to reflect normal human cognition but rather an objective, machine-readable transaction, which may also portend the fate of our sociality.

But reason has always applied to considerations far beyond the realm of the technological and has been of utmost significance in distinguishing valid from faulty information, while it also is fundamental in establishing a priority order among values. Central to any technology's efficiency is its precision, which in this case means the avoidance of operational friction; it is a modern ideal and an accepted expectation for both technological development and rationality. "The very name of the process for achieving the ideal of rationalization is significant: it is given the name of 'modernization,'" notes Edward Shils (1981, p. 288). "Being modern is being 'advanced' and being advanced means being rich, free of the encumbrances of familial authority, religious authority, and deferentiality. It means being rational and being 'rationalized.'" In the industrialized Western world, once a goal has been established and the logical progression of steps leading toward it are determined, any action deviating from its intended path is by current common accord, irrational, wrong, and doomed to failure; it generally is agreed that if a strategy proves successful, regardless of the means employed to achieve it, that strategy is justified.

Success is ample proof of the rightness and righteousness of a planned course of action followed scrupulously; a corporate plan, for example, would include adequate budgeting for fines, penalties, legal suits and other contingencies, so they can be accommodated without undue interruption in proceeding with the planned course. Individual citizens, on the other hand, increasingly define their decisions by controlling their range of thought, which means minimizing the context of ideas. Such are the secure and reliable measures by which the West has charted much of its path and repeatedly tested its economic and technological development. We have established a model for our social understanding, decisions, and action Daniel Bell (1973, p. 307) described nearly half a century ago:

> Much of contemporary social theory has been addressed to the rigorous formulation of rational models of man, in which optimizing, maximizing, and minimizing provide models of behavior that are rationally normative. But we seem to be unable to formulate a "group theory" of economic choice. The impasse of social theory, in regard to social welfare, is a disturbing prospect at this stage of the transition to a communal society.

Well-disciplined rationality offers a relatively secure way to plan events and control the future accordingly in the less predictable, more diverse, and human side of life, for it ordinarily demands the greatest flexibility, not the least, plus a deeper and more protracted quality of thought than the precision, efficiency, and timeliness of technological design. Much like the West's affinity for commodification, we have moved much closer to the adoption of a streamlined reason more suited to the values and purposes of our production/consumption system. We have certified this narrowly-gauged reason as the safest and most reliable strategy for a society that consistently has grown more object-oriented, money-driven, and technology-dependent. Our society is drawn to the ownership of commodities; it claims to be fully satisfied by personal possession of the fiscal resources needed to exploit the extravagant range of choice our present abundance makes possible. But it also is a society that seems to shun nature, of which we are an integral part, and at very least we have decided to distance ourselves from nature. Like many other psychologists, Tim Kasser (2002, p. 90) finds a social counter-balance in this arrangement, writing that "materialistic values are associated with making more antisocial and self-centered decisions about getting ahead rather than cooperating. As a result, others in the community are treated as objects to be manipulated and utilized. Material values also conflict with attention to making the world a better place, and the desire to contribute to equality, justice, and other aspects of civil society." With scant adulteration, the spirit of material competition has migrated from industry to our culture and personal life, where it is considered satisfactory but leaves no time or inclination for critical assessment of the world we are creating, decision by decision. When given an opportunity, we avoid critical assessment.

This status reveals a subtle and scarcely recognizable change of direction away from the path along which human sociality evidently had been evolving for countless millennia. Within a growing mass, the principle apparently is that thought should be concentrated on one's income potential and how to optimize its demonstrability.[12] The combination of abundant objects available for purchase on any day in any marketplace—an abundance enriched by its expanding number of categories, their fine distinctions, and creative combinations—can be disorienting, particularly when intrinsic value and monetary value are confused so easily, as Dennis Ford (2007, p. 232) describes:

> Capitalism, too, impedes our taking intrinsic delight in this life by indoctrinating us with the proposition that value and desirability can be reduced to monetary value. We are seduced into confusing wealth with money, and a person's work is judged, not in terms of its intrinsic rewards, but by its value in the marketplace. Our perception and intrinsic delight in the world is reduced and exchanged for activities and perceptions that are useful or profitable. Our self-worth is bound to our worth in the marketplace rather than our ability to take delight.

The only justification we can offer is that our species has not yet grown accustomed to abundance rather than scarcity, but our species may just be lulled by comfort, too satisfied to apply our extraordinary mental capacities in any other way. The changes in worldview explored in this chapter have caused our culture to reconceptualize knowledge by tailoring it more appropriately, which is the subject of the next chapter.

5

Tailoring Western Knowledge

> We bend to the inanimate with new solicitude. We fear the risks and disappointments of relationships with our fellow humans. We expect more from technology and less from each other.
> —Sherry Turkle, 2011

Influences on the Character of Knowledge

Knowledge is the foundation upon which values and decisions are determined, its continuous differentiation within each individual the source of a rising number of options, and within society an increasing complexity. Beginning after the Second World War and strengthening in the present, the Western conceptualization of knowledge reflects an increasing myopia and channeling, conditions that stem from several specific influences on Western cultural evolution: the acceleration of industrial development; the evident successes of natural science; the cultural preeminence of technology; workplace pragmatism; the facile adoption of strategic quantification; the winnowing of context in judgment; the mounting social tension of presentism; the aversion to knowledge depth; and the hegemony of an industrial ethos. These influences have led to the diminishment of the knowledge foundation for decision, leaving a common knowledge tailored more to the specifications of economic and technological progress than progress toward the realization of human ideals.[1] Foremost among these influences are: the natural science epistemology; technological development; the workplace environment; and quantification.

Natural Science

The natural science epistemology has maintained an impressive and uniform procedure for validating knowledge of the physical world. Because scientific theory requires a wide review of rational, precise testing and detailed, objective reporting by those commanding the requisite specialized knowledge, the essence of science is communication: only when theory passes all appropriate tests is it accepted by the scientific community as new knowledge. Science is an exclusive international community quite distinct from the general population, which has neither the means nor perhaps the will to follow so exacting an order of proof, as discussed in chapter four, so the natural scientists' commitment to their extraordinary ethos renders science its uniquely high degree of credibility.

The natural science epistemological model maintains a strong influence on Western culture, having been adopted for use in virtually all categories of knowledge and having become the more generally applied standard for truth that began replacing religion and aristocracy as early as the fifteenth century (Butterfield, 1957). This epistemological model also has contributed to a perception of the power of knowledge-as-product, which when labeled "information" in the second half of the twentieth century, eventually was to preoccupy much of Western culture. For many generations, industrial decisions about the means to accomplish goals on a large scale have been shaped increasingly by scientific knowledge, whose select principles eventually filtered from the laboratory and workstation to the home and other less structured settings. The West chose the natural science epistemology because of its expected efficient, affective and definitive answers to rational and objective questions, while current-events media publicize the positive side of the model's highly evident successes, often glorifying science, though critics often fail to explain its negative potential or the extent of control necessary to the validation of scientific achievement (Nelkin, 1987).

Technology

As the artificial enhancement and extension of human capacity, technology has been designed and employed since the earliest *Homo sapiens,* and now exists in a great many forms. Because of its social nature, the long path of technological development constitutes the clearest, most understandable material representation of accumulated knowledge, and therefore of stages in social history and human evolution. Its path of development deepened during the final quarter of the twentieth century, however, when digital technologies were more widely acquired by mass consumers of all ages. Technology is tightly interwoven into the fabric of social history though with extraordinarily ubiquitous evidence of that fact in the modern period, for it aligns very closely to Western cultural desires: the modernist need for change; the rapid transition from knowledge to action; self-individuation; and the demand for immediate access to information about current events. Our culture has made these conditions desirable, for we experience change quickly, change being a consequence of the rise in decisions available for the structuring of social life, which now gauges life's quality by its synchrony with technology's rhythm, its ongoing beat of system efficiency. Technological development proceeds at an increasing velocity because, as a strong current in cultural evolution, it builds upon itself, modifying more than creating. In this sense, Zoltan Torey (2014, pp. 105–106) finds technological development analogous to human cognition, writing, "The continual development of science and the increasing sophistication of technology bear witness to an internal process of revision, a reworking of the brain's contents that renders accessible what used to be beyond conceivability." Individuals must be more efficient simply to keep pace with their environment. And when paired with evidently positive outcomes, system function fosters heightened social expectation, this synergy ultimately constituting the sensation of technological momentum.

Technological momentum is the social phenomenon of individual and societal dependence on technology, this dependence having become so routinized and inured that life without it would seem unimaginable. A popular belief holds that technology determines social change, even though the various technologies are designed, produced, programmed, adopted, adapted, and evaluated by human beings. Technological development has played a significant part in changing the social value of knowledge through technology's intersections with several other trends in Western cultural evolution: the spread of a highly pragmatic outlook; the general gravitation toward rationalism and materialism; the rapid fluctuation of economic conditions and opportunities; and the heightened desire to project individual and group identity. The variety of options technology introduces also exerts a remarkable influence on change in commonly-held values, for technology can render easily achievable those tasks formerly judged too difficult to attempt, and can reveal the possibility of a change previously judged so alien to the culture that it could scarcely have been contemplated. Nothing more clearly profiles social evolution than technological development. As both the cultural artifact of power and convenience and the substance of modern myth, technology is fused in the present culture with all other material considerations in replacing the intellect's formerly understood position as the quintessence of humanity; the way we manage technology today, it even displaces much cognition.

The industrialized world's increasing complexity is in large part the result of technological development's capacity to move much faster than our social and intellectual development's adaptation to it, which explains the general preference for information (knowledge-as-product) over thought (knowledge-as-process). Necessary to capitalist industry since its introduction, instrumental knowledge has become essential to modern success far beyond the factory walls, and in doing so has very much benefited from mass-media authority, as sociologist of science Dorothy Nelkin (1987, p. 51) indicates: "The press coverage of new technological developments plays on and probably encourages the public's desire for easy solutions to economic, social, and medical problems." But in a society fraught with competition, technological innovation necessarily is followed soon by the discontinuation of its superannuated but now familiar artifact, soon to be replaced by the next one.

The Workplace

The workplace environment is the organized and pragmatic world in which most Western adults spend a very substantial part of their conscious life, so it is logical that the workplace might also provide new insights into the management of activities associated with home and other social environments.[2] Indeed, starting with the generally accepted natural science epistemology, other strategies, principles, and values designed by industry for industrial purposes also have contributed to the migration of workplace thought and routines, ultimately transforming the societal culture in various ways (Osburn, 2014). Among these changes are three specific criteria for decisions: the criterion of utility, which holds that any idea advanced and any time spent in the accomplishment of work should be directly useful in supporting organizational objectives, otherwise the effort is inefficient, less effective, and to be discarded; the criterion of quantification, which reduces problem-solving to mathematical calculation; and the criteria for attitude and strategy, which the management model exemplifies in achieving only specific objectives.[3]

Quantification

Quantification is the reduction of a problem, condition or situation to its calculable elements by applying metrics to facilitate its management. It follows from the materialist interpretation of the world by presuming that whatever is real is calculable and, therefore, that it is foolish to stray from the truth by mixing the real—meaning technical information—with the ethereal—meaning emotion, feelings, and morality. Lacking in technical reality, the latter are believed to distort the calculation intended to represent the technical system (primarily technological or economic), rendering that system less manageable even though neuroscience and cognitive psychology demonstrate that normal human thought is, in fact, a combination of these knowledge sources (Lieberman, 2013; Gazzaniga, 2011; Damasio, 2010; Thagard, 2010; Johnson-Laird, 2006). In its close association with rationality, quantification not only is appropriate in many settings, but also may be the most efficient, effective and generally satisfactory strategy to follow, yet not in others. Moreover, though quantitative proof of anything may be wholly objective and precise, it also can be objectively and precisely wrong. Quantification is efficient but disregards the human context of situations and conditions, thereby overlooking the depth in thought that leads to understanding. These conditions have displaced much of the value the culture formerly had found in various strains of subjectivity, except where validly proscribed. With natural science for our generalized model epistemology, quantification has become the pillar of strategy in collective decision-making, regardless of its limitations.[4] In formal education, for example, quantification can immediately be seen in the shift of importance accorded content to the higher level of importance accorded methodology, which is designed expressly for a more rationally-delivered knowledge (Osburn, 2014). It is another function to which the demands of accountability and efficiency apply pressure, quantification being much easier to assess and manipulate on the instruction side of the educational transaction than on the learning side.

Evolution Brings New Decisions

Language

The combination of extraordinary mental capacity and phonetic expression through language has proved to be a principal engine of cultural evolution. Language is the vehicle for communicating thought from one individual to another or others in various symbolic forms, speech its earliest and most common manifestation. Philip Lieberman (2013, p. 71) asserts, "Language clearly is the principal instrument whereby culture is transmitted…. Virtually all of the aspects of human behavior that enhance our fitness relative to that of other species are culturally transmitted through the medium of language." Language may be to the human social system as oxygen is to the individual biological system: it diffuses new knowledge, perceptions, tastes, sensitivities, aspirations, feelings, and values in their connection with other knowledge already resident in mind. Without communication there could be no culture as we presently experience it, only an inchoate gathering of individual beings, because the substance of human communication constitutes the essence of cultural evolution. Moreover, Richerson & Boyd (2005, p. 135) demonstrate that primates with larger brains are more likely to use social learning, more likely to engage in novel behavior, and more likely to use tools, suggesting that "social learning allows more-flexible responses to novel environments." Language functions much as the human brain does.

The value of language to cultural evolution is its capacity for sharing thoughts, rendering them useful to the security, satisfaction, and success of the total society and most of its individual constituents, all while exercising and developing the mind, its use determined by the articulator. Biologist and neuroscientist Harry Smit (2014, pp. 22–23) observes that our relatively plastic cognition results from the power of our language: "We are above all language-using animals; *Homo loquens* and only therefore *Homo sapiens*. The ability to use a language is the mark of having a mind, for it is because of language that we are rational animals, are able to reason and can think, feel and act for reasons.... Only humans can pursue goals and explain the reasons why they want to pursue goals."

Meaning is essential to language (Searle, 2010) and speech is not simply the production of distinct sounds to convey meaning, but rather a much deeper, more congenial and cognitive system that depends heavily upon the human penchant to sociality and maintenance of the culture.[5] "The emergence of language arguably is our species' defining characteristic," adds computational linguist Simon Kirby (2007, p. 671). Language is a phonetic system of meanings, honed through the ages to express and communicate any subject's recognized fine distinctions. Language facilitates the organization of individuals into collectives with a variety of bases and interests and stimulates mental activity, the organization of common experience constituting a society (Foskett, 1984). It is through language that ideas both simple and extremely complex can with relative efficiency and ease be exchanged, clarified, and refined through ever greater understanding to nurture learning, which results from the social diffusion of ideas and eventual social change. Like any other major cultural change, however, the emergence of speech, approximately 50,000 to 150,000 years ago, although possibly as long ago as two million years (Buss, 2004), also depended on the cultural readiness of the society into which it was introduced, as evolutionary linguist James R. Hurford (2007, p. 243) explains:

> I have suggested a couple of evolutionary changes that led to the first nearly language-like communication: gradual enhancement of the capacity for learning arbitrary symbols, and of the disposition to combine symbols with deictic gestures to convey elementary propositional meanings.... I suggest, then, that a crucial precursor to the appearance of these proto-linguistic abilities was not in itself a specifically linguistic change, but rather a shift in the normal social relationships between individuals in a group.[6]

Considering the multitudes who have benefited from this communication tool for many millennia of expansion, refinement and adaptation to changing needs, language has proved to be an unprecedented and expeditious stimulus of cultural evolution. Decision is clearly the pivotal concept in this context, for humans are inclined to label and classify just about anything material or spiritual known, every experienced state or condition, every time of past, present or future related to every conceived possibility. And language changes and expands according to human need and desire. In the course of time, word meaning has been refined by innumerable minds to be fuller and to allow greater precision in nuance, because the choice of word—*le mot juste*—is the first step in the communication of meaning, accurately and thoroughly, defining both the sender's intention and feeling and those surmised of the receiver. In his distillation of language function, behavioral and developmental psychologist Lev S. Vigotsky (1962, p. 153) concludes, "A word is a microcosm of human consciousness."

Symbolic phonetic speech more elevated the communication of thought than antecedent modes of communication could ever have achieved, for without language there would be only the simplest culture imaginable among us and the slightest evolution perceptible in our future. Linguistic communication also strengthens memory in the way it connects the most complex concepts, and facilitates memory's expansive capacity in recalling relevant experience, which inevitably is altered as perceptions and conditions change, rendering decisions more practical and powerful. Thanks to this capacity, not only can a specific *idea* be diffused, the entire logical chain of reasoning and feeling can too. This added dimension of experience explains the value of reading, which also permits the reader to adjust the flow of thought at any point and to re-think, contemplate and resume reception at one's own rate of comprehension in connecting ideas and perspectives. Language both written and spoken made possible a much greater accumulation of the culture to be passed along more quickly and in greater detail and nuance through the generations, thereby rendering the substance it communicates more readily to be socially critiqued and altered.

Mass communication technologies now multiply these linguistic capacities. Moreover, just as the current mass-communication media respond to experienced needs and stimulate new ones, they also are harnessed to the mass-marketing of goods and services, thereby tightening the production/consumption system. Sociologist Leslie Sklair (1991, pp. 75–77) paints a striking image of marketing's development:

> The mass media perform many functions for global capitalism. They speed up the circulation of material goods through advertising, which reduces the time between production and consumption. They begin to inculcate the dominant ideology from an early age.... The systematic blurring of the lines between information, entertainment, and promotion of products lies at the heart of this practice.... What it has created is a reformulation of consumerism that transforms all the public mass media and their contents into opportunities to sell ideas, values, products, in short, a consumerist worldview.... The potential of global exposure to global communication, the dream of every merchant in history, has arrived. The socialization process by which people learn what to want, which used to occur mainly in the home and the school, is increasingly taking place through the media of the global communications industries.

The relatively facile reproduction and diffusion of a wide variety of symbols counts among the greatest human powers brought to bear on the stimulation of cultural commodification—a characteristic of modernity—and also responds to the cultural need to accelerate most activities, especially those of social significance (Bell, 1973). The human need for meaning is in large part accommodated by the introduction of language.

Meaning and Worldview

Worldview is a general perception of life, a lens through which an individual makes sense of the environment and his or her place in it. Worldview is the accumulated, synthesized, analyzed, and distilled understanding of events, knowledge, values, things, people, motivations, behaviors, ideas, and perceived possibilities and limitations in life. It includes both individual and social perceptions of the contextual reality, a comprehensive outlook forming the basis on which new attitudes and values are adopted and decisions made. Worldview is the beholder's reality and foundation for further thought and action. It is meaning. Communication among groups, between individuals and through self-introspection is a continuous stimulant in the shaping and reshaping of worldview, and the refinement of its meaning introduces new knowledge, perspectives and values. Michael S. Gazzaniga (2005, p. 135) observes that, because "Our brain is adapted for extreme efficiency … it distorts incoming information to fit in with our current beliefs about the world." Thus, a societal worldview reflects its socially constructed reality, which among other human features includes knowledge, values, sociality, emotion, feelings, morality, the sense of responsibility for others, and the meaning interpreted by all normal humans. The sole reason for communication is to exchange meaning, an explanation requiring no question.[7] Meaning defines the intention, the sense or nuance and the importance of a phenomenon, an idea, an object or a purpose. Meaning is inherent in the concept of worldview. Humanity creates and modifies its own meanings through individual development and the dialectical processes of cultural evolution.

Current Western culture, however, focuses predominantly on novelty, specifically technological innovation. These strains of thought have become the chief purveyors of meaning for the individual human life now disconnected from others by scientism's insistence that, except for its link to personal individuation, which ultimately is an economic/cultural pastime, subjectivity is taboo. Words are the vehicles for exchanging thought in most human communication, but a large segment of the Western mind no longer assigns much belief to the truth of words as conveyances of meaning, such belief having strayed in the ongoing storm of advertising crafted psychologically and ideologically and spewing incessantly from the ubiquitous media. Because the culture is so influenced by the structured communiqué, few words are required, and words no longer require much thought for advertising to convince people of their personal inadequacies in social competition, should they somehow fail to react automatically on cue in the market. In one terse statement, Max Horkheimer (1947, pp. 21–22) summarized this situation three quarters of a century ago:

> The more ideas have become automatic, instrumentalized, the less does anybody see in them thoughts with a meaning of their own. They are considered things, machines. Meaning is supplanted by function or effect in the world of things and events. In so far as words are not used obviously to calculate technically relevant probabilities or for other practical purposes, among which even relaxation is included, they are in danger of being suspect as sales talk of some kind, for truth is no end in itself.

For several centuries, Western culture increasingly has elected the path to decisions requiring the least thought and, therefore, the least context, so its redesign has caused the conscious elimination of subjectivity.[8] Contributing to this strategy is our close association with technology, so it has proved highly influential in our outlook: objective knowledge can be constricted, suppressed and perhaps even lost, but the meaning of emotion, feelings, and social responsibility lasts a lifetime—every normal human's lifetime—through the passing generations. These sensitivities constitute an internal self-messaging center where they can remain stifled unless invoked in judgment, a classification of thought now being removed gradually from the objective sphere of decisions because it demands subjectivity. Contextual human implications are claimed superfluous.

The assumption must have been as it continues to be, that the patterns of scientific decision leading to success in technological and industrial development should perform equally well in all or most other human endeavors. In this view, quotidian life best fits the underlying strategic pattern for economics, science and the capitalist spirit, leaving technology the sole technical dimension of Western life with which the general population maintains some degree of hands-on experience. Indeed, the West is so deeply immersed in technology every day in every way that its presence can be taken for granted, on faith and without question.[9] Natural scientists surely never intended their controlled approach to the understanding of nature to be applied *indiscriminately* to the understanding, explanation, and justification of other aspects of human life.[10] But in an increasingly complex society undergoing continuous change, we often seek understanding in a tactile model, preferably one whose success is familiar.

Human cognition is complex and flexible and includes extraordinarily interactive functions, many of which we employ unconsciously. Of still greater significance, human cognition interacts with the physical and social environments in ways impossible for the cognition of other beings (Boyd & Richerson, 2005). Whether as individuals or societies, we are distinctively animate creatures, forever thinking and feeling, and though we are material we are not exactly things. We are much more.

Reason Streamlined

More compatible with the principle of efficiency, Western conformity to the requirements of technical knowledge has facilitated the adoption of a modernized rationality, but streamlined. It excludes the human features of emotion, feelings, and morality because the original application of this narrowly-gauged reason was intended for application to the purely technical functions of the industrial plan, though later was found applicable to peripheral (human) concerns. This rationality has led to an almost structured integration of humanity and technology, the cultural effect of which has been broad but deep. Similar to criticism later expressed by many others, George Basalla (1988, p. 205) observes that these intellectual eventualities "overwhelm human values and defy human control. Change is possible in the system only if it does not conflict with primary technical values such as efficiency or large-scale integration. Hence, the way we live, work, and play is structured by the monolithic technological order that rules modern industrial society."

We have reduced reason from a perfectly human process of logical understanding, explanation, and clarification to an instrument of action that includes obfuscation. Influenced by the mixture of scientifically-sound objectivity with efficiently-rigid rationality, both of which were first so successful in scientific and technological ventures that the West has learned to perceive subjective thinking as a weakness in and distraction from our maintenance of the economic cycle of development, production and consumption, and even to find subjectivity—our most human distinction—an object of degradation and ridicule. In this environment, attention to our humanity is valued no more than any frivolous human frailty, a wasteful remnant of tradition to be tolerated only in extreme situations because, by forcing the technical system to accommodate non-technical considerations, it supposedly is destructive but most obviously inefficient. Not only do we streamline reason, we also minimize much other thought in the economic interests for which justification is highly self-evident, so the whole strategy becomes part of a tenacious emphasis on technique and immediate result rather than substance and ultimate effect. We neatly strip our non-economic values from our cognition. More than a century ago, sociologist Georg Simmel (2004 [1907], p. 482) commented with dismay on the general integration of this cultural phenomenon:

> This preponderance of means over ends finds its apotheosis in the fact that the peripheral in life, the things that lie outside its basic essence, have become masters of its centre and even of ourselves. Although it is true to say that we control nature to the extent that we serve it, this is correct in the traditional sense only for the outer forms of life. If we consider the totality of life, then the control of nature by technology is possible only at the price of being enslaved in it and by dispensing with spirituality as the central point of life.

Now spread throughout the West, a diminished capacity to reason is the status quo of common sense in disregard of the humanly fundamental cognitive participation of emotion, feelings, and morality.[11] Happiness has become not only measurable but purchasable, as well. Leslie Sklair (1991, p. 41) emphasizes, "The culture-ideology of consumerism proclaims, literally, that the meaning of life is to be found in the things that we possess. To consume, therefore, is to be fully alive, and to remain fully alive we must continuously consume."

Consumerism has weakened much ostensible evidence of the humanity we presume motivates us. It has accomplished this by introducing an astounding abundance into a life that for many millennia had known primarily scarcity, too often painfully and fatally. The mutual dependence of industrialization and consumerism presents options on a scale heretofore unimaginable, including more than things: behaviors, beliefs, attitudes, and identities. Democracy's human traction and humanity's ideal of free will, both of which were concentrated early in the West, support the importance of options, intellectually, politically, and spiritually. Consumerism also relates to the general understanding of Darwinian evolution theory, for as Ian Tattersall (1998, p. 224) observes, "Even as it becomes almost daily clearer that many of our individual personality traits are genetically influenced, often very heavily, our emergent human capacities present us individually with an unparalleled menu of behavioral choices, the basis of our free will. And we make most of these choices for economic or social reasons that have nothing to do with spreading our genes." This is our species' biological motivation.[12]

The ongoing cultural and economic globalization phenomenon is leading the consumer society's spirit into new topographical and cultural territory where a concurrent thirst for democracy is rising. Psychologist Hubert J.M. Hermans (2013, p. 46) rightly emphasizes that "not only different cultural groups are involved in a process of globalization, but also the internal dynamics of the self of the individual person is part of this." If there is an eventuality other than war or vast natural disaster that can drive a modern society into the deep reflection necessary to the reassessment of its situation and the determination of its stance,[13] it would be a fundamental disturbance in the economy upon which the culture is founded because they are joined in their global spread. But the economy has proved itself an untrustworthy foundation for this culture because it is managed by entities driven by the narrowest of self interests. Humanity does continue to pattern the Western culture, of course, but not consciously in humanity's best interest.

Human Values

Human social values and industrial commercial values may at first appear to have very little in common, but as the economic cost to any society's individual members increases, its effect on each almost inevitably requires the re-ordering of the personal values hierarchy and the introduction of new ones. Emotion, feelings, and morality relate profoundly to values, so to separate them from decisions is, quite clearly, to disregard human values, though they constitute the greater part of our normal thought, our definition as a species, and certainly more than our bipedalism. Wolfgang van den Daele (2004, pp. 36–37) describes the current situation accordingly: "The predicament is that such knowledge is dissociated from and external to the instrumental knowledge of nature accumulated through science and technology." When humans are likely to be affected by a decision—which is nearly always—the disregard of our most profound thoughts and commonly shared motivations is foreboding, because it calls for the re-assessment of end and means.[14]

As decisions with human implications are determined to guide technical activities, our social environment has become inimical to our individual subjectivity. Keith Jensen's (2012, p. 317) assessment of the knowledge foundation for decisions reveals, "Philosophers have long viewed emotions as the enemy of reason, though this view has been changing. Early cognitive research tended to avoid emotions as being messy."[15] We have been conditioned to distrust our internal messaging. Common sense and close observation show that strategic planning has proved its value in industry and government, even to the point of its adaptation to managing individuals' personal lives. In industry and government, however, such decision-making exercises have been multiplying sufficiently to affect large populations directly, so the impact of many if not most technical issues is not limited to the immediate technical environment, but spills quite naturally into the social environment. This perception is now sufficiently evident that industrial and governmental organizations increasingly employ or retain technical experts from outside the organization (Fischer, 1990), a practice that has warranted the establishment of special interest groups in voicing the community's perspectives and defending interests of a quite different nature. With each decision, the process becomes more intense, narrow, and restrictive. In these situations, specific concerns relating directly to the technical aspects of a proposed change constitute the ostensible reason for ad hoc expert involvement in decisions. But human values, which today often are perceived simplistically as unquantifiable, and for that reason, negligible components of tradition, also are considered too remote from the technical issue at hand. They are believed of a more individually-oriented and personal nature, perhaps whimsical, and thus quite literally immaterial except as an interfering nuisance. And yet, it is precisely because human values do strike directly at the core of every normal individual that they are so very significant.

Culture Evolves Options

In exercising our options, both an individual's and a culture's predominant considerations are knowledge and values. Their cumulative influence on the course of human evolution follows from the interaction of individuals and groups within a larger population whose culture establishes the norms of conduct for guiding natural selection and adaptation, the principal evolutionary functions. They have been the subject of biological and cultural debate since well before Charles Darwin's time, relating most notably to his 1859 treatise *On the Origin of Species by Means of Natural Selection*. Gradual in its evolution, a culture usually requires many years, decades, centuries, millennia or more to be clearly recognizable, as it is an ongoing product of social mixing that proceeds much more rapidly than biological evolution, which requires no fewer than many millennia to be recognizable. Both manifestations of human change consist of "episodic innovation," as paleoanthropologist Ian Tattersall (1998, p. 238) characterizes them. It is quite possible, however, for cultural evolution to occur with sufficient rapidity to cause stress within the population undergoing change which, originating principally in the West, appears to be the condition in a growing part of the world today. Cultural evolution takes place more swiftly among humans than any other mammal, partly because it is self-derived through accelerated knowledge accumulation and the recognition of change in our own mind. The uniquely human capacity of language expedites and enhances communication among diverse groups, and therefore cultural change. Individual function within the culture exerts considerable influence on evolution's cultural force, because humanity has evolved psychological capacities for simplifying adaptation to human interactions (Damasio, 2010; Sober and Wilson, 1998; Searle, 1995). Extraordinary human cognitive capacities and diverse psychologies motivate cultural evolution directly.

Culture facilitates cooperation among individuals and social groups and is the human phenomenon creditable for much of the change judged as progress. Cultural evolution is a gradual process of change and adaptation that stimulates decision-making, which then initiates a related and often faster-moving cycle of change. Richerson & Boyd (2005, p. 5) clarify this definition, emphasizing, "Culture is information capable of affecting individuals' behavior that they acquire from other members of their species through teaching, imitation, and other forms of social transmission." Culture and biology are mutually influential in their respective evolutions (C. Boehm, 2012; Damasio, 2010; Bowles and Gintis, 2002; E.O. Wilson, 1975). Because the development of human mental capacities follows from a high degree of sociality, it also relates directly and positively to the size and diversity of communities. As Matthew D. Lieberman (2013, p. 28) observes, "increasing evidence suggests that one of the primary drivers behind our brains becoming enlarged was to facilitate our social cognitive skills—our ability to interact and get along well with others." Moreover, social interactions consume about eight times the energy expected solely from cranial capacity (Dunbar, 2000), a proportion that appears to grow in conjunction with human group expansion.[16] The human cognitive system is the primary engine of cultural evolution.

Controlled Influences on Options

Having earlier identified a few of the fundamental and most common obstacles to be encountered in the process of making decisions, we turn now to the key sources of influence diverting attention from human values.

Science and Technology

The news media are highly influential in conditioning our Western deference to the natural science attitude, for the social acceptance of science as a model for human life, generally, also is the most reliable foundation from which to launch any joint effort on a common trajectory. Dorothy Nelkin's (1987, p. 172) research is convincingly clear on this point:

> Science writers, in effect, are brokers, framing social reality for their readers and shaping the public consciousness about science-related events. Through their selection of news about science and technology they set the agenda for public policy. Through their presentation of science news they lay the foundation for personal attitudes and public actions. For they are often our only source of information about the technical choices that significantly affect our lives.

Nelkin also observes that the scientific community has broadened its influence by adopting standard public relations strategies from the corporate world in order to gain sympathetic and supportive public attention. She contends, moreover, that the news media accommodate science's need to secure corporate and governmental financing as well as public admiration, trust and favorable public policy. Having become an increasingly integral part of daily personal life, technological development is similarly a beneficiary of the close relationship of science and news media in this scenario.

Corporate Objectives

Corporate power, leadership and policy at the global level has developed commensurately with the corporate need to strengthen its potential for goal achievement, which has been accomplished to the point that the corporate world now competes with state powers and often exceeds them. But Alford & Friedland (1985, p. 48) find the challenge runs even deeper than this assertion suggests. They write, "Corporate power increasingly challenges democracy, reducing the impact of political participation and biasing the democratic process." Drawing on the American experience, Robert Reich (2007, p. 209) concludes that capitalist strategy and spirit have invaded the democratic political process, for "Large companies have hired platoons of lobbyists, lawyers, experts, and public relations specialists, and devoted more and more money to electoral campaigns. The result has been to drown out voices and values of citizens." Intended to be easily adaptable to a variety of circumstances, corporate strategies and spirit can be adopted by any group defending its position or attacking another's.

Knowledge Tailored

We now adapt to the contours and corners of our technical environment rather than our social environment, our human side. Because knowledge is our culture's foundation, we have tailored it by depth, time, and context.

Depth

Since the latter part of the twentieth century, the significance of an individual's fitness to assume employment in the workplace has been that person's ability to shift knowledge and skill quickly and agilely from one specialization to another (Sennett, 2006). Such flexibility has become one of management's most valued qualifications for current and prospective employees, so knowledge depth often is not sought as much as the ability to make a successful transition from one knowledge classification to another. A criterion now raised to highest level, this industrial strategy entails concentration on present activity and relative disregard of job experience, life experience, and potential. Thus, in his comparison of young adults of the 1970s with those of the early twenty-first century, Richard Sennett (2006, p. 79) finds that "both groups are university-educated and ambitious, and that the striking difference between them is the focus of their ambitions: The group from the earlier generation thought in terms of future strategic gains, the contemporary group in terms of their immediate prospects." Commitment to either the quality of work produced or the employing organization's likely destiny in such an environment is believed irrelevant and therefore of dubious immediate value, present function being of first if not sole importance.

Presentism

The high priority assigned to profit partially explains the knowledge foundation's diminishment in making human decisions, efficiency being among the most significant contributors to the profit margin. But the spirit of capitalism can invade territories well beyond the factory site to affect the general citizenry's quotidian life, where it instills a relentless sense of "presentism." A dominant concentration on the present moment, presentism follows logically from the growing belief that the past is useless and worthless if it is not easily translatable to success in immediate conditions and situations. The industrial primacy for profit connects directly with the quantitative and other symbolic values of money and, as presentism sustains the spirit of competition and progress at a high pitch, the whole package conjures the uneasy sense of alienation and anomie often ascribed to twentieth- and early twenty-first-century Western culture. Gilles Lipovetsky (2005, p. 50) observes several related consequences of presentism, noting particularly that "the race for profits leads to the urgent being prioritized over the important, immediate action over reflection, the accessory over the essential." And competition, which most clearly is a market-oriented capitalist concept that is felt generally and understood in the current economy, is rampant throughout the culture, from getting and spending to the display of individuation, whether of individuals or groups. But it confuses end and means. In short, the efficiency required to be competitive indicates in a most direct way that time is of the essence.[17]

Accompanying these complications are the fundamental facts that progress, as defined today, is inimical to tradition and tradition is anathema to progress. This situation creates a confounding individual and social condition, for tradition has long been the foundation of any society's stability through change. If the past no longer is believed of value to the present and the future too remote to be charted through its specifically unknown but generally expected changes, then attention must fall to the present. In this regard, the single most significant change experienced is the focus of attention, at the center of which is money, for our culture has adopted the values system originally established by industry for the market. George Soros (2000, p. 185) is blunt about this aspect of the West's cultural evolution, concluding, "It is no exaggeration to say that money rules peoples' lives as never before." Our culture is most comprehensible in money's unique value, because it is acceptable that a minimal amount of time may be lost if there is a reasoned expectation of achieving our most obvious goal, which is the swiftest acquisition and accumulation of money. As a wholly quantitative value, money is wholly understandable.

Context Winnowed

The conditions outlined above lead quite logically, and in the name of efficiency, to a winnowing of context in the knowledge foundation for decisions. The evident intention is to maximize system value by reducing or eliminating system connection with its non-essential environment. Yet the fact remains that every situation, every contested issue and every idea, decision, and plan is part of a context, an environment including non-technical situations. The context of decisions leading to action has been diminished, however, pursued increasingly and with unrelenting purpose as a means to accelerate the cognitive processes an environmental change inherently requires. While this strategy for progress may cut many corners, they are found most dependably in the subjective dimensions of context, perhaps because subjectivity is more meaningful in narrative than numeric form, thereby failing to meet the rigorous standards of rationality, objectivity, and efficiency industry has determined them to be. Emotion, feelings, and morality are treated much like context and are to be invoked only when elevated—by some external force—to an urgent necessity. According to this logic, the historical and experiential aspect of the knowledge foundation for decisions has very little or no place at all, as they must concentrate instead on present and prospect, specifically as regards their technical problems and opportunities. "As the work of historians makes clear," writes Frank Fischer (2009, p. 195), "intentions contribute to making things happen and, as such, are inherent to the description and explanation of the causal mechanisms underlying political and social phenomena." But lacking subjectivity also means lacking a sense of narrative movement, and that "events in time are disconnected, experience is not accumulated," Richard Sennett (2006, p. 183) explains in his criticism of industrial, cutting-edge management. Otherwise a most significant dimension of human life, experience is no longer a valued source of knowledge.

On the other hand, the context of actual human life is situated at the nexus of systems individuals share through their social and physical environments, and everything has the context of its connections, making context the very basis of understanding. Dennis Ford (2007, p. 122) writes that "all knowledge claims or facts are only intelligible in their own context. This natural dependency on context is evident in everyday experience.... Facts, as well as meaning, require contexts." To find the centrality of context and the connections among objects and ideas is to discover their relevance to a given situation, and therefore their relative value. In a culture dominated by the ease of manipulating objects and ideas to create their utility, however, knowledge of context, or just becoming aware of context, requires a highly conscious effort, the effort to understand, which leads toward a mental state achievable primarily, if not solely, in knowing the deeper levels of inclusiveness. Knowledge pursues an ideal extending far beyond that of accurate information, for understanding is the perception of the significance the values system requires in forming judgment. Quality of judgment is critical to any individual's physical, social, and psychological survival; it stems directly from a sound understanding of the environment in relation to the individual's values and their priority ordering. Judgment proceeds from the ever-rising but always elusive state of understanding, and is the pivotal function of decision. Necessarily, decisions of almost any kind are determined in a context whose center is the subjective self, while the manifestation of poor judgment in decisions results most likely from inadequate knowledge of context.

The internet opens a vast potential for learning, having quickly demonstrated its sweeping influence on communication among most of the peoples of our planet. Yet, despite the greater learning potential it places at the disposition of individuals and institutions around the globe, its communication of information—the trigger for thought—evidently produces minimal effect on continued knowledge development and may be a deterrent. In the internet's infancy, philosopher Alexander Bard and social theorist Jan Soderqvist (2002, p. 200) found that,

> The most sought-after and therefore most valuable information of all on the net is that which concerns networking itself: how to construct and administer your network in the most intelligent way.... The arena is crooked and events are unpredictable. Round every corner there is a complete surprise. What was relevant yesterday will seldom have any relevance today.

A natural continuity of human life has become rare and almost unexperienced. The decision to forego the rich and varied intellectual stimulation to which the internet so easily connects its vast clientele's preference for immediate engagement, has become part of the more general Western trend toward method and away from substance.[18] "Like it or not," concludes social theorist Heather Menzies (2005, p. 4), "the medium itself exerts a bias toward superficiality and human disconnection even while connection and being in touch, technically speaking, have never been easier." Power, competition, and method are again the principal attractions.[19] A safe speculation is that, if such a bias emanates from the medium itself, it would follow from several conditions uniquely prevalent within it: One condition would be the infinite number of participants this communication mode can accommodate; another, the degree of anonymity it provides each participant; and a third negative condition would be the irresponsible and apparently thoughtless spontaneity the internet encourages.

Subjective Knowledge

The kind of knowledge at issue in this essay is subjective, most often referred to as information, but it certainly does not displace technical knowledge any more than technical knowledge can displace subjective knowledge. Its function is not to solve technical problems but to invoke considerations relative to the technical interface with human beings and to guide examines reason in a manner that maintains a satisfactory human homeostasis. We occupy two fundamental environments, the physical and the social. To severely weaken the social environment by diminishing or losing our subjective knowledge permanently would be to diminish or lose our humanity. The following chapters are intended to validate this conclusion, the next one examining the extraordinary freedom our mental capacities make possible, and the motives and responsibility complementing it.

6

Freedom, Motivation and Responsibility

> The social group is the survival vehicle of its individual members.
> —James R. Hurford, 2007
>
> Self control is the price of admission to society.
> —Matthew D. Lieberman, 2013

The Self: The Composite Human

A culture normalizes its constituents, so each unique individual and complex mind experiences continuous renovation leading to a more complex psychology. The process renders human behavior quite varied and difficult to predict, as neither the individual nor the culture is ever a finished product, so an understanding of our own species is manifest only in the evolutionary path humanity carves through time. Given humanity's seemingly unlimited possibilities, this chapter introduces the concept of the self and addresses the fundamental issue of whether human motivation is dominated by self-interest or by a commonly inherited concern for the commonweal. It begins the essay's summary of findings that both motivations apply, the ultimate or underlying human motivation being, as Darwin claimed, the survival of our species.

Self-Interest and Others

Zoltan Torey (2014, p. 122) writes that the experience we call "self," "is the natural by-product of the language-equipped brain's routine functioning."[1] There is no self without others in mind, so it is extremely unusual and difficult, if not impossible, to imagine the self as the sole sentient entity to exist. As Ty Solomon (2015, p. 14) reports, "Most identity scholars argue that difference or Otherness is central to identity, since it is through the marking off of difference that the boundaries of the Self are defined." Furthermore, common sense and reason suggest that some measure of self-interest is by nature necessary if the self is to survive—let alone flourish—in an environment largely social and usually competitive. Neuroscientist Antonio Damasio (2010, pp. 267–268) supplies a logical explanation of the self in maintaining balance through individual and cultural change:

> The self focuses the mind process, it imbues the adventure of encountering other objects and events with a motivation, it infuses the exploration of the world outside the brain with a *concern* for the first and foremost problem facing the organism: the successful regulation of life. That concern is naturally generated by the self process, whose foundation lies in bodily feelings, primordial and modified. The spontaneously, intrinsically feeling self signals directly, as a result of the valence and intensity of its affective states, the degree of concern and need that are present at every moment.

Each individual's motivation necessarily stems from the perspective of self, each continuously engaging in introspection and thoughtfully experimenting as situations and conditions change.[2] But since the debate is at least two-sided, introspection also reveals some properties of social dialectic.

There is no single model for the human being or perhaps for any other species, the principal difference residing in the fact that humans simply are far more complex and versatile and consequently manifest a greater range of possibilities, which also indicate the considerable potential of an individual's influence within any given culture. Roy Baumeister (2010, p. 34) observes, "The ability of the human self to alter its own states and responses, and to bring them in line with conceptually meaningful standards such as laws, norms, moral ideals, and many more, is vitally conducive to culture." A culture functions as it does because, in concert with others, the individual human cognitive capacities integrate rather smoothly by dint of their inherent sociality, influencing other individuals in their continuous adjustment to and alteration of the environment.

There is ample evidence that throughout modernity, people increasingly have concentrated mental energies on the immediate projection of self within the culture, often leaving longer-term existential concerns unattended. A substantial part of our culture's evolution, however, has accumulated enough consistency in our cognitive capacities that we retain responsibility for our species and other beings, primarily because *Homo sapiens* could not otherwise have evolved so progressive a path—thus far. Reflecting on the relationship of self and society, G.H. Mead (1934, p. 315) contends, "The individual who identifies himself with the group has the sense of an enlarged personality." An evolutionary perspective on humanity uncovers the value that becomes most evident in the concept of self, for the ideal of self-understanding is fundamental to understanding others and to social responsibility. There almost always is something for the individual to gain from the presence of others or just from an awareness of the relative ease of access to them. But the more widely accepted model of "Economic man" rejects the notion of humans as extraordinarily social beings who may even be altruistic by nature. Instead, this model claims that we are indomitably self-centered and even selfish individuals, able to behave otherwise only when intent on garnering support from others for our own cause. Particularly during the past century and a half, this belief has served the purpose of those who perceived in the model its personal advantage for themselves, a perception that continues to cloud our social environment.

Materialism, according to cultural sociologist Celia Lury (2011, p. 214), is a feature whose "consumer culture is a particular form of material culture in which the capacity to exercise consumer choice has become central to personal or self-identity," as she explains:

> "Consumer choice" is indeed one of the most important means by which our society thinks about individual agency and autonomy, and makes judgements about individuals.... From this point of view, the sociological significance of consumer culture is to be found in the fact that the individual is not judged by him-herself or by society in terms of how well they carry out their duty or responsibility in relation to some wider collective or external morality ("the family," "the community," "the greater good of all" or "God's will") but in terms of how well they exercise their capacity to make a (consumer) choice.

Such a life is structured by the collaboration of industry, government, and agents of finance, mass-marketing and mass consumerism. Thus, philosopher Seumas Miller (2010, p. 294) notes, "Politicians these days sometimes talk as if the market were an intrinsic good, that material well-being is good in itself and independent of its outcomes in terms of human being—market fundamentalism."[3] This democracy-oriented arrangement, crafted carefully to inspire and support a sense of individual freedom, also promotes the immediate interests of the economy underpinning our society.

Freedom

Regardless of any nation's governance philosophy or style, all citizens enjoy the freedom of thought introspection provides, and although it can help in understanding problems and decisions, introspection also can introduce new internal conflicts. The sense of free will yields further decisions, a consequence of freedom requiring some kind of internal order or balancing constraint.[4] Morality furnishes such constraint by issuing recognized feelings, so it also is a source of deep inner conflict that incurs the cost of internal debate and restless nights. Alluding to this uncomfortable situation, Mary Midgley (1994, p. 106) observes that,

If freedom and morality are indeed closely linked in this way, it is perhaps a rather paradoxical fact that the first effect of freedom should be to put us under these new constraints. Our freedom is exactly what gives us these headaches, what makes possible this moral thinking, this troublesome kind of search for priority among conflicting aims. By becoming aware of conflict—by ceasing to roll passively from one impulse to another, like floods of lava through a volcano—we certainly do acquire a load of trouble. But we also become capable of larger enterprises, of standing back and deciding to make lesser projects give way to more important ones. That, it seems, may be why moralities are needed.

Because humans possess the complex and powerful mental systems our incomparably high degree of sociality requires, normal Western life presents many complexities. But, because of the human capacity to perceive this freedom of thought, and to cope with the added dimension of the burdensome responsibility it introduces, humanity has a conscience, the constraining force of morality in conflict with many other motivations occupying our introspection.

Motivation

This essay refers frequently to the human faculty of reason, the logical concatenation of knowledge leading toward explanation and understanding. But reason is not the sole mental process for motivating action or further thought, the principal others being the emotion and feelings inherited genetically by all normal humans. Closely connected with emotion and feelings are values, which when linked together convey deep personal meaning, attachment and authority, influencing the internal deliberation that leads to action.[5] "Few deny that emotions can be motivating," according to philosopher Carla Bagnoli (2011, p. 62), adding, "Many recognize that emotions may account for the motivational appeal of moral reasons, and some argue that emotions provide moral reasons for action." Clinical studies reveal this connection with morality while also noting the absence of such a pattern in psychopaths, who nonetheless can be quite rational (Joyce, 2006). The deepest emotions and feelings pertinent to the present essay are those leading to the constructive social acts of sympathy, empathy, compassion and altruism, for without appropriate feelings there would be precious little concern for others, and no morality (J. Taylor, 2011), therefore not much humanity, if any. Nonetheless, we stifle our subjectivity most clearly in decisions, for "capitalism is a culture that puts humanistic values and ways of thought at peril; indeed, humanistic values and ways of thought are progressively dismissed or relegated to either the legal or the purely private, subjective realms," writes E.M. Adams (1997, p. 130).

Empathy: Emotion and Feelings

Empathy is the recognition of another's condition or situation and the capacity to experience similar emotion and feelings, which are universally human and dependent upon the Theory of Mind features discussed in Chapter 2. This emotional stimulation is compassionate when the observer decides to aid the one undergoing an emotional experience, and when such aid is provided at serious cost to the observer it is an act of altruism. Empathy, compassion, and altruism share a primary concern for the *suffering* of others rather than for the *cause* of the condition or situation. Primatologist and ethologist Frans de Waal (2009, p. 80) gauges the significance of compassion in his conclusion, stating, "If identification with others opens the door for empathy, the absence of identification closes that door," suggesting that a negative action such as humiliation will be forthcoming. Emotion is especially significant in human evolution, but particularly in the evolution of human sociality because without it, cooperation could never have developed to the extent it has.

Empathy, compassion, and altruism combine with reason and imagination in constituting the foundation for human cooperation, itself an act usually considered far more emotional than rational, but an act ultimately derived from the human capacity to perceive in the mind of others a favorable attitude toward cooperation, and to act accordingly when possible. This level of cognition is as significant to cooperation as cooperation is to both cultural evolution and the maintenance of an ultimately harmonious society. Human emotion flows from compassion, according to moral philosopher Lawrence A. Blum (1994, p. 178): "By transcending the recognition of social inequality [emotion] promotes the sensed experience of equality in common humanity." Emotion and feelings are among the most significant foundations of human culture, as they convey the encouragement necessary to cultural adherence. Moreover, they bolster the individual and collective sense of social responsibility. Henrik Høgh-Olesen (2010, p. 249) succinctly captures this idea in his metaphor of the special niche we humans have built into our environment:

> As humans we simply are each other's means to the common goals, and the *human niche*—that is, the physical and social environment that we have adapted to throughout history—is a niche characterized by considerable inter-dependence, collaboration, closely knit relationships, intensive gift-giving, reciprocity, extended sharing of resources and services, and radical self-sacrifice.

These spiritual features are the standards of religion and morality, religion being at once an individual, personal belief and a social means of supporting it, particularly as religion also contributes to the maintenance of sociality and order by strengthening morality.

Religion

"Religion is a species-specific human universal," writes evolutionary psychologist Ara Norenzayan (2010, p. 68). Religious spirituality responds to the questions and feelings most people experience while also meeting other individual and group needs, such as helping to cope with life's challenges, both quotidian and extraordinary.[6] Religious spirituality accomplishes this general objective by alleviating stress and anxiety but is not an evolutionary adaptation, according to Norenzayan (2010, p. 58). He explains that religion is rather "a recurring byproduct of the complex evolutionary landscape that canalizes the cultural transmission of religious beliefs and behaviors into convergent yet culturally distinct pathways. This means that religious beliefs are the product of cultural transmission constrained by evolutionary psychology."

Religion emerged in the association of prehistoric humans, collaborating in ever larger groups while generating an unprecedented complexity that has placed new demands on mental capacity in the brain's neocortex. This site is particularly noteworthy because it is the part of the brain that coordinates higher-level thought, including sensory perception, the generation of motor commands, spatial reasoning, conscious and abstract thought, language, and imagination (Gazzaniga, 2011). Introducing a logical theory for religion's emergence, Ara Norenzayan (2016, p. 123) posits, "If modern hunter-gatherer groups clue us to the ancestral conditions, even in a limited and oblique fashion, then we can conclude that these beliefs started as rare forms of cultural beliefs." Norenzayan (pp. 138–139) summarizes how this may have proceeded:

> Taken together, the cross-cultural and historical evidence points to a converging pattern. As groups expand in size and in social complexity, religion acquires a moral dimension. Gods become more powerful, interventionist, and demanding of hard-to-fake commitment. Rituals become more frequent, routinized, and in the service of transmitting dogma. Once belief-ritual complexes begin to take shape, other commitment devices are added to the mix by the processes of cultural evolution: synchronous movement (song and dance), practices encouraging self-control (including habitual suppression of self-interest and other socially undesirable behaviors) and a sense of fictive kinship (treating co-religionists as if they were brothers and sisters). Packaged together with supernatural monitoring and extravagant displays of faith, these "cultural gadgets" further ratchet up level s of cooperation and social cohesion in prosocial religious groups, and turn anonymous strangers into moral communities.

We humans are extraordinarily curious beings with many questions, some of which can be especially persistent when existential. Among the reasons for religion's continued strong social support are the anxieties that surround our understanding of human mortality and our heightened general awareness of the negative treatment people continue to inflict on each other, in conjunction with religion's appreciation of justice, its concern for the well-being of others, and its explicit statement of morality. In explaining this continued support, anthropologist Scott Atran (2005, pp. 316–317) observes that religion meets a common need because "science treats humans and intentions only as incidental elements in the universe, whereas for religion they are central. Science is not well suited to deal with people's existential anxieties—death, deception, sudden catastrophe, loneliness, or longing for love or justice. It cannot tell us what we *ought* to do, only what we can do. Religion thrives because it addresses people's yearning and society's moral needs." Commodity consumption alone is proving not to be the panacea for the West's general dissatisfactions, but may instead contribute to them.

Morality

The concept of morality comprises individual and societal judgment of human character as determined by observing behavior and inferring intention; it is closely associated with dignity. In terms of good or bad, right or wrong, morality is the system of principles and values most cogently applied in the assessment of one's own behavior as well as that of others, ethics being the dimension of morality that applies particularly to the practice expected of various professions, a code of behavior, although it also is associated with the assessment of conduct within the general social context. Morality, then, is the cluster of both inspiring and constraining thoughts held by all normal people, however they may act.

Learned at a very early age and continuing throughout life, morality's guidance always is accessible for consultation in making relevant decisions in any social setting. It occupies a unique place in our thought, says Michael Ruse (2012, pp. 175–176), explaining, "Moral ability is innate, but we have to learn how to use it, and once acquired it is difficult to change it. It is the same as learning English or French. Perhaps you can push the analogy a bit further, suggesting that there is some kind of deep universal moral grammar and that growing up in a particular society you learn to apply it in somewhat different ways." With its focus on the agent's stance toward others in any situation and under any conditions, morality can lead to the most challenging kind of internal reflection and debate, the consequences of which can be evolutionarily significant at the societal level, as G.H. Mead (1934, pp. 386–387) explains.

> Of course, there have been evolutionary changes that took place without individual reaction. But moral changes are those that take place through the action of the individual as such. He becomes the instrument, the means, of changing the old into a new order. What is right arises in the experience of the individual; he comes to change the social order; he is the instrument by which custom itself may be changed.... Values come into conflict with each other in the experiences of the individual; it is his func-

tion to give expression to the different values and help to formulate more satisfactory standards than have existed.

Central to the direction of human evolution, the concept of morality continues to be a subject of much scholarly and scientific controversy.[7]

Moral standards for human conduct are derived culturally to form principles of support for several aspects of our consciousness: others' attention focused on one's own behavior; one's attention focused on the behavior of others; one's inference of another's judgment, or the societal judgment (reputation) of one's own behavior; and one's moral self-assessment. Morality functions within societies much as it does within individuals, meaning that both individuals and societies tend to be labeled according to their estimated moral character. Awareness of morality entails a complex and layered network of reflexive mind-reading, centered on the quality of effort contributed by all toward societal well-being, and it specifically includes evaluation of one's worthiness of either condemnation or praise. This consideration raises the general level of self-consciousness, but primarily for any individual who is making a decision about behavior or has just acted on it. Morality is a highly complex system to which normal humans are closely attuned, for we are concerned about our own social standing, past, present and future, and it either supports our dignity or places weakens it. Frans de Waal (1996, p. 217) writes, "Morality is as firmly grounded in neurobiology as anything else we do or are."

There are, of course, those who monitor their own deceitful subterfuge, which they may manage without attracting too much attention and most likely are able to accomplish in the future—but without seriously jeopardizing the trust and social standing usually necessary to their chosen path through life. This group includes some who seem to relish the sense of duping others by flaunting moral principle. Confusing the question of why some people may follow their moral guidance more habitually than others is the fact that such principles lend a special rationality to decisions of the most common kind. Identifying the significance of morality to human thought, evolutionary psychologist Dennis L. Krebs (2011, p. 259) notes, "Research indicates that utilitarian moral judgments stem from higher-order cognitive processes than deontological moral judgments do, and that the latter are more highly influenced by emotional reactions than the former are." Regardless of our intentions or actions, there should be no doubt about the importance we humans ascribe to morality, for it always is active in our mind.

Why Morality?

When hunting became an organized and intensive way of life, about a quarter million years ago, its practice demonstrated on a large scale the value of human cooperation. Cooperation made good sense in this life-sustaining but life-threatening enterprise, just prior to the rise of anatomically modern *Homo sapiens,* some 200,000 years ago. This is the chronological frame cultural anthropologist Christopher Boehm posits as the period during which a strong moral sense arose to meet the need of cooperative hunting, a sense that could render the effort relatively safe as well as productive. Boehm (2012, p. 163) reasons that this event evolved "to a very significant degree by social selection, guided by highly consistent social preferences." The plan was supported by methods of enforcing individual responsibility for others drawn from existing socially-derived standards of conduct. In this scenario, the conscience evolved from emotions stimulated repeatedly by the humiliating experience of social punishment for failing to perform satisfactorily. Boehm (p. 168) writes that, "the genes involved in self-protective self-assessment and self-control could have been strongly supported by punitive social selection." Each individual had to contribute skill and effort dependably well since the welfare of many was at stake, meaning that one's reputation also was at stake. Boehm (p. 171) further indicates that, in the oral traditions of the earliest civilizations, "the question of how humans acquired a shameful sense of right and wrong is addressed so frequently that I would have to number the instances in the thousands, and these stories can be colorfully different—yet strikingly similar." Any notion of heroism extant at the time would have been solidified. This sequence of cultural change and its ancillary requirements may well mark the beginning of the strong feeling of morality and social responsibility that evolved into the morality individual conscience now guides in the interest of society. It is one of humanity's most distinguishing characteristics.[8]

Morality may also have been a central current in the cultural watershed of other key human universals, including the concept of justice and the development of religion, language, narrative, and mythology (Suddendorf, 1999). Furthermore, writes Dennis L. Krebs (2011, p. 200), "New brain structures enabled early humans to form and manipulate ideas in their minds, which mediated the expansion and refinement of their ability to learn, to remember, to plan, to reason, to engage in creative thinking, to predict the behavior of others, and to understand what others are thinking and feeling." Two aspects of this intellectually productive segment in our cultural evolution are of particular significance to the present essay. One relates to the prosocial capacities these new brain structures strengthened; the other is the brain's malleable composition, which enables the incorporation of both new and recently developing features, plus a sample of those established at primitive stages of human biological and cultural evolution, not solely the rewired parts of the brain. Krebs (p. 216) also provides a condensed explanation of how the culture may have managed to accommodate morality:

The mechanisms that give rise to moral emotions were selected in ancestral environments because they induced early humans to behave in ways that increased their inclusive fitness. A sense of moral duty probably originated in the emotions and motivational states that disposed early humans to behave in prosocial ways. This sense helped them reap the long-term benefits of group living. A sense of pride and guilt probably originated in reactions to the social approval and disapproval of others. These senses reinforced prosocial dispositions, helped people resist temptation, and induced them to repair damaged social relations. A sense of justice probably evolved to uphold systems of cooperative exchange.

The self is aroused by the known or supposed existence of other selves because, owing to the benefits of cooperation within a society, there is for any individual a highly pragmatic self-interest in the welfare and attitude of others in that society. Anthropologist Peter I. Bogucki (1999, p. 27) summarizes, "Ego is at the center of anyone's social sphere," which also means most clearly that self is the core of human dignity. In referring to Adam Smith's socio-economic theories in the eighteenth century, evolutionary psychologist Randolph M. Nesse (2010, p. 146) explains the function of social selection in evolving humanity's extraordinary capacities for cooperation and culture: "Individuals pursuing self-interest make thousands of social choices. These choices are the invisible hand that domesticated our species. Each lifetime recapitulates the process; tiny social cues act on mechanisms shaped by selection to detect and respond to them, steadily but firmly rewarding increasingly prosocial behavior." As observed earlier, punishment acknowledged instances of failure to contribute toward prosocial behavior. Like most other beings, we humans have always focused on ourselves as individuals among others, and on our conspecifics as distinct from other species.[9] People acknowledge our sameness as members of a particular species among others species, but also our distinctions as individuals among conspecifics. Language constitutes the most common and natural manifestation of exchange among selves within society, but even in that ordinary context, James Hurford (2007, p. 168) emphasizes, *"A form of communication exists because the producer of a signal normally gets some benefit from it."* A self is interested first in self because the self has invested heavily in that entity, which is a perfectly normal way to proceed in life; to be perceived as extremely self-oriented, however, or to care nothing about others, is abnormal and understood negatively as such by most others. We individually possess internal forces that function to keep our species on an advantageous track. The common courtesies we exercise daily may not appear especially important per se, but they are symbolic reminders of our significance as humans, of our dignity, and of our unique responsibility.

There are, however, and have long been other interpretations of how and why such an otherwise complicating and distracting consideration as morality exists at all, interpretations arising most frequently in connection with religion's part in maintaining humanity's guide to behavior. But Michael S. Gazzaniga (2008, p. 165) finds morality at the earliest stages of human life, which strongly suggests that it is embedded in our genetically-inherited information: "The fact that babies are able to discriminate between their own cry and other infants' cries suggests that they have some innate understanding of the difference between themselves and others."[10] And most scientists conclude similarly about morality's place in humanity (H. C. Barrett, 2015; Kenrick & Griskevicius, 2013; L. Barrett, 2011; Krebs, 2011; Damasio, 2010). Religion has maintained a high level of persistence in societal attention to prosocial behavior and the protection of others that some of our other cultural penchants may have weakened, and it also has instilled a strong sense of morality that could easily have migrated to those not committed to any religion.

Functions & Benefits of Morality

Morality is one of the prosocial features the restructuring of the brain's response to growing pressures accommodates in coping with conflict. It has been a normal part of human life through at least the past fifty millennia of increasing cooperation among intelligent and strong-willed individuals who also have accumulated a knowledge base for managing a priority-ordered, yet flexible, system of values. Ranked highest among reasons for the human being's long maturation process is the prosocial dimension of thought any normally functioning adult requires. Decisions and other judgments rendered by social beings depend heavily on an understanding of human motivation, particularly as technical knowledge grows more complex and presents more frequent conflict with the human values guarded by emotion, feelings, and morality.

Morality is a source of motivation and control very distinctly separating humans from other beings. The conscience may cause individual frustrations but also provides overriding social benefits that affect us positively as individuals and, in the long term, more evidently as a species. Influence of the conscience flows from individual self-assessment stimulated by both our inherited information and our learned knowledge, so the social environment can assess our individual character according to widely understood standards. Our character and intentions are inferred by others from our behavior and their own self-understanding. Conscience reflects the social acknowledgment that our species has established norms for behavior and that our culture refines them, all of which humans uniquely possess the capacity to contemplate.

Rules of Human Behavior

Applying to all normal people, moral rules must be flexible, adaptable and immediately understandable in the course of nuanced and always-changing conditions, but without jeopardizing their social value. Therefore, such qualifications complement our human psychological apparatus, as David Sloan Wilson (2003, p. 28) explains:

> [M]oral systems include an open-ended cultural dimension in addition to an innate psychological dimension. Our genetically evolved minds make it possible to have a moral system, but the specific contents of moral systems can change within groups and vary widely among groups, with important consequences for survival and reproduction. Far from leading to the caricature of genetic determinism that limits the capacity for change, our innate psychology creates a capacity for change by setting in motion a process of cultural evolution.

The moral system facilitates cooperation on large and small scale, lending the capacity to plan and execute social change with minimal disruption in individual lives. Moral philosopher Jacqueline Taylor (2011, p. 257) indicates one of the most significant values of morality in her following assessment, "Our capacities to admire and value one another for our moral dispositions and moral effectiveness, and to develop pride in such dispositions and effectiveness, play a key role in helping to create empathic and caring individuals." This value connects directly with human dignity. To be truly meaningful and lasting, it is logical that a moral system would evolve from the ground up, in both expressed and tacit agreement about how we humans should treat each other. Harry Smit (2014, p. 191) indicates that humanity possesses not only a natural penchant toward sociality but also a specific penchant toward the rules of engagement: "The use of language enables us to follow rules: they constitute reasons for doing things and inform actions within rule-governed practices. I have argued that the ontogenesis and evolution of rule-governed behavior is an example of the development of a complex, linguistic skill. Moral behaviour evolved as an extension of this skill."

Underlying our natural attraction to establish and demonstrate acceptable behavior is the strength of our cultures which, although falling short of legal authority, contribute to cultural authority and lend it an adhering quality that supports its influence. Whereas the assessment of intention is the essence of moral judgment, and as such bears much weight, the assessment of behavior is more malleable and dependent upon surmised intention. Therefore, compared with social guidelines such as conventions, customs and traditions, moral rules are more complex, being "unconditionally obligatory, generalizable, and impersonal insofar as they stem from concepts of welfare, justice, and rights," writes philosopher Shaun Nichols (2004, p. 5). In view of morality's various degrees of severity, its commitment to written codification could quickly become a knot too tight to be unraveled—especially when its fine degrees of infraction are considered. Yet, morality is understood universally in the absence of a written record; it is the bulwark of our cultures.

Moral Judgment

While humans who are considered normal may exhibit many differentiating features, we also share a natural capacity to both *perceive the presence* of a moral issue and *identify its nature*. "It is moral perception which does that individuating or construing of the situation, thus providing a setting in which moral judgment carries out its task," asserts Lawrence A. Blum (1994, p. 42), and it is evident that moral reasoning depends very heavily on Theory of Mind capacities, primarily the reasoning relative to emotion and feelings. Because a cognitive capacity exists for making both these often subtle distinctions and distinguishing among levels of the infraction's severity, the perception that a given situation includes a moral dimension to which the relevant principles apply, so a judgment can quickly be determined about both the severity of the infraction and the quality of the agent's character. The perception that facilitates distinctions between infractions that are conventional social misconduct and those of moral content—even in determining their relative degree of severity—has been integral to human social life for so long that it is embedded in the cognition of modern humans at a very early age: the capacity to make these distinctions is part of normal human psychology.[11] Learning the distinctions between proper and improper behavior can easily be traced to the mother as a model, according to Christopher Boehm (2012, p. 235), "along with a primitive capacity for self-recognition, innately based dominance and submission tendencies, and also a strong resentment of being dominated."

James Krebs (2011, p. 208) asserts that research in neuroscience implies that "making moral judgments requires at least two processes—a logical assessment of intention, and an emotional reaction to the assessment—with each of these processes mediated by different, but interacting, brain circuits." Any normal person today understands that people do continuously make moral judgments about others' conduct and their inferred intention, while we also make our assessments of *self* on the same basis—particularly about moral implications. Such judgments result in largely conflicting emotions and feelings. At stake is the perception of character, which indicates that prosocial behavior is of considerable importance to us individually, even when we may behave otherwise. The moral system is complex, for its punishment ranges in degrees of severity from the very serious, which is doing harm to a fellow human (causing pain and suffering), to not very serious at all, and therefore is easily forgiven and perhaps forgotten. Yet, the moral system is almost automatic for normal humans of all ages, from toddlers to the elderly. Ultimately, the general society benefits from this human capacity, though it persistently challenges every normal individual.

Impact on Our Species

Whether relatively simple and primarily manual functions or highly complex intellectual challenges are involved, morality continues to be essential in collaborative ventures, which now occupy most aspects of Western life. Throughout human evolution, morality also has fostered an ever-greater cohesive quality within each society, strengthening the sense of community and detailing a more widely shared understanding of how humans can live together harmoniously and productively as individuals, thus to thrive as a species. Logic suggests that had this mode of life not proved successful throughout continuous group selection, it could not have become the common behavior it now is. Morality has long been the social preference for conduct, despite those relatively few individuals who exploit peace and harmony solely to their own benefit. Specifically, Christopher Boehm (2012, p. 169) finds, "Today, this social selection continues to do two things as far as our gene pool is concerned. One is to reduce innate dispositions to bully or cheat. The other is to keep our conscience in place as a means of self-inhibiting antisocial deviance that can easily get us in trouble." Moreover, scholars generally agree that the perception of morality is a significant criterion in mate choice (Krebs, 2011; Nesse, 2010; Tiberius, 2008), which suggests the essential reason for humanity's continued support of morality. "Even in the most dire situation," writes moral philosopher Richard Joyce (2006, p. 9), "morality clings on—or rather, humans cling on to morality." Since most normal people find value in their own sociality, and because they understand that most of their conspecifics perceive morality similarly, they are mindful of its place in human life; each, of course, also knows that social penalties apply when one fails to behave accordingly. "Human societal organisms rely critically on moral systems to define appropriate behaviors and to prevent subversion from within," concludes David Sloan Wilson (2003, p. 37), adding, "Moral systems have an innate psychological dimension but also an open-ended dimension that allows human history to be seen as a fast-paced evolutionary process with cultural rather than genetic mechanisms of inheritance." Morality is not limited to guarding against infractions, however, as it also rewards those who act on empathy, particularly altruism, as well as those who are dependably reciprocative and fair. They are the ones who may become recognized heroes when accounts of their positive behavior circulate far and wide, quickly spreading a lift in spirit Daniel Goleman (2006, p. 53) says "may be catching. When someone sees an act of kindness, it typically stirs in them the impulse to perform one, too. These social benefits may be the one reason mythic tales worldwide are rife with figures who save others through their courageous deeds."

Nature and nurture can function together seamlessly in humans because of specialized mental capacities highly dependent upon the unusually deep human memory. Thus, morality is a complex and powerful guide for both individual and social conduct, yet easy to comprehend and employ comfortably to one's benefit. More than that, morality is so closely interwoven in the cultural evolution of humans that it can be argued the heart of humanity. We control our own individual behavior, most often according to the influence of our long-inherited and frequently-exercised conscience.

Conscience, the Moral Compass

The conscience helps ensure a high quality of social relationship and responsibility, so moral judgment arises immediately upon the perception that an act of moral significance is about to occur or already has. It is the oversight of human consciousness that keeps us moving in a socially healthy direction, although not without individual inner conflict. As a special dimension of humanity, conscience is an internal set of feelings about one's own intentions and actions as right or wrong, good or bad, and is our basis for judging others' witnessed behavior or inferred intentions, as well as our own in interpreting others' supposed assessment of us. The conscience functions much like an interior dialogue, by balancing the likely advantage of any option with the moral costs inherent in the context of others' likely judgment of our options. The advantage it offers is a sense of pride, while the cost is a sense of guilt or shame and the likely indignation of others. At least since the age of hunting and gathering, all normal humans have possessed a conscience, its significance defined in Christopher Boehm's (2012, p. 176) conclusion, "Basically, we've moved from a wolflike or apelike 'might is right,' fear-based social order to one also based on internalizing rules and worrying about personal reputations. This was enough to make us unique in the animal kingdom." And it is enough to demonstrate an evolutionary path toward improved social motivation and responsibility. The attention humanity accords reputation may arguably be morality's most valuable function, as it forces a higher level of mutual understanding.

The English noun "conscience" derives directly from the French meaning and spelling but ultimately from the ancient Latin *conscientia*, connoting consilience, a convergence of principles and concepts reflecting varied perspectives in a comprehensiveness that bears a particularly powerful effect. In the Roman Empire, the concept of conscience was social, its foundation in opinion not religion. The word's frequency increased during the Enlightenment and has since continued as a secular basis for principle, independent of religious association. Ara Norenzayan (2010, p. 64) theorizes the merger of religion with the concept of conscience:

> The idea of supernatural agents, a byproduct of mundane cognitive capacities, was culturally transformed into *morally concerned supernatural policing agents*. This idea became culturally widespread, as it allowed for further expansion of human cooperation beyond the constraints that marked the old strategies of kin selection and various kinds of reciprocity. The omniscience of supernatural agents greatly extended the social accountability of human beings to all times and all places. Moreover, these omniscient agents could track the transgressions of as many individuals as needed. The consequence is that the tragedy of social defection was contained: in a group committed to the existence of supernatural moral watchers, there is always someone watching you.

This combination of secular and religious support in natural selection has embedded morality securely in the individual and social mind as a unique motivational mechanism (Joyce, 2006).

Morality today occupies a substantial part of the human mind. It is realized in behavior to varying degrees and in differing ways understood not as accidental but as conscious and deliberate functions. The conscience nags, advises, challenges and torments with its demand, which most often is unsolicited for self-scrutiny, but can also supply the encouragement of pride. These events remind us of a duty or responsibility to others and of the certain shame, guilt, and damage to reputation likely to follow when the valued standards for conduct are not met. Christopher Boehm (2012, p. 172) summarizes the practical function of conscience:

> Broadly, a conscience provides us with a social mirror. By continually glancing at it, we can keep track of shameful pitfalls that threaten our reputational status or proudly and virtuously chart our personal progress as group members in good standing. But more than intellectual self-knowledge is at stake, for as a practical matter we're continually trying to cope with our own powerful, well-evolved "appetites," which so often are likely to land us in trouble with our groups. These run all the way from dominance tendencies to material greed and sexuality, and expressing them antisocially can create serious practical problems in everyday life.[12]

We humans are sufficiently social beings to be driven to care very much about how our conspecifics perceive us, to ponder the possibilities and, more often than not, to conduct ourselves as we know we should.

Emotion initiates the feelings conscience arouses, just as reason guides consequent behavior. Conscience thus adds a significant dimension to our thought, our behavior, and even our place in society, because it means continuous attention to the reconciliation of our own aspirations, desires, wishes, needs, and even with those of others. This is consilience, and by doing otherwise we pay a price commensurate with the nature of the offense. Humans are imperfect creatures, quite possibly because our extraordinary cognitive capacities—particularly our imagination—can lead us to stray from the straight-and-narrow, the conscience being a faithful reminder of our human frailties. It is a firm but not rigidly structured mold that often curbs radically negative action and reaction in quotidian life. The human mindreading faculty is, again, of considerable value in this activity; having an idea of others' perceptions of our own actions or intentions aids in predicting the social reception of our conduct, leaving us better informed to plan goals and strategies for optimal success. In this process we sharpen our own definitions of right and wrong, good and bad about our intentions and conduct, and we usually have an opportunity to reconsider. Consequently, the conscience is a tool for maintaining and furthering the given society's coherence, which it does by shaping societal character and ensuring continued cooperation. This can be seen in the historical evidence of altruism and prosociality, even though from a strictly objective perspective such acts may initially appear somewhat irrational; but they represent a long-term view not often manifest in the current Western culture. In this context, free-riding and selfishness may not be eliminated but are contained at a manageable level, often constituting little more than a disappointment for others. The conscience is one's own personal guide for conduct, to be followed or rejected but at least pondered, according to one's own psychology and understanding of the context. It is an example of decision determined on a foundation of the best information available at the time, which trusted social relationships quite often can help supply. Freud (1994, p. 43) concludes that the conscience maintains the decision by which "Civilized man has exchanged some part of his chances of happiness for a measure of security." The conscience is attentive to the implications our decisions bear for humanity; it is the greatest support of our social responsibility.

Morality as the Essence of Humanity

Just as morality depends upon a normal human mind, a successful social life depends upon adherence to the moral system. For that reason, Mary Midgley (1994, p. 152) asserts, "Conscience simply cannot be fitted into the Enlightenment classificatory system that divides thought radically from feeling." Feelings do continuously participate in our thought (Johnson-Laird, 2006), making it extremely difficult if not impossible to dismiss them. Reason, emotion and feelings function together and in concert with all other knowledge. They are integral aspects of every normal human mind because they are the products of long-evolved capacities to respond to the challenges and opportunities of their dynamic, increasingly complex and meaningful social environments. Attitude and behavior are primarily the products of decisions, which also change with new knowledge and a re-ordered values priority, so everyone makes countless moral decisions every day, accumulating to define individual character as variously perceived by others, all of whom occasionally commit moral transgressions. Such transgressions are not usually committed unconsciously, however, for normal people have a conscience that weighs the estimated consequences of these actions, most of which arguably have accumulated toward the decision judged of greater moral significance within their context; otherwise, we surely would long ago have brought human life on Earth to its end.

Distinctions in the gravity of our moral infractions are assessed on an intricate sliding scale but without requiring much time or effort for interpretation, as the code is understood thoroughly and widely, its lifetime of learning having begun shortly after birth. Demonstration of commitment to the moral system is quite significant because it defines human character in an act essential to the social judgment of individuals, leading to one's reputation. Reputation is at the root of concern for many of the self's and others' decisions, individual character understood by others primarily because of their own moral feelings about themselves and others. In Richard Joyce's (2006, p. 222) perception of this human capacity, he writes, "[Natural selection] is a process that has made us sociable, able to enter into cooperative exchanges, capable of love, empathy, and altruism—granting us the capacity to take a direct interest in the welfare of others with no thought of reciprocation—and has designed us to think of our relations with one another in moral terms." Ultimately, the extent to which an individual's character is judged moral or not, good or bad, is founded on that individual's actions, surmised intention alone being a less sound basis for judgment, though often the only one available.

Reciprocity and Moral Commitment

Morality's most evident human benefit is its influence on one's associates, for morality encourages reciprocity, a ubiquitous and strengthening dimension of cooperation. Very often a tacit agreement based simply on common understanding, reciprocity establishes bonds between individuals and among groups to create the quality of environment necessary to any society, though people may scarcely give much thought to the implied commitment the concept conveys because it is so common an occurrence.[13] "The biological function of morality is to enable individuals to maximize their benefits from interactions with others by upholding fitness-enhancing systems of cooperation," writes Dennis Krebs (2004, p. 321). Morality is the foundation for all forms of reciprocity, a general impetus to the sense of social responsibility for non-kin as well as kin. When witnessed by others, knowledge of positive moral acts spreads, contributing to the perceived character of the morally committed person and associated reputation. Moral reciprocity is sufficiently significant in human evolution that it connects directly with the urgency that evolved the human capacity of speech.[14] Indeed, reciprocation may be the most common basis for judging character and spreading related information throughout the culture, as Richerson & Boyd (2001, p. 204) observe in their conclusion that "humans certainly appear to be very efficient decision makers when it comes to detecting defectors on social contracts." The availability of such evidence can either establish or destroy good reputations, for there is general agreement on the considerable significance of honoring or failing to honor commitments, however they may have been established.[15]

Altruism

Extreme reciprocity and moral commitment to others are acts of altruism, manifest not just in self-abnegation but also self-sacrifice. As Keith Jensen (2012, p. 305) emphasizes, "The important point is that people are not only self-regarding. They appear to exhibit genuine concern for the suffering of others." Self-sacrifice is altruism's distinguishing feature, an act of compassion accompanied by varying degrees of self-sacrifice in meeting another individual's need. Focused on altruism's self-sacrifice, the concept has been at the center of scientific and scholarly debate since Darwin's time.[16] Again, legendary heroes usually are models of altruism.

Altruism stems from feelings of empathy, having evolved with the culture most evidently because of its utility and perhaps its necessity in conveying this undeniably influential human capacity, its record covering millions of years (Buss, 2004). In matters of decision, altruism is of special significance for a species as naturally preoccupied with reputation and the conduct of individual and social life as humans tend to be. Facile symbolic communication has provided the means to introspect in detail about the conditions of one's own life, which always includes emotion, feelings and the compassion that motivates altruism, a cherished trait well-recognized around the globe. Christopher Boehm (2012, p. 180) observes that the most fundamental moral advice about treating others as one would prefer to be treated belongs to all cultures:

> This brings us again to the golden rule, which seems to be expounded in all human cultures be they recent and complex or ancient and "Paleolithic." Some form of this prosocial dictum is found in the ideology of every institutionalized religion, and as a generalization it has found its way into certain formal philosophies of ethics, as with Kant. The essence of this dictum seems to combine elements of altruism and personal self-interest because in part it's a way to convince *others* to behave more generously.

Conscience conveys meaning for any normal person and is the most vigil of moral monitors, yet informal because conscience is individual and internal. Organized more formally, however, the beliefs and feelings encouraged in religion present morality in an unequivocally prescriptive/proscriptive spirit.

Social Relationships & Responsibility

Among the many individuals with whom we communicate regularly, we have developed social relationships with some that are sustained through interactions over a relatively long period, often through particularly meaningful experiences. Such social relationships are cultural by-products, re-enforced as a core aspect of morality maintaining harmony within groups of all size. At least in their long-term degree of value to our species, they are unique to humans; moreover, interpersonal relationships constitute a sound basis for empathy, which can develop into altruism. Social anthropologist Bronislaw Malinowski (1931, p. 641) explains the seamless merging of empathy with the self, the culture, morality and social relationships:

> Culture entails deep changes in man's personality; among other things it makes man surrender some of his self-love and self-seeking. For human relations do not rest merely or even mainly on constraint coming from without. Men can only work with and for one another by the moral forces which grow out of personal attachments and loyalties. These are primarily formed in the processes of parenthood and kinship but become inevitably widened and enriched.

Evolutionary and developmental psychologist David F. Bjorklund and psychologist Anthony D. Pellegrini (2002, p. 267) define this category of social interaction, writing, "Relationships are interactions between two individuals over time. Different relationships reflect different histories where individuals have interacted with each other in the past and anticipate doing so in the future. Common relationships include attachment between mothers and their children, sibling relationships, friendships, and romantic relationships."

Parents or early guardians, whether prehistoric or modern, head the list of those who care for infants in establishing the mold for the child's future sympathy and empathy in diverse contexts, so most individuals have experienced this emotion to some extent from an early age, as has our species since the earliest stages of its evolution. This experience is carried forward with the individual's progression through life, earning new friendships along the way and perhaps beginning a family for which to care and exercise responsibility. Because it is expected that cultural groupings contribute directly to the spread of sympathetic and empathetic feelings to foster a sense of responsibility, this context has conditioned humanity to optimize the evolution of symbolic language. When people began communicating linguistically, they could engage in extended, deepened and detailed conversation with others, and when the substance of those exchanges developed a more sophisticated character, they began to expect it from others. By pooling information of all kinds, including a full range of emotion and feelings, the social dialectic could proceed in an ever-widening social circle. Cognitive scientist Peter Gärdenfors (2003, pp. 213–214) identifies the development of "self" as the major influence in spearheading the evolution of extraordinary human cognition:

> My main thesis has been that the appearance of an inner world has made possible the emergence of more advanced forms of thinking. Higher cognitive capacities such as planning, self-consciousness, free will, and language presuppose such an inner world. During the development of thinking, humans have achieved an ever-higher degree of *independence* of what happens in their current surroundings. The activities of the brain have become detached from the direct control [by] the senses. Thought can lift and fly its own way.

We humans can detach our thought from the immediate environment to engage in abstract thinking. Individually and socially, we can analyze our own conditions, states and situations, rendering all the present cognitive human capacities, including emotion and feelings, much more richly realizable as we optimize them via symbolic language, spoken and written.

There is no self without at least a sense of others' existence, even if only one other, and special among others are those relatively few with whom a friendship develops. The value of friends is the comfort, support and closeness they afford, conditions accompanied by feelings of trust and obligation, both of which are reciprocative. Friendship presents safe ground for participation in the conflicts and resolutions essential to developing the skills and attitudes necessary to a healthy and advantageous social environment. In this connection, Bjorklund & Pellegrini (2002, p. 287–288) report research in childhood friendships, showing, "When friends disagreed, their ultimate solutions to the dilemmas were more mature than when nonfriends disagreed. In other words, healthy social conflict between friends resulted in greater growth in social knowledge than did conflict between nonfriends." They also find that during adolescence, friends replace family in providing the commiseration and advice needed, and that "the result of this close association is that friends are both models for and reinforcers of group behavior." Among the many values of these relationships is their sound basis for the development of empathy, which fosters altruism.

As important as interpersonal relationships are, however, the research literature in recent decades reveals that they have been under considerable stress in Western culture, reflecting a condition now prevalent in the consumer society (Hidaka, 2012). The mass production of commodities requires mass consumers, so consumption is an activity displayed most diversely in urban settings where consumers are clustered. Therefore, seeing a loss of close human relationships in these urban groupings of the late twentieth and early twenty-first century, Peter Gärdenfors (2003, p. 212) reasons, "Rather than a Gemeinschaft [a community], the urban world creates a *Gesellschaft* [an anonymous society] that is based on economic and political relations. In such a society we do not have a personal relation to most of the people we meet. It is no longer necessary to be ashamed of how you behave. This leads to the disintegration of the social identity." Much in this change of spirit is owed to the ubiquity of decisions confronting individuals every day and almost at every moment, decision itself often constituting the confusing distraction of abundance leading to stress. Leaving little time to appreciate personal relationships, we trade humanity for economic and politically-oriented social concerns. Integral in this turn of worldview, is the increasing speed of change that most of contemporary Western society witnesses, which also is owed to the number of tasks that now can be accomplished—and are expected to be accomplished—during any given segment of time. A heightened consciousness of change draws attention to time's passage and its declining availability for the many things left to be done, decisions to be made and plans to be set, causing the value of time to rise high among life's pressures. This is the state of presentism, meaning the past is gone and therefore worthless, while the future is too obscure, ambiguous, and complicated to contemplate, so there truly is no time like the present; it is the dominant thought replacing tradition.

The continued rising prominence of technology and technological development plays a central role in this fixation on time, as technology almost automatically requires human adaptation. Life in general, then, is experienced in an intense, precision-oriented environment where technology's predominance is increasingly evident, and change is our one reliable constant, positioning time at the forefront of consciousness; we are continuously aware of its rapid passage and disappearance, meaning lost opportunities and possibilities: time is money, time is a commodity, and time is easily and forever measured, allowing little place for interpersonal relationships because they cannot be squeezed into an agenda where, in any case, they would be relatively anomalous and unsuitable to material valuation. Economic Man has become the faster and more precise Digital Man. Sociologist and philosopher Jean Baudrillard (1998, pp. 198–199) offers the following assessment of this consumer society:

> The system is built upon a total liquidation of personal ties, of concrete social relations. It is to this extent that it becomes necessarily and systematically productive of relationship (public relations, human relations, etc.). The production of relationships has become one of the key sectors of production. And because they no longer have anything spontaneous about them, because they are produced, those relationships are necessarily fated, like all that is produced, to be consumed (unlike social relations,

which are the unconscious product of social labour and not the result of deliberate, controlled industrial production: these are not "consumed" but are, in fact, the site of social contradictions).

The pressure on lives compressed into ever smaller units of time has encouraged an influential proportion of Western society to discount the value of interpersonal relationships. But when this trend is considered from an evolutionary perspective, it suggests only a skeletal understanding of the role time has played in whatever progress we may have achieved up to the present in our evolution, though this change has been and remains a matter of individual and social decision. Ultimately, the industrial ethos has influenced our social ethos even though our evolution, heretofore, has been moderated largely by emotion, feelings, and morality.

Industrial Influence

Employing an impressive proportion of the total Western population, industry offers the products, services and most of the financial resources required by individuals wishing to acquire them, and industry is the modern economy's principal engine. It both stimulates and feeds the population's consumption. It comprises not just factories, as it did for the most part prior to the twentieth century, but also conglomerations of corporate factories and similarly organized service industries, which together assume much of the power than formerly was controlled by the state, if not more. Social historian Harold Perkin (1996, p. 186) crafts the telling comparison: "The principal instrument of domination is no longer the imperialist state but the TNC [transnational corporation]," a trend that since has only grown more pervasive, powerful, and persuasive. Consequently, the population is removed further from any sense of responsibility normally assumed within a democracy. But the sheer power of corporate presence and magnitude, implication and consequence are only the most evident objectives industrial development has achieved.

An equally significant aspect of this tidal-surge resides in the arrangement whereby the corporation operates in an environment quite remote from the mass population, which often finds it an amorphous, anonymous and impenetrable entity, a condition to which the public has become rather accustomed. Moreover, the welcomed flow of commodities aids in muffling any concerns that may lurk beneath the societal surface. In short, industry, the vast enterprise of production and service employing the majority of Western citizenry, has created the economy and made it the focus of public attention, at once the source of so much joy and grief, hope and dread for so many. But the entire industrial enterprise is controlled by a relative handful of individuals. By comparison with pre-industrial times, industrial development has given Western society great satisfaction, above all with its most evident benefits of a reliable source of income, a regular occupation, an ever-expanding choice of livelihood and an infinitely vast set of decisions to be made among goods and categories of goods, believed by many not merely to enhance the quality of life but to fulfill life's purpose. Furthermore, industrial growth has given human time a specific tangible value in the form of money. Money holds the value of greatest significance, being the value of values and the common denominator of all things material, spiritual, or intellectual. Industry has instilled a closely-attuned consciousness of and firm belief in competitive production and service, which in the lives of the public translates into a highly competitive culture. Similarly, industry also has filtered a more scientific premise throughout the mass public, along with other strategies, principles and values favored industry's own quite remarkable organic existence. These include the scientific ideal of objectivity, the concentration on time as an economic value, the exclusion from functional design of any consideration that can be labeled irrelevant to technological or economic system function, and the planning of human activity as integral to a system imagined as wholly mechanical.

But the present system evinces one fundamental problem not immediately perceptible throughout industry, the economy and the Western culture: it is the evident lack of a strong and convincing sense of responsibility for how the entire production/consumption system functions in the best interests of the population rather than in the best interests of just those relatively few situated among its economically top tenth, which leaves the huge remainder with their hope for improvement solely from the invisible hand. Anthropologist Craig Dilworth (2010, p. 450) clarifies this careless responsibility:

> Conventional development theory and practice is *capitalist (bourgeois)* development theory and practice. To conceive of development as indiscriminate economic growth is to opt for the view which most suits the capitalist class, since it is in their interest to maximise the amount of capital being exchanged, and not have to bother about whether capital really ought to go into things that are appropriate but not very profitable, and not into things that are inappropriate but profitable.[17]

Corporate ownership, which consists primarily of the principal investors, does not manage operations any more than operational management controls ownership, so the control of industrial wealth has for a long time been exercised with a minimum sense of social responsibility; it is a logical outcome of corporate development (Berle and Means, 1931). Responsibility for anything other than profit, upon which management depends for expansion, and ownership, which depend upon earnings, is inconsistent with an efficiently-run and effective economic system. If the major investors seem most often the winners in this economic puzzle, which no longer presents much of a financial gamble, this is explained by political economist Robert Reich (2007, p. 126), who finds that "markets have become hugely efficient

6. Freedom, Motivation and Responsibility 133

at responding to individual desires for better deals, but are quite bad at responding to goals we would like to achieve together." One can infer that the current code in this culture and this economy is the pursuit of self-interest, or as Adam Smith would have it, the ultimate and best way to serve the common interest. Reich (p. 163) cogently summarizes what may be the public concern in this scheme:

> Our voices as citizens—as opposed to our voices as consumers and investors—are being drowned out. We may even be losing confidence that what we have to say as citizens is important. This is not because big corporations have conspired to drown out or marginalize our citizen voices but chiefly because corporations are engaged in escalating competition for political outcomes that advantage them over their rivals.

Feeling like helpless bystanders, individuals may simply no longer care about the directions their society determines or their possible outcomes.[18] Or they may believe themselves lacking in the capacity to understand the highly technical (economic and technological) issues and situations and can see no options. Do they rationally decide not to spend their time on such issues? Do they believe the responsibility lies elsewhere? Do they feel completely removed from what is happening and how and why it happens? Any of these questions, but probably all and more, may apply. The immediate reasons for these possibilities of decision, which bears the potential for social evolution, are most readily perceptible in the principles of technological development, for they become central to Western industry, the present economy, and the general ideological environment. This is the topic of the next chapter.

7

The Western Ideological Environment

> Note that it's just as much a myth that cultural evolution inevitably leads to progress as it is that genetic evolution does.
> —H. Clark Barrett, 2015

The Technological Presence

Most consumers, as both the production/consumption system's ultimate benefactors and beneficiaries, are well aware of the social impact science, technology and the economy wield, for consumers are expected to understand their responsibility for the system. When the system fails to function as intended, it becomes the source of general disruption and intense frustration for all.

Early industry was tied to the authority of knowledge, because it was critical in bringing a new reality to industrial production and making a clear connection between the workers' combined effort and their standard of living, reflected primarily in general economic growth. Such recognition in the West has progressively been integrated in the social mind for the past several centuries, as technology's dominant presence and the economy's looming significance in all aspects of contemporary society is scarcely avoidable.[1] Observing that today "the material world is currently being altered at an uparalleled rate," archeologist Nicole Boivin (2008, p. 231) proffers this explanation:

> Not only has global capitalism led to the creation of an overwhelming and unprecedented diversity of new material objects and technologies, whose effects on individuals and societies continue to go largely unstudied, but traditional material landscapes, artefacts, and bodies are being transformed faster than ever before. The human material story is also, and increasingly so, a tale of environmental degradation, resource depletion, and the loss of traditional technologies, practices, and ways of life, as well as the destruction of heritage and archaeological sites.... As we watch technologies

spread faster and further than ever before, we see material ways of life disappear that may have greater emotional, moral, health, and social value than those with which they are being replaced.

Technological Development

Technological development demonstrates rationality in action, because reason requires functional precision for the increased efficiency and predictability of system function. Although tolerance often is advantageous in social management, it is anathema to the precision and efficiency of technological management and therefore not tolerated in that setting. Indeed, technological function increasingly has served as the model for human cognition, for technology so clearly and convincingly showcases efficiency's potential.

As the West generally aspires to this potential, so do the similarities between mechanical and human function increasingly capture our imagination, and have for at least the past half millennium; together, they fairly constitute objective data's ongoing eclipse of our subjective information. Therefore, by thoughtlessly applying the natural science epistemology to the humanly critical functions of general decision-making, our current dependence on technology contributes to an already unnatural condition, exemplifying a social phenomenon Robin M. Williams (1979, p. 31) refers to as culture's "creation" power, which he describes: "A new standard or belief is developed out of experience and becomes effective, at some level, in regulating behavior." Successful strategy in one branch of knowledge can, therefore, become the model for strategy in others, as demonstrated by the migration of natural science epistemological strategies to other classifications of knowledge that include human motivations and functions. But humans differ from machines: humans are designed for different purposes; built of different materials; relate to distinctly differing environments; and are subject to different and changing motivations, most of which are formed internally within each of our society's constituents.

When applied to human function, the technological model of functionality encounters singularly human complications because humans require appropriate motivation. Nonetheless, the principal complicating factors in our society often are treated either as mechanical parts with a poor fit or simply ignored in the name of efficiency, because people are expected to be *more resilient than machines and much more accepting of abuse.* The thought that people trust technology more than other people (Turkle, 2011) is today perfectly believable. The rationality accompanying the automatic reaction to apply technology to general problem-solving eventually shapes human action to fit the specific technology's carefully-designed purposes. Meanwhile, however, the combination of objective and subjective cognition constitutes the more natural flow of human thought, each mode dependent on the other and leading to an outcome recognizable as human rather than an outcome more likely expected from a different species or a robot (see Chapter 4, note 6). "With the computational metaphor in place," says Louise Barrett (2011, p. 118), "it became almost inevitable that the brain would be seen as the equivalent of computer hardware, with cognitive processes operating like the brain's software: an idea that has permeated modern Western culture at all levels." Yet, normal human cognition is dual-track, incorporating both objective and subjective thought and balanced by reason; it has been successful in shaping human holistic thought to incorporate the problem's context as well as its core.

Mechanical Thought

A product of human thought, technology's functional logic is humanly perceptible and understandable. But because of significantly critical distinctions between mechanical programming and human cognition, our understanding of technology is of little help in our interactions with other people, particularly in understanding them. The normal human mind is motivated by a variable but vast array of accumulating objective knowledge, which nonetheless is nuanced by emotion, feelings, and morality to find meaning for us in the continuous influx of new objective knowledge, since the totality also is influenced by ongoing environmental change that may be quite subtle. But technology is subject only to its programming and the physical effects of motion through time. In the West, therefore, we have determined to minimize our knowledge foundation for decisions by adopting a rigidly mechanical brand of reason, most often in formal settings but increasingly in others. We now proceed directly in a carefully-charted vector from goal-setting to its anticipated successful achievement, avoiding whenever possible any non-technical entanglements with the array of uniquely human conditions, situations, and feelings that stubbornly prove much less amenable to predictability, precision and strategic management than economic and technological challenges.

Technology Molds Worldview

Because technology's purpose is to change the way things are done, its key position in industry and the economy is quite understandable, as is the system's influence on the culture. The earliest indication of large-scale social change had arisen from the high visibility of rapidly-spreading industrial production sites and technology's displacement of human labor. But as this was occurring, the workplace also was creating new functions and responsibilities, management eventually emphasizing not only *which* functions were to be executed and in which order, but more often the *manner* in which the workers were to execute their redesigned responsibilities. Particularly during the nineteenth century, and in conjunction with the general goal of efficiency, this emphasis evolved into a heightened attention to worker discipline (Clark, 2007), for the intention was no longer for workers to be creative or skilled but rather for them to avoid causing product damage or destruction, an expectation formerly reserved for the design of precision machinery (Lilley, 1966). The idea that workers must be professionals rather than craftsmen was an historic change when it went into effect, but today represents an innovation of even greater dimension, as Western production and service industries are established within global cultures unaccustomed to maintaining a state of mind prescribed by management. And since modified employment responsibilities tend to join technology with humanity ever more closely in functionality, such employment extends the demand for machine precision to the workers' personal attributes: humans now are more often expected to accommodate technology's precision than technology is expected to compensate for that human failing.

Owed to the increasingly rapid innovations made possible by natural science epistemology in the early days of industrialization, the West began to express its collective notion of progress and its implied positive direction for human history primarily in terms of technological innovation. Technology's path defines human progress, as Michael Adas (1989, p. 60) illustrates in this interpretation of technology's cultural value and its deeper social implications, when they first arose in the seventeenth century:

> The Europeans' recognition of the superiority of their precision tools and instruments was connected to a further and more fundamental revelation. European travelers and missionaries began to sense that even their ways of thinking and perceiving the world were fundamentally different from those of any of the peoples they encountered overseas. Perhaps the most striking examples of this realization were linked to changing European approaches to time and space.

Adas shows that technological development soon became the basis for identifying and judging relative degrees of "civilization" around the globe, most apparently when the later harnessing of electricity caused a remarkable new wave of novelty to flood the West.[2] By the closing decades of the nineteenth century, new technologies had become favored household items, making change perfectly evident to an even broader segment of the population. And new standards for the quality of life developed when home construction standards were invoked and luxuries such as mass-produced carpeting and draperies were made affordable, while practical appliances such as telephones and machines for home laundering added time-saving convenience to quotidian life. Moreover, radios brought current news and entertainment into the home which, owing to electricity, could be illuminated even throughout the night. Following from its new and growing societal dependency, technology soon was the measure of the lives supporting industrial development and the general economy. Having eventually become thoroughly integrated and increasingly complex, technological systems now make industrial production and the economy either fall or rise, stop or go, all while altering the general population's outlook. Technology stimulates imagination by bringing change to quotidian activities and extending perceptions beyond the initial purpose of any specific invention.

Though change of this kind may often prove ephemeral, it proceeds in an ongoing flow that cuts to ever-greater depths, much as the gradual but steady flow of rainwater erodes the landscape in new patterns. But technological change continuously alters and refines functionality, producing the maelstrom of innovation the Western culture has come to demand; moreover, this occurs in the known today and the anticipated tomorrow not in the vague, distant and evasive future promised by other cultural forces, pre-eminently religion, and most certainly not by tradition. As economic health now garners the reverence formerly accorded religious belief and practice, historian of American foreign policy Walter Russell Mead (2007, p. 15) finds change per se accorded a status at least as revered in the West as religion, an appraisal he perceives to be spreading throughout much of the world's population:

> The English-speaking world—contrary to the intentions of almost all of the leading actors of the period—reached a new kind of religious equilibrium in which capitalism and social change came to be accepted as good things. In much of the world even today, people believe that they remain most true to their religious and cultural roots by reflecting change. Since the seventeenth century, the English-speaking world or at least significant chunks of it have believed that embracing and even furthering and accelerating change—economic change, social change, cultural change, political change—fulfills their religious destiny.

In the nineteenth century, only the simplest and least penetrating comparison with other nations was required to strengthen the general sense of change as a highly desirable condition of life, for it reassured the West of its natural orientation toward progress, now understood as the purpose of change. While cultural change may most often have been associated with notions of progress, however, its absence in nations came to mean something quite different: static conditions were perceived as primitive if not regressive. Michael Adas (1989, pp. 196–197) describes the broader socio-historical background of this general Western conclusion:

> Individuals who through education and hard work had risen above their modest family origins placed a high premium on improvement, a term that is ubiquitous in nineteenth-century writings on colonial areas. Change was not only good; it was essential for the civilized. Stagnation and decadence were associated with barbar-

ians; "primitive" and poorly developed material culture with savages. The history of civilized peoples was a tale of progress, of continuous advance; that of barbarians, a dreary chronology of endless cycles of decline and recovery.

The kind of knowledge recognized, required and rewarded in the putative consumer society is the technical knowledge most readily relatable to the common economic good and an improved general quality of life most readily associated with individual social competition, international societal competition, and the social Darwinist drive to individual success. The latter also reflects a distinct change in worldview Margaret C. Jacob (1997, p. 52) summarizes in her example from British history. She writes, "By 1660 and the end of the first phase of the English revolution, the prosperity of the English state came to be seen as linked—at first tentatively and then decisively—with the development of science and technology. The linkage between prosperity imagined and science improved, with technology aiding both, remains part of the Western vision to this day." The new worldview was destined to prompt further cultural change.

Industry and Commerce

Capitalism and industry developed concurrently, because the combined commercial monolith requires extraordinary funding for expansion and the continuous upgrading of both production and service industry technologies necessary to the maintenance of competitive advantage. By the mid-nineteenth century, transportation had opened a growing field of interest for the discoverer of natural laws and greater possibilities for the inventor of technologies, both having become entrepreneurs in funding their own work. Intensive activity had hastened the earlier, more gradual emergence of a new type of individual to become central in moving industry ahead by marketing ideas, for entrepreneurs need the help of others in financing, developing, promoting, and protecting economically useful new ideas on a much larger scale. Consumption fuels capitalist enterprise, so market investment soon drew the wealthy classes into its new mass scale intended for buyers at nearly all levels of financial means, including the potential of those employed in the rapidly-growing number and variety of new industries.

Science Is Knowledge

The Western frame for viewing and understanding the world had been constructed first by European scientists—then called natural philosophers—from Copernicus (1473–1543) and Galileo (1564–1642) through the encyclopedists of the eighteenth century, when intellectual leadership encouraged its development (Jacob, 1997). René Descartes (1596–1650) is prominent among those rare leaders who combined the scientific, mathematical, and philosophical insights valued by the influential voices of the day, as well as by the general public whose mind had been freed to contemplate the many treasures thought surely to lie buried, awaiting their discovery in a new world of those individuals' making. Margaret C. Jacob (1997, p. 49) also finds, "A quick survey of Cartesian literature for the laity reveals the intentions of its authors and the general tendency of Cartesian science to promote order in the state as well as in commercial development." She summarizes (p. 37) Descartes' key contribution to the effort:

> Descartes offered the first intellectual syntheses of modern thought to rest entirely on the individual's ability to know nature mathematically and experimentally. With knowledge, Descartes promised, came mastery. You can do things because you think. His discovery of the uses to which science could be put laid a new foundation of orthodoxy, both political and religious. Scientific enquiry became a viable alternative, a way of rejecting both the fashionable skepticism of Montaigne's generation and the scholasticism of the clergy and the schools. Descartes's reliance on the self, disciplined by his method, could establish an entirely new metaphysical foundation for doing science, or for practicing one's religion, or for giving allegiance to authority of church and state.

There would be advantages for virtually everyone. When knowledge and values change, perspectives do too, so a deep cultural evolution grew apparent relatively swiftly in Europe, as the seventeenth century neared the eighteenth and social concern for the good of all became more evident.[3]

Because news of scientific and technological advance raised the expectation that change was in the making, such news spread quickly. But those who were unable to read, or who for other reasons decided not to be informed, further distanced themselves from the ever-larger segment of the public who did determine to benefit from the rich flow of new ideas. At the same time, however, illiterate industrial workers also lost their employment due to explicit written instructions that necessarily accompanied the predictably more-complicated technology (Veblen, 1914). The phenomenon of knowledge became both a focus of public attention and a source of national pride when organized and explained for the general public in the German *Grosses volständiges Universal-Lexikon aller Wissenschaften und Künste* (1732–1750), which claimed to contain all the knowledge available in its day, as did other knowledge compendia. They too were produced under the leadership of recognized European intellectuals and published concurrently, foremost among them the French *Encyclopédie* (1751–1772) and the English *Encyclopædia Britannica* (1768). Reliable scientific and technological knowledge was thus made accessible to the increasingly literate public who recognized the value of epistemological authority. As engineering knowledge grew in importance so did the engineering population, sufficiently by the late eighteenth century that influential professional societies were established. Engineers became acknowledged social leaders, for the general population was animated more consistently by reports of invention, production, and related change circulating in the news.

By the nineteenth century, scientific ideas were deeply integrated in the European educational experience (Smith, 1972), preceded or supplemented by the informal acquaintance those who had witnessed such power first-hand in industry were able to provide in the normal course of socialization. Accustomed to at least several generations of elevated living standards and recognizing itself as the consumer of mass production, the general population began to assume its position as a significant entity of singular importance and evidently crucial to the whole vast enterprise. The maintenance of mass production depends on an expanding market and a regular upgrading of technological systems, both having become necessary in attracting and maintaining a flow of investment sufficient for corporate advance. And the transformation was swift: whereas it had taken about two centuries for the Western citizenry to accept the scientifically-discovered and proved knowledge that the Earth circles the Sun not the reverse, technological wonders were much more readily visible and tangible and therefore more credible, and even acceptable to the ego—although not necessarily the production workers' ego—so an understanding of technology's primacy in the world spread more quickly. In this context, sociologist Robert MacIver's (1937, pp. 456–457) assessment, "Social evolution is, in short, the process through which our social systems reflect technological advance" seems well justified.

The Industrial Mold

The influence of industrial strategies, principles, and values is central to understanding the Western social transformation of the past several centuries. In his study of time's cultural significance, social historian Patrick Joyce (1987, p. 24) observes that, although industry rendered a clear distinction between work time and leisure, "the transferral into the area of leisure of values emanating elsewhere, especially from the world of work," is more remarkable. Applying primarily to an individual self-consciousness concentrated on others' assessment, the influence of work experience reaches beyond industrial strategies to accomplish tasks. Richard Sennett (2006, p. 112) points to an example: "the equation of occupational prestige with self-direction and autonomy more than with money or power. Merit in the work world is judged on this basis." The intensity of these and other workplace considerations is manifold amid the unrelenting stresses to increase efficiency in the industrial setting, and it becomes an ever-present source of the human stress emphasized throughout this essay. Today's Western worlds of work and leisure account for the high level of self-consciousness related specifically to time, its value and rapid passage.

Quite significantly at the forefront of the industrial workers' mind is the mutual dependence of production and consumption, for the growing number of employees returning home from work each day is quite impressive, rendering them de facto emissaries of the industrial ethos. As organized work became the Western consumer society's norm, these individuals developed similar routines and expectations. Virtually the entire population now is guided in its daily processes by the mass-media influence sponsored principally by industry via commercial advertisement, an expected "part of the narrative space through which we make sense of the world," writes sociologist Chris Rojek (2000, p. 101). "As such it is equivalent to the family, education and the community in accessing information and building identity formation."

Still another new source of cultural authority emerged from the democratic principles and ideals fomented in the fervor of eighteenth-century revolutions in France and America. Noting that "*Vox populi, vox Dei* (the voice of the peole is the voice of God) became the ruling maxim of more and more of American life," historian Daniel Boorstin (1973, p. 450) might well have added western European life. The people's voice, which the mass-market media came to promote as the most rational and suitable justification for purchasing anything, amplified this cultural draw, leading to the frequent public opinion surveys and statistical reports now employed so liberally to aid in guiding our decisions toward the desired status for our normalizing culture: we know what to purchase by their numbers, which are the price per item and the tabulation of those who already have acquired the product or are speculated to do so. Such a guide to social success can spare a busy population much of its time and effort otherwise committed to making a more complex decision about other possibilities, because reason dictates that need should be satisfied now, not later: complicated thought should be circumvented or eliminated or at least constrained, for it can be if it follows properly contrived reason.

The Social Environment

The West's present social structure reflects several centuries of development in science, industry and technology, which today are deeply embedded in our consciousness, worldview and consuming culture. Though this society's competition for individual position and attention is fairly intense, it functions surprisingly smoothly, further indicating that a high degree of sociality does still undergird modern life in the positive force our collective subjectivity generates.

Subjectivity and Balance

Subjectivity is critical to human balance, our homeostasis. Our nature is to think continuously of ourselves because we also have the capacity to perceive ourselves among others. And there is no sociality without subjectivity, for there can be no thought of others without thought of ourselves and no thought of ourselves without thought of others. In the course of cultural transition, however, a vapid objectivity has developed in our cognitive process and now almost overshadows subjectivity's value. Emotion, feelings, and morality are among our most human capacities, but are suppressed by an externally-induced and mechanically-regimented rationality. The movement to ban subjective qualities from formal decisions promotes primarily, if not only, commercial and state intentions. It has achieved considerable success by strengthening the belief that objectivity is the sole rational route to success, which is measurable by accumulated capital and the things to which only money can provide access: money is the pass-key to the world. These lessons have become so deeply engrained in the Western population that they also apply liberally to most if not all aspects of contemporary life, where human subjectivity and responsibility have faded from the cultural picture and our cognition no longer achieves the effect of panoramic enlightenment, but instead, the effect of workhorse blinders. Subjectivity is the timeless universal feel of humanity, yet has been all but replaced in formal settings by technology's power, the economy's material abundance, and a higher level of attention to the rationality of a loosely-adopted and thoughtlessly-applied scientific epistemology that manages to ignore other pertinent scientific principles.

It may be that emotion, feelings and morality, which normally rank high among humanity's motivations, are thought outmoded; or that people should be modeled only according to the tangible realities of the material world that would exclude its immeasurable, ethereal ideals; or that we are motivated purely by a radical brand of reason that must be kept unsullied by any hint of subjectivity. In the present environment, then, the meaning of human life becomes a much less significant part of our identity, for it is the individual's identification with materiality that counts, quite literally. The inevitable encounter with decision overflows with thoughts of the efficiency a staunchly objective attitude requires. We have willingly relinquished attention to an otherwise desirable social harmony and personal peace. Or have we just given up? The most significant act of thought any humans can engage in is introspection, a highly subjective function introduced in Chapter 2 and recalled here by Roger Smith (2007, p. 121):

> The difference between natural science and human science knowledge is not that nature remains as it is as a result of knowledge and humans do not, or that humans are forces in the production of knowledge and stones are not, but that humans have reflected, used language and created culture, including the present kind of discussion of it. This is a humanistic presentation of the existence of special and, as far as we know, unique capacities in being human. At the centre of these capacities, however, is reflection, and it is the central insight, and difficulty, of the philosophy of the human sciences that this very reflection has turned on itself, questioning, and thereby altering, its own identity.

But there is no knowledge in the absence of thought and very little thought, if any, in the absence of emotion and feelings, because self is always on our mind (H. C. Barrett, 2015; Brady, 2013; M. Lieberman, 2013; Gazzaniga, 2011; Damasio, 2010; Johnson-Laird, 2006; Sober and Wilson, 1998), because sociality always has been central to human worldview and motivation (M. Lieberman, 2013; Gazzaniga, 2008; de Waal, 1996). Are the leaders of our production/consumption system fearful of humanity's natural and most positive motivations? By aligning ourselves so closely to the technical components of our knowledge we excise from the system our most human characteristics.

Cooperation

Small and large-scale cooperation has been highly successful among humans because we are motivated by a potent mixture of reason, objective knowledge, understanding, subjective information, and other cognitive features necessary in gauging the essence of others' mind and potential. This spiritual niche is unique to human beings in meeting the demands of an increasingly complex social life while also maintaining the cultural stability and internal harmony useful to the purposes of physical, intellectual and spiritual cooperation within the species. It is essential to our species' longer-term stability and harmony: our individual and organismic homeostasis. Our early ancestors engaged ever more frequently in collective activities beyond the family structure, most evidently in cooperative endeavors related to the common good. In fact, Dennis L. Krebs (2011, p. 247) contends that humans learned to concentrate on the long-term positive side of collaboration rather than its negative side, which helps explain our relative facility for this most significant social technology.

> [T]he morality of acts, and even more so the morality of people, is rooted more in the motives and intentions that guide behaviors than in the consequences they produce.... Viewed from the perspective of evolution, there is little reason to expect people who behave in prosocial ways to be driven by the motive to foster the greatest good for the greatest number or by any other lofty moral goal, because prosocial dispositions

did not evolve to enable people to achieve such goals—they evolved to enable people to maximize their long-term genetic gains by delaying gratification, upholding their groups, and joining with others to advance their adaptive interests.

A premise of this book is that a normal person understands that, ultimately, we are all in this together, and for only an extremely brief moment in human history. Primitive human groups routinely confronted existential challenge, so cooperation in the special mental effort demanded by mutual understanding and the decisions and planning of purposeful group activity, most often would have been the vehicle for determining principal goals, the strategies best suited to them, and even the individuals who could best apply the tactics. The assemblage of varied knowledge and diverse perspectives was found to provide the most effective foundation for decision-making, so James Hurford (2007, p. 295) theorizes that the social group became "the survival vehicle of its individual members." Most adults today know that cooperation entails the complications of clear explanation, mutual understanding, patience, tolerance and often compromise, because cooperation brings the added potential and challenge of diversity in perspective, skills, experience, psychology, and temperament. In the long term, therefore, the only way collaboration can be successful is if it also works to the advantage of each individual in the group. Strategic organization and process—management—plays a significant part in making any cooperative venture successful, of course. But humans are extraordinarily adaptable, and in this instance our earliest antecedents modeled collaborative effort on the family, which offered a common experience applicable to other circumstances (Hurford, 2007). Cooperation's requisite sensitivities and positive inclinations are as old as humanity itself, today constituting a multifaceted and sophisticated human capacity. The most successful long-term venture in cooperation arguably is the human design, adoption, and maintenance of a code to guide human behavior: it is morality, introduced in Chapter 6.

The Place of Morality

As readily recognizable aspects of morality, the conditions of trust and fairness today constitute a highly significant social dimension of human life. Trust in others is foundational to morality and essential to the continued strategy of cooperation. Of central importance is the inference of individual character, which quickly appears on the local gossip agenda to establish one's reputation and sense of dignity (Bontekoe, 2008). People tend to avoid cooperation with untrustworthy individuals or groups whose reputations follow from the assessment rendered by those with previous direct experience. Trust and fairness make successful cooperation possible and so have become an ingrained set of social principles, as James Hurford (2007, p. 325) explains in his clarification of their significance:

> In summary, there is evidence of a sense of fair play, of what is an equitable distribution of resources, in primates, including humans. Behavior conforming to this sense of fair play increases the closer we get to Western everyday norms of commerce.... These phenomena are relevant to the evolution of language insofar as they show a common psychosocial thread, from non-human primates to humans, indicating tacit awareness of group norms of cooperative behavior.... Linguistic behavior is typically trusting behavior. As a speaker, you trust the hearer not to use to your cost what you tell him. And as a hearer, you believe or do what the speaker says. Trust by one party is an inference of trustworthiness in the other.

Everyone is expected to mesh synchronously with the incessant advance of the production/consumption system, which now apparently is believed our sole true support through life's increasing ambiguities. In short, social order and change now conform to technological order and economic progress because expecting them to adjust to ours is unthinkable. In the competition between human morality and system functionality, decisions tend to fall more favorably on the latter, for they more clearly represent progress. There need be no other human order or goal because human elements are believed sufficiently embedded in our scientific, technological, and economic protocols to carry us along. Craig Dilworth (2010, p. 396) similarly characterizes our globalizing Western outlook, writing, "The increasingly dominant worldview of today is that of Western society, with its belief in the validity and importance of modern science, its emphasis on economic growth and technological development, and its view of humans as primarily socio-psychological entities, and only secondarily if at all as biological entities." Nature is expendable.

Morality is particularly important to humanity because of the mind's plasticity and other special features, and because humans are as distinct from each other as our unpredictability suggests, having evolved in large groupings adapted to a relatively liberal self-governance. Assistance is delivered to normal individual minds via the conscience, which guides our social behavior by monitoring it and reporting to us. An extraordinarily high degree of sociality is the foundation of humanity's capacity for self-governance at various levels of behavior, and is owed primarily to morality and its ever-attendant conscience.[4] Formal divisions of the total population are governed by laws, codes of conduct and etiquette in a more regulated manner, but individuals tend to behave in the best interest of others, even though personal experience does unfailingly include aberrations by individuals and groups, duly noted as exceptions. The logical extension of this long evolutionary movement in self-governance is our underlying concern about the well-being of humanity itself, a category of attention that transcends the individual and even the culture, pointing to a sense of responsibility for the commonweal.[5] The normal tendency toward concern for humanity's well-being is illustrated most clearly in the recognition of human dignity and human rights, discussed in Chapter 1.

Humanity protects and advances morality for the species' well-being, moral behavior stemming from empathetic sensitivities that make possible a general interest in others. Individuals belonging to diverse human societies of all sizes usually comport themselves according to the rules, regulations, and laws of human design and monitoring, whether at work or leisure, a generalization validated by the noteworthiness of its exceptions. Rational thought guides human behavior, for rationality evolved by conscious decisions to restrain selfish instincts. Violations of the rules, which most often are extremely complex when their judgment requires the alignment of infractions with specific categories of morality plus the *degree* of infraction, is registered in others' reaction, but often equally and sometimes more forbiddingly within the offender's own conscience. Cognitive psychologists and neuroscientists agree that all normal humans possess a conscience (Krebs, 2011; A. Damasio, 2010; Spelke, 2007; Fiddick, 2004; Gärdenfors, 2003). Even though it may be despised as the great, unsleeping goad and therefore does not determine every action, the conscience does always warrant close attention—otherwise, it could not have earned immediate recognition and negative connotations. As a combination of reason and emotion, the conscience has been and continues quite arguably to be the most consistently dependable means of individual self-control in humanity's long-term best interests, because it is society's self-monitoring device. Most importantly, the conscience bears deep human meaning and value and therefore is a highly significant contributor to sound judgment; it has served its purpose even when leaving no trace in subsequent behavior.

As individuals, we are interested first in ourselves, our survival, our own well-being, social success, and personal future. But in view of humanity's special features for cognition, communication and cooperation, individual representatives of the species also exhibit a profound affinity for and concern about their conspecifics, often in a deeply caring sense and in the long term. This outlook belongs to a highly significant dimension of humanity, though the more recently established material world of abundance and choice does pose a formidable challenge to these fundamental motivations. The present Western culture highlights an aspect of sociality weighted overwhelmingly toward one specific *instrumental* value of other people, which is the reflection by material means of the individual's own identity within the social environment. It interjects competition into a society of individuals who want what others have (Schwartz, 1986), and this competition among individuals and groups invites differentiation of a personally judgmental nature. Our current conformity by acknowledgment of difference rather than similarity follows logically from material considerations and new kinds of decisions, which are both causes and effects of human evolution, and they relate directly to morality. Within the general framework of the production/consumption system, individuals seem to judge themselves and others increasingly by the degree of their progress toward achieving individual goals, which may be the new basis for moral decision. If so, this unwritten and much simplified guideline would state that integrity is determined primarily, if not solely, by the congruence of an individual's actions with that individual's goals, regardless of the nature of such actions, because the end justifies the means and collateral damage is not part of character judgment.

Such conditions can be perceived to arise most prominently in the cultural attraction of technological development, as sociologist and philosopher Jacques Ellul (1980, p. 109) suggests in his statement: "Conformity to technology is now the true social conformity. The technological system omits from its scope things that used to be the object of great concern by society (e.g., the identity of moral conducts)." Observation suggests that Ellul's assessment has increased in validity since he formulated it almost half a century ago. But of greater significance, he interprets this condition not as an added cultural feature but as the *displacement* of a cultural dimension, for it appears to be displacing our responsibility for humanity.

Individual and Social Responsibility

A diluted sense of responsibility indicates a lessening of human sociality, which in recent decades has begun to shed some of its traditional connotations to assume a decidedly newer one.[6] This reconceptualization reflects a change in worldview incurred by turning our societal focus away from humanity's well-being and toward the well-being of our production/consumption system. It may be one ramification of the change to which Robert Reich (2007, p. 5) refers in writing, "The last several decades have involved a shift of power away from us in our capacities as citizens and toward us as consumers and investors." In this transfer of power, he observes the loss of citizen power to corporate power, stemming from the increasingly close connections among merging corporate entities and their aggressive bonding with governments around the globe.

Cultural sociologist Roberta Sassatelli (2006, p. 236) perceives the concept of consumption "less as a private sphere where the consumer can think only of him/herself and be freed from the constraints, worries and burdens of political and productive imperatives, and more as a public domain defined by consumers' freedom to voice their own moral commitments in order to change politics and the economy." But she attenuates (p. 227) her hopeful reasoning with the thought that consumer choice is "capable of expressing consumer sovereignty only if consumers do not lull themselves with the sirens of the Smithian tune [meaning the 'invisible hand,' which translates into twentieth and early twenty-first century 'trickle-down economics'], but take full responsibility for the environmental, social and political effects of their choices." The problem with this interpretation of consumer power is that Adam Smith's portrayal of the free market—which today may seem disingenuous—has become so firmly ensconced after almost two and a half centuries of moral cushioning, that it is well anchored in the comfortable security it provides our social and political leadership, while the mass of Western society appears to have withdrawn from the struggle. Enough of the population has been soothed, rather mysteriously, that an innovative brand of inertia rules the day.[7] Self-imposed individual limitations are intended to mesh without grating in the system's technical apparatus and causing our widely-agreed and uniquely admirable cognition to be constrained.

Self-Consciousness

The present system could not have evolved without a strong cultural self-consciousness to support moral conscience and its demanding introspection.[8] The eighteenth-century sensation of modernity made cultural change more noticeable, even well within the parameters of a single lifetime, only to speed by ever more quickly as the decades rolled on. In recent decades, nearly all aspects of the social environment have been evolving with such velocity that the world has become almost a foreign place for many, stimulating an even greater intensity of self-consciousness. It may not be surprising that the natural response is to withdraw into oneself, to reconnoiter and reassess through more careful introspection, including others' viewpoints, desires, fears, and intentions. Theory of Mind capacities are essential to successful human cooperation in making decisions, and the West accentuates this state of mind by the individual projection of a desired image employed to display choice in fashion, fad, leisure interests, residence, means of transportation, and anything else believed commodifiable. Learning their distinctions in monetary cost relative to the individual's valuation of purpose requires time and effort; but when reflected in simple monetary calculation, such time and effort are much easier to monitor. As a large part of our complex shopping experience, distinction among groups relates to a value that may even exceed that of individual distinction. Biochemist and cultural critic Colin Campbell (1987, p. 89) theorizes that "individuals do not so much seek satisfaction from products, as pleasure from the self-illusory experiences which they construct from their associated meanings. Consumption's essential activity is thus not the actual selection, purchase or use of products, but the imaginative pleasure-seeking to which the product image lends itself." If so, the manufacturer participates in this consumer activity by anticipating and responding to need with its further stimulation and expansion of the onlooker's range of interest, which is accomplished through the attention generated in highly significant social dialectic, from goal-setting to successful achievement created by mass-media advertising to maintain the tempo. Of special interest in this connection, psychiatrist Jeffrey M. Schwartz and science journalist Sharon Begley (2002, p. 338) note that "attention is the mechanism by which the mind effects the expression of volition." Attention is necessary to the consumer's assurance of the distinction's social recognizability, for it magnifies, amplifies, and extends the stimulation such distinction exercises, at the same time highlighting the individual's status as a decision-maker.

Time-Consciousness

When industry assigned time a monetary value, money gained considerably more cultural prominence and a new significance in the individual's assessment of self-worth: its calculation suddenly had been raised high in our consciousness. Among the many things money can buy is a person's time, now assigning quantitative significance to human life. Time is ethereal and fleeting, yet clearly is also much more subject to order and management than ever before, now subject even to ownership: is it my time or company time, and am I using mine to optimal advantage as I'm expected to do when at work? Sociologist John B. Thompson (1995, p. 36) explains the context of this incentive to sell segments of one's life:

> As individuals were increasingly drawn into an organized, factor-based system of employment, the experience of the flow of time became increasingly linked to the time-keeping mechanisms required for the synchronization of labour and the organization of the working week. As time was disciplined for the purposes of increasing commodity production, there was a certain trade-off: Sacrifices made in the present were exchanged for the promise of a better future.[9]

Whereas religious obligation may formerly have called for the postponement of personal gratification in favor of warranting its greater reward at an unspecified later date, a more pragmatic exchange can now similarly be a useful strategy. Thus, industry turned toward time's exchange value to lure a very substantial portion of the population away from rural life and nature to its barren factory sites, which tended to locate in considerably more complex urban centers where resource transportation and product distribution were more efficient, thereby increasing the size of urban populations and further diversifying them. And since population density and diversity affect cognitive development (see Chapter 5, note 17), it also can heighten the sense of life's pace.[10] Decisions often introduce new demands on time, a relation to which automobile manufacturer Aurelio Peccei (1977, p. 21) refers somewhat romantically as "the orderless, torrential character of this precipitous human progress." Time is situated at the crux of determining the efficiency and rationale for establishing a rigorous objectivity, not just in industrial production and service but as well in much of the general society's quotidian activity. Not yet in complete control of time, Western society has deferred to it as one of the few natural elements to which humans must adapt, so when push comes to shove, human values accede to the pressures of time. Change brings new decisions, together placing more demands on time; then, as time is the sole element in modern life that does not exist in abundance yet always seems to diminish, it rises higher in the human consciousness and often predominates, all to negative effect. Time is scarce because that is precisely how it is felt. And some cultural characteristics make time pass ever more swiftly, such as our concentration on efficiency and innovation or our acute awareness of the general abundance related to our decisions, which rapidly change our perception of possibilities. Among the many other new complexities to occupy daily life, time's swift passage has become the most reliable element of nature's substratum, and this environmental force has progressed with a tenacious self-consciousness throughout Western society, while also propelling the culture, decision-by-decision, toward today's consumer society. Time-consciousness is an intensely personal experience that surely contributes to the more widespread stresses experienced daily.

What Are We Thinking?

A life of shopping in a world of increasing plenty suggests that enough money circulates among the population to make the system work as intended for most producers and most consumers most of the time. Meanwhile, industry's expansion to accumulate greater profit from further expansion and its requisite technological upgrading is mirrored in the culture's need to extend horizons through a more diversified commodification. But just as economic and technological rationality has migrated to the mundane quotidian by following carefully guided decisions leading in new directions, so has the relative importance of money, even to the point, as business magnate George Soros (2000, p. 56) observes, "that economic and especially financial values have come to dominate our lives." Money increasingly substitutes for values of any other kind, including quality. Money is the value of values. For those making their living in production and service industries, journalist and educator Max Lerner (1968, p. 186) wrote more than a half century ago that money had transferred workers' "interest and life energies from the making of goods to the making of money with which to buy and enjoy the goods." His conclusion is now applicable to any occupation. Since our drive for money is perfectly rational it therefore is perfectly understandable and acceptable, but it also places an uncomfortable stress on other values by altering some priorities and challenging the very presence of others. In the consumer society, qualitative values such as friendships, the natural environment, or simply the human capacity for introspection, cannot compete with quantitative values, especially money. Our narrowed sphere of reason makes this clear.

Motivation both individual and societal is realized in the increasingly accelerated and voluminous flow of innovation, creating a self-conscious opposition to the concepts of durability and stability. This is because anything believed durable has joined the principal obstacles in modernity's path, so anything traditional ranks high among them. Considered together, change, decision, immediacy, efficiency, comfort and convenience, along with the ease of social success for the moment and the acquisition of the most or the latest at the lowest price, constitute the critical criteria in a world defined by its commodities, their varieties, and the range of decisions they represent. What transpires in this consumer society is something not just highly social but primarily social, so the problem is not that we have become less socially oriented; the problem is that we have diminished our sociality and are showing signs of further diminishing it. Trends of the past five decades are social only because goods produced on a mass scale ultimately are purchased by consumers to become just the most recent tools for cultural competition, which may be displacing the establishment and maintenance of significant human relationships. This may be "that when people feel the emptiness of either material success or failure, they often persist in thinking that more will be better, and thus continue to strive for what will never make them happier," as Tim Kasser (2002, p. 74) finds, which is not an uncommon diagnosis (M. Lieberman, 2013; Kenrick and Griskevicius, 2013), but virtually everyone's spare time increasingly limited. Or we think it so or make it so. Consumption has many social outcomes, most of which condone the seduction and adoption the materialist attitude over the idealist, and it also facilitates the complex cultural system's continued evolution through adaptation in individual and collective decision. In this environment, social critic Raymond Williams (2009, p. 22) warns that consumption "ratifies the subjection of society to the operations of the existing economic system." Which has a cost.

Who's Minding the Store?

Industrial and government management has established a pattern for strategic planning that has not yet prescribed how this pivotal human act should proceed in other environments, but the general population has adopted some of their attributes. John Kenneth Galbraith (1978, p. 334)

7. The Western Ideological Environment   153

comments on this de facto model's features that have been acquired liberally, raising questions:

> The question arises whether the planning system, in absorbing economic conflict, ends all examination of social goals. Do its techniques of control—its management of market behavior and its identification with and adaptation of social goals—serve also to minimize social introspection? In brief, is the planning system monolithic by nature? And also very bland? To what extent does a society draw strength from pluralism of economic interests, which, in turn, sustains pluralism of political discussions and social thought?

Industrial and government intentions to emphasize the values of planning for their respective constituencies likely have exerted a positive societal influence in many ways, but the narrowed focus our leaders tend to relate to humanity's supposed mechanical functions undermines and detracts from the way people think, feel, and live *as human beings*. Reflecting on his own similar conclusion, Frank Fischer (2009, p. 22) writes about formal education that "professionals neither learn much about broader social and ethical implications of their occupations nor are they earnestly counseled to take them seriously." In planning our lives together, then, we are left to our own devices, which in view of our extraordinary cognitive capacities surely would be appropriate except that we soon encounter so many minor distractions and impediments that the proverbial trees quickly obscure our panorama of the forest. We telescope our worldview.

At the twentieth-century's midpoint, journalist and literary critic Lewis Galantiere (1950, p. 541) made public his troubling observation about industrial development. He noted that the capitalist spirit was indeed responsible for much impressive development following the Second World War, but also that for a longer period, "Since the end of the Middle Ages, since the rise of the centralized monarchical power, the trend of European capitalism has been away from a sense of responsibility to the community and towards exploitation of the community." Daily news of international affairs indicates this trend's continuation and its application at least equally to the Americas, suggesting that the model for success industry has established may not be the best one for human social conduct. With today's societal stability expected to be achieved almost entirely by maintaining the economic status quo—which clings so desperately to technological development and economic expansion—the Western culture most often is eager for change. Contributing to this draw, Langdon Winner (1986, p. 39) observes, "In our times people are often willing to make drastic changes in the way they live to accommodate technological innovation while at the same time resisting similar kinds of changes justified on political grounds." We have permitted the fanfare and psychological adjustment accompanying technological and economic attractions to overwhelm our attention to the deeper social and human values we still share, in fact, more profoundly.[11] There is a paucity of evidence that the full range of knowledge pertinent to these issues is brought to the table when the decisions to be made are likely to have an effect on large segments of the population, as well as on our planet itself. But this lacuna becomes conspicuous only when its *eventual* consequences are contemplated, which is relatively rare and much too late. Our decisions often carry quite negative social and psychological repercussions, even though relevant information via our genetic heritage has been available for ages to alert virtually everyone to the possibilities of such outcomes.

The principal reason for our failure to benefit fully from this information is that our human subjectivity does not follow simple instructions automatically, as programmed robots do; instead, they enter our thought to mix with extant information and knowledge in creating human meaning. Though our cognition is designed to sort through the normal combination of objective and subjective knowledge, we nonetheless are learning to suppress the subjective part when that seems to be the politically acceptable thing to do. We may do this only out of concern for the negative image our response would otherwise project, thereby indicating our naïveté. Emotion, feelings, and morality often seem to be considered something other than information or knowledge, although it remains unclear exactly what. Thus far, our evolution consistently has been motivated successfully by the combination of all human mental capacities, not just the select mode of thought tailored to achieve external narrow goals that exhibit a progressive tendency toward specificity and exclusivity.

Our Present Basis for Decisions

Sufficiently repeated and accumulated, Western decisions have construed a challenging reality for our culture and the individual lives it embraces. We persistently have designed and developed our knowledge and value systems to conform to the technical specifications modernity most prizes. This process has led to the emergence of many new kinds of decision because easy access to cultural choices has become an accepted sign of success in our individual and social life's management. In ever more complex situations, and under changing conditions offering many competing possibilities, Western decisions of the past century or more have proceeded by sifting our options through a special funnel designed to expedite its flow of preference. The procedure may not lead to absolutely exclusive options but does offer their varying degrees of difference by pairing values the consumer society can determine according to the following guidelines:

Technical knowledge of any kind over all other knowledge
Efficiency over thoroughness
Avoidance over experience (theory over empiricism)
Immediate utility over durability
Technique over value or substance
Specificity and precision over context
Microscopic vision over panoramic vision
Change over stability
Change over nature (including human nature)
Alteration of environment over adaptation to environment
Materiality over spirituality
Now over future
Objectivity over subjectivity
Quantity over quality
System over individual
Things over people
Science-directed epistemology over human-directed epistemology
Distancing oneself from life over embracing it
Short-term gain over long-term gain
Consideration of the moment over the lifetime
Result over experience (arrival at destination over the voyage)
Action over understanding
Answers over questions
Lifestyle over life experience
Representation of phenomena (in words, pictures, models or mathematics) over the actual phenomena

In her treatise on consumption in the United States, sociologist Juliet B. Schor (1998, p. 21) writes, "One problem with the national discourse is its focus on market exchanges, not quality of life, or social health." Most clearly, her statement describes a Western narrowing of thought. One reason for this mental channeling has been our preoccupation with physical objects, the orientation having become an idée fixe crowding our time in ways that permit the justifying convenience of avoiding personal and social challenges. Then they eventuate into an even tighter tangle of inefficiencies to include the more complex and truly major human issues made more obscure by the dense and overwhelming flurry of minor ones. There is a good possibility that we make many of these decisions unconsciously, their volume having become so inured it seems the natural, unquestionable state of the world. Or we may perceive the major issues to be the responsibility of a state agency or social institution and therefore not our problem as individual citizens with our own private lives to manage.

There is no society without individuals, who conveniently are overlooked by the reported population averages and medians, though the concept of a "quality of life" reflects all aspects of any individual's life, material and spiritual. We can quite easily produce statistics to prove our scarcely questionable material success, so they are the facts to which we first resort in answering any question about the quality of our life. And who can rationally argue against efficiency? Thus, the final assessment may be immediately reassuring but soon loses that value, because something about it seems not quite right. Our sense of that quality is subjective, of course, meaning that it reflects a combination of the reasoned and emotional sides of our being, invoking both our objective and subjective modes of cognition because it really asks how we *feel* about life, which we have learned is a politically unwelcomed mixture of the material and the ethereal. It is easy to fool ourselves, and we get plenty of help in doing just that. Robert Reich (2007, p. 99) surely is correct in his observation: "Today's economy can give us great deals largely because it punishes us in other ways. We can blame big corporations, but we've mostly made this bargain with ourselves." We have achieved this state of being decision-by-decision accumulating their weight, but like a snowball, the more it rolls on, the larger, heavier, and more self-guiding it becomes. Our current existential condition has not arisen simply because of scientific, technological, industrial, or state coercion: our decisions have produced it.

As a society, we probably have an excellent understanding of the technical, objective side of our problems, but we most definitely have lost sight of the subjective side, the part about our values and our humanity, the part we share. In the long term, our culture has become our own individual worst enemy. We have created a situation cultural historian and critic Stuart Ewen (1976, p. 220) anticipated with unerring prescience nearly a half century ago, as the tip of this iceberg was just beginning its surface into The Titanic's full view, dead ahead:

> The cultural displacement effected by consumerism has provided a mode of perception that has both confronted the question of human need and at the same time restricted its possibilities. Social change cannot come about in a context where objects are invested with human subjective capacities. It cannot come about where commodities contain the limits of social betterment. It requires that people never concede the issue of who shall define and control the social realm.

The point is that there need never have been any diminishment of a whole category of our thought, arguably the category most distinguishing us among all other beings. There is no valid reason to believe that science, technology, industry, or the economy would logically be antagonistic to the subjective dimension of human life, because *we* created *them*. But their close alliance was *introduced on so massive a scale and with such dazzling speed, its totality supported by a strategic concentration of management expertise, per-*

suasive mass communications, and discriminate intelligence-gathering capacity only capitalist industry commands, that the population simply was unprepared to assimilate it with equal speed and understanding, and therefore control. Humanity never had experienced so well-organized and magnificently powerful a behemoth, one capable of causing the West's population to assume responsibility for not only the creation of an overshadowing mass production/consumption system, but also its infinite sustenance. In this most significant sense, the industrial revolution peaks today. Its grand procession of social conditioning and normalization has convinced us that our society will collapse if technology cannot develop unrestricted and the economy cannot grow infinitely, both unfettered by human values and ideals.

Described in preceding chapters, the current confusion in our conceptualization of knowledge is the consequence of several centuries of societal concentration on the material aspect of our human life, its emphasis on an objective stance and a corresponding diminishment of the subjective qualities that define our humanity. No doubt we, and our forebears, foolishly thought we were taking the easy way out, if we managed to think about it. And this does make sense in an environment changed so rapidly from one of scarcity into one of abundance. Though our culture remains strong and more genuinely diverse than ever, its evolutionary momentum is diverted from foundational considerations by more externalized, specialized, narrow, tangential, and immediate ends so objective, in fact, that they have very little to do with humanity's collective potential and only the slightest hint of what that potential might yield. Dennis Ford (2007, pp. 217–218) is insightful in describing this displacement:

> The dominant, sacral mode of knowing in the modern era—science—is an expression of our motivation to control. Knowledge is defined as that which contributes to that control. If knowledge does not lead to control and pragmatic results, then its status as knowledge is suspect or dismissed altogether. The world we see through the instrument of science is thus restricted and limited, a partial truth that reflects but one of many possible motivations. Change the motivation and you change the world.

Owing to uniquely human mental capacities, we can imagine and create a considerable part of our world, and can enjoy an unequaled potential to do so freely. It would seem, then, that we humans have some degree of responsibility for the quality of our life and that of others, as well as for the planet upon which we dwell. This responsibility is the subject of the next chapter.

8

Human Stability and Balance

> We can no longer, it would seem, depend on the gradual undesigned adjustment of social institutions to our changing needs.... The great mechanism is thrown out of balance too easily and does not recover it spontaneously.
> —Robert M. MacIver, 1937

Well-Being, an Evolved Value

Well-being is a positive state of mind, a reasoned and felt psychological contentment with the overall conditions and course of one's personal life, making the human capacity to assess our own thought more significant than we may first believe.[1] It constitutes our homeostasis. Though we may seldom control life's negative events in a pragmatic sense, we often can control our reaction by buffering them with a positive outlook.

Indeed, if there is a single human feature serving as the basis for a general state of well-being, it surely resides in the remarkable human flexibility for adaptation—preeminently psychological adaptation—to changing circumstances, situations, and conditions. Negative events are to be expected, but ultimately and most often it is the manner we determine to respond to them that controls our state-of-being. Antonio Damasio (2010, p. 294) explains, "Biology and culture are thoroughly interactive. Socio-cultural homeostasis is shaped by the workings of many minds whose brains have first been constructed in a certain way under the guidance of specific genomes. Intriguingly, there is growing evidence that cultural developments can lead to profound modifications in the human genome." Our capacity for adaptation to environmental change demonstrates the extraordinary value of human sociality.[2] Humanity evolves according to patterns established socially, patterns from which ideals and wishful thoughts arise naturally. Each of us is unique, yet each also participates in the species' ongoing evolution.

Valerie Tiberius (2008, p. 155) observes a special kind of self-control some individuals are able to manage, having either inherited or developed a special attitudinal mechanism: "Psychologists have shown that optimists have all sorts of advantages in terms of health, happiness, and success in their chosen pursuits." And simply knowing that change is possible and human beings can set it in motion, even according to a detailed, rational plan, is reason for hope, which is a highly significant human feeling that evinces a remarkable persistence in the West (Sharot, 2011). Shared by all normal people, our subjectivity joins us together in many more similarities than differences in developing and maintaining strong cultures.

Well-Being and Sociality

A psychological state valued highly by all normal humans, well-being is elusive and not readily recognizable, making it a concept extremely difficult to define in any but the most general terms. Well-being is affected by all aspects of life, but for humans it can change as suddenly as our values priority, and without apparent reasons, well-being stems primarily from our sociality, a common human denominator. An understanding of the key role the social environment plays in our worldview is essential to maintaining a positive state, and because we are always evolving, individually and socially, no society may ever achieve perfection. But any human society must have ideals it can pursue toward a better quality of life, for without them there is no hope.

Philosopher and ethicist Sissela Bok (2010, p. 124) finds that happiness studies have grown to an unprecedented abundance around the globe in recent decades, and specifically that "on average, individuals thrive on having adequate social contacts and suffer when isolated.... Some psychologists even regard social contacts as the one factor without which happiness is not possible." Given the significant power of sociality in motivating human evolution, such a conclusion is quite logical. Sociality is variously involved in our fleeting psychological ups and downs that contribute to our natural resilience and adaptive capacity to return to a neutral or normal range, according to Bok (2010, p. 145):

> It is this process of adjusting emotionally to circumstances bringing good or bad luck that psychologists now refer to as "hedonic adaptation." Adaptation is what allows organisms, from molecules to humans and entire species, to respond to changed circumstances—as when our bodies regulate temperature, hormonal flows, immune responses and much else to achieve a better fit with such changes. We could not survive without being able to adjust in countless such ways, most of them beneath the level of consciousness. At a still higher stage of abstraction, systems, including organ-

isms, attempt to maintain the equilibrium of homeostasis in response to disturbances from the outside. Like all organisms, we humans are programmed to seek to maintain homeostasis to the extent possible.

Emotion and Feelings

It is abundantly evident that emotion and the bodily feelings it generates are strong motivations blending with rationality to be socially useful in guiding our behavior.[3] Because humans are affected by a sensitivity to others, the emotions and feelings this consciousness generates are of far more significance to collaboration and planning than may be indicated by the priority we often accord them. Antonio Damasio (2010, p. 56) explains this in his terse account of how and why we came to be who we are, which is much more than Economic Man:

> [T]he defining aspect of our emotional feelings is the conscious readout of our body states as modified by emotions; that is why feelings can serve as barometers of life management. This is also why, not surprisingly, feelings have been influencing societies and cultures and all their workings and artifacts ever since they became known to human beings. But long before the dawn of consciousness and the emergence of conscious feelings, in fact even before the dawn of minds as such, the configuration of chemical parameters was already influencing individual behaviors in simple creatures without brains to represent those parameters.

It may be a consequence of our relatively sophisticated system of agreements, rules, and laws that we sometimes accede to the thought that emotion, feelings, and even morality are no longer necessary, and can be ignored. But they do constitute a large part of our durable, shared knowledge, occupying much of our thought. In accord with many other psychologists and biologists, Peter Hammerstein and Robert Boyd (2012, p. 319) contend that "emotions play a crucial role in human decisions. They may sometimes lead to irrational behavior but at the same time enable us to maintain cooperative institutions essential for human sociality." Emotion is a principal factor in guiding our attitude through change and anticipating the possible outcomes of decisions. Paul Thagard (2010, pp. 148–149) finds, however, that like other emotions, happiness may be temporary, "but goals and the meaning that derives from them can be enduring.... Hence a meaningful life is not just one in which all our goals are satisfied, but one that provides reasons for doing things." The current emphasis on aspects of our knowledge best suiting both the Economic Man model and our economic/technological structure renders us considerably less human, for this approach to life depletes our cognitive apparatus by an entire dimension and degrades human values.

The Place of Morality

As the existence of others confirms our own, we want to be able to get along well with them, especially when our reputation is concerned, because it usually is in our best interest to do so. In his emphasis on the essence and complexity of morality, David Sloan Wilson (2003, p. 27) observes this warning from a clinical perspective:

> [O]ur ability to function as groups may require sophisticated cognitive mechanisms that appear effortless only because they are automated. Decades were required to understand the neurobiology of vision, and a similar effort may be required to understand the neurobiology of moral systems. The concept of an innate psychology of functional groups is not just a radical conjecture of evolutionary biologists. It is supported by some of the most distinguished research programs in the social sciences.

Critical to human sociality is our morality, as sociality is morality's reason for being. It represents a degree of individual control over others' assessment of us and our contribution toward their quality of life, since the quality of our own individual life and that of our cultural associates are to some extent bound together. The presence of sociality, congeniality, dignity, and morality may often be taken for granted today, and very likely have been for a long time, but their absence is noted immediately and most often regrettably. Quite commonly, therefore, in production and service industries of the latter twentieth- and early twenty-first century, the posting of vacant employment positions to be filled according to appropriate qualifications specifies not only the position's technical requirements but also the social requirements of good communication skills and the ability to work well with others; in the long term, these qualities constitute the foundation for getting things done properly and in a manner that strengthens corporate culture. Such desiderata may easily be recognized but are measured only with considerable difficulty and interpreted with uncertainty, for they are complex, comprehending continuous thoughts of morality and trust, all of which are essential to any organization's health.

Regarding the place of these human needs within our consumer society, Frans de Waal (2009, p. 221) concludes, "A society based purely on selfish motives and market forces may produce wealth, yet it can't produce the unity and mutual trust that make life worthwhile." The most imposing feature of Western culture during the second half of the twentieth century and the first quarter of the twenty-first is the economy, because consumption is its engine. But the question always arises about the extent to which money is ultimately essential to our well-being as individual humans, rather than as cogs in the mechanism of a poorly-measured progress. The remainder of this chapter summarizes the principal features humanity has evolved to support our individual and societal bid for well-being.

Fairness and Justice

Critical to the balance of our knowledge foundation for decisions is the character of other individuals directly involved in the process. Not mechanically driven, people do cheat, mislead, freeload (ride free), and otherwise practice deceit and commit moral infractions, some more than others, some more consistently, and some more adeptly. But the good news is that every normal human is aware of this problem because all have experienced similar temptations quite often, if not many of the actual infractions, Hurford (2007, p. 253) justly observing, "If language were not used most of the time for honest purposes, deception using language would not be possible." Moreover, most are endowed with a morality that triggers their respective emotion, feelings, and judgments. How we respond to these signals is determined by individual human psychology, which is influenced primarily by the social environment and its highly complex and always changing conditions, but also by our physical environment.

The appropriate balance of knowledge for decisions includes a substantial component of attention to the fairness and justice we expect, even though we know this expectation comes at the cost of some outcomes. Consequently, the goal of fairness and justice constitutes a highly significant part of rational decisions. Legal philosopher John Rawls (1957, p. 653) establishes a strong link between these two qualities: "The fundamental idea in the concept of justice is that of fairness.... Essentially justice is the elimination of arbitrary distinctions and the establishment, within the structure of a practice, of a proper balance between competing claims."[4] Rationality is always critical in decisions, but in *collective* decisions it also is a matter of practicality, claims Warren Quinn (1993, p. 46):

> It is special by being the virtue of reason as it thinks about human good. A virtue isn't a virtue because it's rational to have it. A good action isn't good because it's rational to do. On my view, the only proper ground for claiming that a quality is rational to have or an action rational to do is that the quality or action is, on the whole, good. It is human good and bad that stand at the center of practical thought and not any independent ideas of rationality or reasons for action. Indeed, even in its proper place as a quality of practical reason, rationality is validated only by the fact that it is the excellence, that is, the good condition of practical thought. Even here the notion of good has the primary say.

Rationality can distinguish between competing factors to determine an appropriate balance, but given the infinite number of decisions we render in a lifetime, very few if any are made solely on the basis of rationality (Skyrms, 2014; Hammerstein & Stevens, 2012; Thagard, 2010; H.C. Barrett, 2008; Johnson-Laird, 2006; Gazzaniga, 2005; Janicki, 2004; Nesse, 2001; Bateson, 2000; Sober and Wilson, 1998). It would be more useful to acknowledge this truth. Like knowledge of any kind, reason itself is neither good nor bad, its value dependent upon application. And many decisions, whether judged good or bad, are determined by thought processes other than pure rationality—if the state of pure rationality is even possible.[5]

Values and Valuation

Value is a cognitive function founded on both cultural experience and genetic inheritance. We value knowledge highly because it is absolutely essential to our motivations, so the study of human evolution directs special attention to knowledge. Tooby, Cosmides, and Barrett (2005, p. 329) further explain this conclusion, writing, "From an evolutionary-functional perspective, knowledge is the total set of regulatory discriminations in the organism that allow its actions to be generated and adjusted to mesh successfully with the variable features of its world." Our mind reconciles our knowledge to our environment; we must have knowledge to evaluate things, conditions, ideas, people, and possibilities, and we know what we value in a rough order of priority, always learning more about relative values in the course of associating with others and in conjunction with our many decisions. Individual internalization of cultural values, though usually invisible and very subtle to others, is a most significant part of maintaining the continuity individual and social stability require. Antonio Damasio (2010, p. 108) connects the role of emotion with that of values, writing, "Emotions are the dutiful executors and servants of the value principle, the most intelligent offspring yet of biological value."

Among other meanings of the verb "to value," those pertinent to human consciousness and rationality are caring for, feeling sympathy or compassion toward, and thoughts of acting altruistically.[6] Normal human beings experience such sensitivities quite commonly, having done so for many millennia because we value them. They occupy a uniquely important place within our social values by rendering possible and fostering the extraordinary sociality and cooperation that should properly be credited with the rapid success of human evolution. Group benefit is a human value for which we have social preferences aligning with our culture's values (Tomasello, 2009). Doing the right thing is a publicly recognized good but also is rewarding intrinsically, and although violation of the established social rules relevant to value usually leaves the violator with a poor self-assessment; following those rules has quite the opposite effect of stimulating pride. Experience with our conscience helps with the internalization of values by motivating thought about our own morality and that of others (Boehm, 2012). These human features have withstood the test of countless individuals and societies through many thousands of centuries. As a proven human value, morality is a profound part of our nature.

Altruism

Altruism reflects a prevailing human spirit that elevates humanity's general welfare to a much higher level of attention and protection than most of our other proclivities. We think often and deeply about ourselves but most frequently about ourselves within the social environment, whether constituted by one other or millions. Self-interest, therefore, is not the sole guiding motivation for human beings, because the concept of humanity means a great deal more than the Economic Man model can explain, even though it does continue to frame the commonly held Western self-image; there often seems a remarkably cynical side to the optimism we muster. Ultimately, concludes Matthew D. Lieberman (2013, p. 96), "Because we have been taught that people are self-interested, we conform to this cultural norm to avoid standing out." And such an understanding supports rationalization. Humans do manifest a consciousness of others, considerably exceeding any other motivation, as David Sloan Wilson (2007, p. 217) indicates in emphasizing its centrality to *all* forms of life: "There is no doubt whatsoever that the problems of altruism and selfishness addressed by Darwin in his passage on human morality, and which have traditionally been studied in insects and social vertebrates, also exist in microbial organisms."

Humans frequently exercise cooperation at higher intellectual levels than ordinarily is expected from a commitment to reciprocity, and can even include the personal cost of self-sacrifice for the good of another or an entire group, most often in the absence of prior agreement. We immediately recognize an altruistic act and surmise its motivation, for it is considered extraordinary and admirable.[7] Its difference from other categories of human social conduct is precisely that it is not governed, as are other behaviors, only welcomed and sometimes questioned because of the personal risk and sacrifice the concept connotes. Although unusual among other animals, altruism's potential is understood to be a natural quality of humanity, an ideal, even though not undertaken by every individual. C. Daniel Batson (2011, p. 229), reasons that,

> If the roots of human altruism lie in generalized parental nurturance, then ... altruism is woven tightly into the fabric of everyday life and not simply decorative fringe. It is neither exceptional nor unnatural but a central feature of the human condition. Rather than looking for altruism only in acts of extreme self-sacrifice, it should be manifest in the everyday experience of people like you and me.

Sober & Wilson (1998, p. 304) similarly trace the elements of this human potential to both the earliest millennia of humanity and the first moments of individual human life: "The quality of the mother-child bond appears to be a crucial predictor of the empathy and prosocial behavior that the child exhibits later in life. This suggests that when selection favored parents who took care of their children, it thereby favored children who provided help to others. If parental care is motivated at least partly by altruistic motives, the same may be true of helping that is directed to nonrelatives."[8]

Reason

Two and a half centuries ago, however, the spirit of modernity grew to what must have been an unprecedented social prominence, given the spirit of the times on both sides of the Atlantic. It was strengthened in the environment of science-oriented industrial development and accompanied by a new set of tests for value that determined a belief in modernity for the sake of modernity, a value per se: we prefer to think that whatever we Western humans have become must be good, because we voluntarily created it by decision. In this instance the pronoun "we" definitely does not mean all of us individually, but instead, "Our institutions have engaged in a continuing process of reverse adaptation, in which things are reshaped to suit the technical means available," as Langdon Winner (1986, p. 174) writes. We have been shaping and reshaping values according to technical standards (primarily economic and technological), in order to fit the narrowing gauge of tolerance in decisions, which like everything else must be accomplished according to the tested and widely-accepted industrial model. Values must be precise and systemically effective, and above all efficient. To the extent that the materialist society meets these standards, it has been able to achieve its crowning endpoint, because money is the common denominator for measuring human success and the satisfaction with life we presume it stimulates, magically if only momentarily. The great abundance of things accessible to the population has become an extension of the human condition, as things endow us with meaning and to some degree a sense of immortality, which may only constitute a more picturesque detour around our mortality's stark inevitability.

Abundance symbolizes our worth, for we understand it to be the principal source of individual human potential. And it is perfectly in the spirit of modernity that we so highly value individual autonomy, for our current epoch focuses more consistently than any other on the display and distinction of self, thereby functioning conveniently as the organizing principle for other values now globalizing.[9] Such distinction presents a particularly easy way to perceive that the act of decision itself has become a high-ranking value, almost on a par with money. Given this level of importance, however, the greater number of our decisions distance us as individuals from some of our long-held values, mostly by removing our distinguishing human features of emotion, feelings, and human relationships; moreover, we yield attention to morality primarily when it raises ethical questions, since in many cases they border on law or a license to practice. Neil Postman (1992, p. 31) sees in this cultural change a "separation of moral and intellectual values," which he perceives as "one of the pillars of a technocracy."

The technocracy is a modern invention. Entirely rational, it proceeds on course almost beyond the competition of any organizing philosophy, because in a world of staggering abundance and unprecedented opportunity for individual life, as David Potter (1954, p. 51) pointed out several generations ago, "No person can possibly deal with all these decisions on their merits or even on an *ad hoc* basis; he must constantly have at hand a set of readymade values which can be applied in disposing of most of the choices automatically." Eliminating some of these values has become the simpler and thus the more efficient decision-making process. But it eliminates only those values not directly participant in technical function—the values whose absence is most likely to be felt only in the long term—for many non-monetary values are now so generalized as to bear significance only for the indefinite, distant future. Threatened and gravely weakened in the contemporary value system are the individual and societal feelings of well-being, which most often are not provable, quantifiable, or demonstrable in any way credible to the modern mind.

The West's self-conscious separation of subjective from objective thought is unnatural and at best extremely foolish, because to be fully self-realizing, we humans require unqualified acknowledgment of our total mental context and capacity *as humans*. Mary Midgley (1978, p. 296) claims "You cannot even be rude or unconventional unless you know what you are doing, and that means knowing what things count as." That is, knowing their context, meaning, and value. Emotion, feelings, and morality constitute information inherited from a very long succession of ancestral trial-and-error experience. Furthermore, we also reinforce them with lessons learned from early childhood and refreshed throughout the rest of life. They are elements of meaning human beings generate to facilitate their action in realizing goals, and they contribute significantly to human judgment as well as to sociality in maintaining humanity's stability through change.[10] Other mammals also experience emotion and feelings, but we humans complement our subjective motivations with a level of rationality, which by all accounts is extraordinary. Human judgment is naturally and inexorably subjective because humans are highly subjective beings with an unequalled capacity for objectivity. The mind's greatest potential for humanity is realizable only by drawing upon the full range of cognition we manage as a means to finding the most advantageous balance of objective and subjective knowledge in varied situations and under changing conditions. Humanity is well equipped to make decisions and plan for a general state of well-being, but must consistently create the opportunity to do so, for such an opportunity may not otherwise arise. *Human values must be a de facto part of collective decisions.*

Cooperation

Because the human mind determines priorities in the thought leading to knowledge, valuation, feeling, motivation and action, it is to be expected that we focus on the self, our primary and principal point of reference. But since sociality is integral to our ever-more varied endeavors and occupies a prominent place in our accelerating evolution, we humans are distinguished from all other species by the extraordinary degree of attention we direct to our conspecifics. We are well prepared to work productively with others, even in disagreement, having done so increasingly throughout our species' evolution but with a very rapid increase in such experience during the most recent twelve millennia.[11] Cooperation has become so common an experience, in fact, that management consultant Edward M. Marshall (1995, p. 4) finds it "the way people naturally want to work." A social life means living amid conflict, because each of us has our own self and our own worldview to which we compare competing thoughts. The theory of rational choice, says social psychologist C. Daniel Batson (2011, p. 208), rests on two assumptions about rationality and value: "The rationality assumption is that humans will choose the action that is most likely to get them what they want. The value assumption is that what they want is to maximize self-interest." Distinction between the rational and the irrational is not complicated, it is rather a distinction between what is rational or irrational *for the longer-term condition of self,* a distinction Robin Dunbar (1999, p. 194) clarifies:

> Social life is founded on cooperation: to live in large groups and gain the ecological and other advantages that they provide, organisms must be willing to forego at least some of their immediate desires in the interests of keeping the group together. This tension between the immediate returns that derive from satisfying one's selfish interests and the longer-term benefits (to self) that derive from the advantages of group-living invariably places the stability of large groups in jeopardy. In effect, unless at least some individuals are willing to give way to the interests of others, the pressures of self-interest are likely to cause large social groups to fragment.

Whether cooperation occurs among large diverse groups or two similarly disposed individuals, it still is an arrangement whereby time, effort, and knowledge are shared in such a way that those involved will ultimately benefit from their contribution, doing so to an extent that is greater for each participant than can possibly be yielded by one lone individual. This arrangement is advantageous in the long run, though under almost constant challenge by those relatively few who would shirk their responsibility; some reassurance of a positive experience is required for the collaborators' continued willingness to participate.[12]

Humanity's high degree of psychological preparedness for thinking and planning in concert with others stems from several capacities: the ability to perceive the larger picture, which is a highly distinguishing human feature; a normally strong sense of self; and the continuous motivation to monitor and regulate one's own course toward success while also monitoring that of collaborators, which is another set of features distinguishing humans in a life highly dependent on social success.[13] Central to this monitoring and regulating system are the bodily feelings whose origins are primitive, but which also have evolved with humanity and are adaptable to the respective culture's current environmental conditions. Their invocation to act relates to mental acuity, but Boyd, Richerson, and Henrich (2005, p. 273) conclude that "human intelligence is only a part, and perhaps only a small part, of being able to create complex adaptive behaviors. In fact, we think 'intelligence' plays little role in the emergence of many human complex adaptations. Instead, humans seem to depend upon socially learned strategies to finesse the shortcomings of their cognitive capabilities." Such strategies help guide the self in group-acceptable directions, so the group also has devised strategies to safe-guard its integrity.

Under normal conditions, these strategies are imposed culturally rather than physically, since morality and conscience are the principal socially designed and administered regulating authorities. Boyd, Richerson, and Henrich (2005, p. 261) also find in both field and laboratory work: "Models of moralistic punishment lead to multiple stable social equilibria and to reductions in noncooperative strategies if punishment is prosocial. As a consequence, we believe, a growing reliance on cultural evolution led to larger, more cooperative societies among humans over the last 250,000 years or so." These cultural forces continue today, particularly as various technological enhancements in communication have removed many of the barriers formerly imposed by time and space.[14] It is noteworthy that this policing activity is a *combination* of individual and social vigilance with consequent action. The common understanding of morality, rules, and laws is indicative of the extent to which the importance of cooperative and moral behavior is recognized in the twenty-first century, and that this trait accrues to the advantage of each individual when most others adhere to its spirit. Morality, rules, regulations, and laws acknowledge the complexity and unpredictability of individuals, for each differs psychologically from the others within a society whose culture is embroiled in continuous change. Pierre Bourdieu's (1977, p. 83) explanation of "habitus" depicts the interlacing of concepts uniting humanity. He writes that habitus is "a system of lasting, transposable dispositions, which, integrating past experiences, functions at every moment as a matrix of perceptions, appreciations and actions and makes possible the achievement of infinitely diversified tasks, thanks to analogical transformations of schemes permitting the solution of similarly shaped problems." Humanity has learned to analogize experience. A culture usually evinces tacit recognition of the molding features of "habitus" by assuming an active part in the development of acceptable behavior and character, which reflects as well the fact that everyone is a product not only of parental but also ancestral minds, evolved over countless thousands of years and now situated within a complex society whose culture more swiftly grows more complex.

The assurance of cooperation in a relatively stable society could not function as successfully as it does without the special cognitive features endowing humanity with the extraordinary powers of communication and social understanding elaborated in preceding chapters. Such cognitive capacities, particularly those dependent on Theory of Mind features, are highly conducive to the cooperation flowing from both individual and group competition for success. Aside from the knowledge and skills our associates possess, what we need most to know about them in decision-making are the less obvious aspects of their character: Do they fully understand the significance of collaboration? How honest and dependable are they? Will they do their part in the group enterprise or are they free-riders?[15] Anthropologist Chris Knight, anthropologist and cognitive scientist Robin Dunbar, and social anthropologist Camilla Power (1999, p. 6) summarize the most relevant applications of these special human cognitive features:

> We humans have minds which appear well-designed to read other minds from cues provided by eye movements, facial expressions, tones of voice and other bodily signals. Correspondingly, we can anticipate the effects which our movements may have in shaping others' thoughts about what we are thinking. From this, it is but a small step to the deliberate and deceptive manipulation of information. An implication of "Machiavellian Intelligence" theory [mindreading] is that it was humans' increasingly sophisticated capacity for deceiving one another which eventually gave rise to that entirely novel level of representational activity which we call "symbolic culture." Social deception exercises a capacity which is fundamental to symbolism—the ability to hold in mind simultaneously both a "true" representation and also its "false" counterpart....
> To signal deceptively is, in principle, to concoct an imaginative scenario.

Much research documents the strong human penchant toward socialization and cooperation, for it consistently and vividly is etched in human cultural evolution. Morality and conscience explain much about the impressive coherence of human culture, but specifically that we are well conditioned to cooperate in group decision, planning and execution, even in quite large groups, as we share a reflexive capacity for mutual understanding and a have developed a variety of ways to represent our ideas. Scott Atran (2005, p. 311) observes, "Humans have a metarepresentational ability to form representations of representations. This allows people to understand a drawing or picture of someone or something as a drawing or picture and not the real thing," which are necessary in systems modeling. Comparison with other species demonstrates the following: "Intentional cooperation in non-human nature is rare, if it exists at all," as James Hurford (2007, p. 254) confirms. Reciprocity is a special form of cooperation whereby one agent does something for another, often with only a tacit understanding that the favor will be returned at some future time, one good turn deserving another, in a give-and-take experience now commonplace.[16]

Balancing the Foundation for Decisions

This essay's core contention is that emotion, feelings, and morality are at least as valid a part of the human knowledge foundation for collective decisions as the price of shoes. Their signals are not something separate and therefore dismissible when inconvenient; they are neither the irrepressible animal instincts of the utmost primitive humans nor some strange kind of modern social handicap. Modified through evolution, they are sophisticated alerts whose purpose is to aid in determining the best course of human action, a purpose consistently grown more critical to humanity as our life has become dense in its complexity and as industrial corporations have developed powers heretofore totally unknown to humanity. The problem is that emotions and feelings are beginning to be recognized only when they can be economically useful and advantageous in competition, the most obvious examples being the commercial marketing of commodities, life insurance, and human dreams. Though our genetically-inherited information is an ongoing part of all human thought, it now is expected to be suppressed in critically significant thought, unlike other kinds of knowledge, such as information related to technological objectives and economic constraints or opportunities, which are considered challengeable solely on their technical basis and in those terms; and there can, indeed, be serious consequences. "It is now recognized that evolving organisms also change their environment. Plants breathing out oxygen is an example," writes Hurford (2007, p. 248) "Before plants, there wasn't all that free oxygen in the atmosphere." Carlo Rovelli (2016, p. 75) assesses the value of our inherited information:

> Our moral values, our emotions, our loves are no less real for being part of nature, for being shared with the animal world, or for being determined by the evolution that our species has undergone over millions of years. Rather, they are more valuable as a result of this: they are real. They are the complex reality of which we are made.

The function of reason, therefore, is not simply to control emotion and feelings but to be attentive to them when an understanding of the nature of circumstance and condition rationally indicates either their benefit or harm to individual and society. Combined with our unique cognitive plasticity, these internal forces sustain human sociality, cooperation, and balance for our successful evolution and the quality of our life. Social philosopher Talbot Brewer (2011, p. 286) emphasizes that "emotions organize our patterns of awareness so as to make it tempting to affirm that things really are the way the emotion portrays them—to believe, that is, that the emotion really is warranted." Humans most evidently are biological not mechanical, so it is unreasonable to treat our cognitive features as machinery or to expect our conspecifics to react mechanically. We are much more than that. Shedding light on the human decision-making process, Zoltan Torey (2014, p. 22) observes, "Situated functionally between the sensory side and the motor side of the brain is the organism's decision-making center, the brainstem. This is the home of biological values and of the apportioning of reticular activation for those motor responses it senses to be in the organism's interest."[17] From another perspective, Frank Fischer (2009, p. 274) describes a major distinction related to our decisions:

> Rather than causes that govern actions per se, emotions serve to orient actors to the external conditions confronting them. Motivating and mobilizing thought and action, in short, precedes deliberation. Only after actors have oriented themselves generally, can they determine particular strategies. While the action of choosing is the task of deliberation, the emotionally conditioned orientation indicates the general direction and thus the acceptable alternatives that might be discussed.

This essay has covered a lot of territory, so the next chapter concludes with a review of humanity's evolution toward our culture's present state. Finding our present situation truly unprecedented, only humanity acting in human interests has the power to regain our former course. The chapter is about doing just that: restoring human emotion, feelings, morality, and humanity to our decision processes, both individual and collective, and protecting them.

9

Invitation to a Stance

> We have to ask ourselves, therefore, What kind of learning process will increase the probability of futures that are favorable to human betterment and diminish the probability of futures evaluated as involving human worsening, particularly those that are catastrophic?
> —Kenneth E. Boulding, 1985

Our Evolved Social Environment

No force other than industrialization has ever generated so broad yet so profound a change in human life in so brief a time—for better or for worse, and evolutionarily—as the West has experienced throughout the past half millennium. Humanity could not have been prepared for change so broadly sweeping yet so profound. We have neither adjusted to it nor gained control over to it to human advantage, but we do now need at least to act responsibly. Louise Barrett (2011, p. 76) warns that "An abnormal environment can disrupt normal development as effectively as can a mutant gene, if not more so, but with major consequences for behavior." This is what we have experienced.

Documented throughout this essay, research in cognitive psychology, neuroscience, and evolutionary psychology consistently supports several conclusions pertinent to the irreplaceable significance of our diminishing emotion, feelings, and morality. Human cognition is distinct among all creatures not only because of its rationality, but also because of the unique human capacity to perceive our potential for collaborative physical and intellectual activity and thus to experience quotidian life fully. Through collaboration, the diversity among individuals can be optimized in our extraordinarily strong cultures to encourage individual human potential by maintaining a high degree of sociality. In conjunction with reason and objective knowledge, our leavening subjective features are essential to human cognition, rendering technical change acceptable to and functional for our species, as subjective information and objective knowledge most naturally function together in managing the equilibrium necessary to humanity's distinctive cognitive system and diverse way of life. Together—and only together—subjective and objective thought have constituted a sound knowledge foundation for the decisions and planning necessary to the maintenance of individual and social life fulfillment in a manner most closely suited to human beings. Since the emergence of *Homo sapiens*, our subjective features have enabled us to benefit from the rich corpus of knowledge discovered, created, utilized, accumulated, and communicated by all our generations of both diverse individuals and cultures. Demonstrated throughout humanity's evolution, our individual and societal self-understanding, self-monitoring, and self-regulating are predominant characteristics of our identity. Essential to our nature, they are situated at the forefront of normal human thought.

Beginning in the natural philosophers' workshops of the fourteenth and fifteenth century, those physicists and chemists established a systematic strategy for understanding the physical world; it soon was adopted by the fledgling production industries whose leadership maintained strong interests in personal profit as compensation for their financial and psychological risks in raising the general standard of living. Appropriate industrial strategy required adherence to a strict and narrowed objectivity, which eventuated into a model for the management of individual and societal human life beyond the factory. Throughout industrial development, Western populations increasingly demonstrated an affinity with technology, and as the successive adoptions of these consistently improved instruments rolled by, the population could perceive, and was encouraged to perceive, distinctions between nature and humanity, positing human beings not as part of nature but as separate from and superior to it. Similarly, but over a longer duration, the principle of objectivity, which is absolutely fundamental to natural science, distanced scientists intellectually further from their direct observation of natural phenomena by interposing various technologies between themselves and their objects of study. In the nineteenth century, electronic technologies removed the scientist further from their visual understanding and, therefore, the public's understanding of science, a condition also applicable to technology just prior to the twenty-first century, when hand-held digital technologies captured cultural attention. Twentieth-century physicists, who had been inclined more and more toward the objectivity of mathematics than the subjectivity of observation, removed themselves even further from public gaze, leaving natural science more of a public mystery than it ever had been, while also diminishing the value of public knowledge explainable by any process that might hint of subjectivity. We do continue to have individual access to knowledge generated by individual subjective means, but its application is not to be mixed with reason in formal decisions, for doing so has become politically incorrect, at best. Such processes are expected to be founded solely on facts demonstrable quantitatively.[1]

Humanity Distanced from Nature

Industry has kept a thumb on the Western evolutionary scales by distancing humanity from nature, but Steven Mithen (1990, p. 262) reminds us, "We today are just as much part of nature as Paleolithic or Mesolithic man."[2] We have evolved with a physical body containing a brain, a neural system and five bodily senses, so in that regard we are as natural as any other mammal. Nonetheless, having established clear demarcations between mind and body, humanity and nature, much of the Western population appears to believe otherwise, and is expanding the distance between nature and us. Our brain is the interpreter of its direct connections with both body and nature, constituting the principal connection between our physical and social environments via our senses (Gazzaniga, 2011). Despite this simple truth, throughout the past five centuries of cultural evolution we have not simply strayed from our place in nature but rather have shunned it, largely because of nature's putative inferiority to humanity's technical prowess, a supposition reinforced by the pride we show in our capacity to alter the physical environment, even when it is accomplished with little evident thought except as related to economics. Ironically, by determining this course we dismiss our nature and our humanity, avoiding the most obvious human responsibilities for our species and our physical environment. Either we have forgotten or have determined to forget that the mind functions according to "The close relationships of body and brain," as Antonio Damasio (2010, p. 92) asserts, which "are essential to understanding something else central to our lives: spontaneous bodily feelings, emotions, and emotional feelings." Our disengagement of emotion, feelings, and morality from our evolutionarily critical decisions is a de facto disregard—if not rejection—of the most profound values each of us holds individually, jeopardizing individual and societal well-being.

Any serious discussion of humanity includes emotion, which then leads to our feelings, and beyond to the morality reflected in our conscience, because most of our social environment experiences these pressures, which are unique to humans by their intensity of significance. Such sensitivities do normally participate in our cognitive processes, constituting the individual and societal knowledge foundation for decisions, but rarely if ever are they expected to be the *sole* deciding factors in any decision. They remain as significant a part of this intense and pivotal activity as the given issue's technical aspects, and though they bear special meaning, no single part of these processes is necessarily dominant.[3] "We're used to having our emotional decisions overruled by our rational, thought-out ones, and sometimes, vice versa," according to David Gelernter (2016, p. 117), but "The emotional system is usually much faster, since its conclusions are reached unconsciously." Because of emotion's relatively hasty path to decision, reason's more analytical properties are expected to help in arriving at a sound judgment, its *social* goal being the achievement of human cultural equilibrium, any organism's or species' ultimate goal. Thomas Suddendorf (1999, p. 223) gauges the significance of emotion and feelings in his pregnant assertion "That 'to feel' is the essence of consciousness is reflected in the everyday use of the word. Losing consciousness means more than being unable to think or reason, it means being unable to feel.... [S]ensations or feelings are the product of active neuronal processes separate from those producing perception." Their sources are separate but they function together in a single cognitive process.

The invocation of values stimulates the human inclination toward sociality and includes a sense of responsibility. Natural to our high degree of sociality, every normal human engages in subjective thought, for if individuals were not at all moved by the value of self, humanity surely would have gone extinct ages ago: the self's survival is preeminent in an environment fraught with mortal danger, and each individual's potential is enhanced by the value our species places on humanity. Frans de Waal (1996, p. 88) explains this value as one not to be taken for granted but protected and nurtured:

> Despite its fragility and selectivity, the capacity to care for others is the bedrock of our moral systems. It is the only capacity that does not fit the hedonic cage in which philosophers, psychologists and biologists have tried to lock the human spirit. One of the principal functions of morality seems to be to protect and nurture this caring capacity, to guide its growth and expand its reach, so that it can effectively balance other human tendencies that need little encouragement.[4]

As a society we do maintain institutions charged with responsibility for the well-being of others, which may, however, also have easily permitted us as individuals to be dissuaded easily from following our internal inclination toward caring about our conspecifics.

Adam Smith's notion of the invisible hand reaching out empathetically from the market cosmos is hardly to be counted upon in truly difficult times, which are experienced much more frequently and profoundly by the general population than are easy times, and they often proceed as though beyond human control. In such instances, it falls to humanity (which comes down to individuals) to assume some responsibility for societal vigilance and protection, as caring about others is a long-evolved human trait, as Sober & Wilson (1998, p. 336) indicate:

> As the most facultative species on earth, human beings appear willing and able to span the full spectrum from mercilessly exploiting their social partners to sacrificing their lives for others. This stunning plasticity of behavior must somehow be orchestrated by

proximate mechanisms that probably include altruistic ultimate motives, but certainly include much more, such as emotions, moral principles, and other mechanisms that we deliberately set to one side to make headway on the subject of psychological altruism. To the extent that behavior has evolved by group selection, multilevel selection theory will be required to understand the full architecture of human motivation.

We care about others because we have the cognitive capacity to imagine ourselves in their situation, whether positive or negative. Without it we would behave like wildebeests, gathered together at the shallow river's edge in idle observation of the crocodiles busily disemboweling them, one by one. To judge our subjective features as somehow inferior to or less useful than the cognitive features we do so proudly recognize and value, primarily our objective rationality and our versatile communication capacity, is a foolish mistake and ultimately self-defeating.

The Distinction of Human Decision

Decision-making is a highly self-conscious and intensely-concentrated mental action normally expected to follow from the thoughtful weighing of often conflicted knowledge, the complex process leading to a judicious determination founded on the best information and thought available at the time. But the current Western knowledge foundation for this activity has been thrown off balance by a strong bias that is unnatural in its favoring of humanity's technical side over its more natural tendency toward subjectivity. This compartmentalization contributes to a purposeful disregard of the features most expressive of our humanity, invoking instead their separation primarily, if not solely, to advance the narrow purposes of a specific segment within our population. An unquestioning modernist faith in the objective natural science epistemology, fueled as it is by narrative images of industrial, economic and technological success, has swayed the general acceptance of an almost exclusive reliance on the rationalized goal of effectiveness through technical and human efficiencies. In this context, however, the rigidly objective attitude of natural science proves not to be a clarifying force for human thought patterns but rather a disruptive distraction, for it too often creates misunderstandings, ill-will, and negative human conditions throughout the culture, too often life-threatening conditions. Our decisions are now much less likely to benefit from our full mental capacity than they may have been just two or three centuries ago—despite the expansion of democracy.

The establishment of planning and decision-making groups charged with identifying the best possible outcome will always encounter both logistical and psychological challenges, if for no reason other than the great diversity among assembled perspective and psychology, but the knowledge foundation on which a decision is to be made must first be adequate to the task. The human organism is a system orchestrated by the brain with connections to body and environment, so to pretend that the proposed system works poorly or well, better or best on only a partial knowledge foundation is to ignore the generally proved and accepted premise about that foundation's high level of significance. And it raises this question: for whom does the knowledge foundation for decision work poorly or well, better or best, in both short and long term? Craig Dilworth (2010, p. 398) synthesizes the historic background for much contemporary conflict:

> Development through the centuries has, if as yet incompletely, created systems that give citizens the opportunity to influence and control their governments. Large international concerns on the other hand, which operate only according to their own short-term goals, lack inbuilt homeostatic checks. We have no insight into their operations, and thus cannot connect them to sensible paths that are of use to *everybody*.[5]

Decision-making is the critical human act that sets the stage for group selection in adapting to the changes produced under variable environmental conditions. Decisions are crucial, for they follow from complex thought processes capable of generating considerably more possibilities than habitual or instinctive actions alone can generate. This is primarily because, while possessing a complexly integrated and flexible brain in continuous development, a multi-faceted mind, an unusually deep memory, an extraordinary set of social sensitivities, an individual yet long-evolved psychology, and a versatile symbolic capacity for communication, we humans are particularly attentive to the effect of decisions not only on ourselves, individually, but also on others. Therefore, we quite naturally incorporate a wide range of complicating considerations when pondering our decisions. Their range of possibility is complemented by a cognitive capacity that includes a creative imagination in the coordination of knowledge and values by scanning and assessing the surmised outcomes a decision likely could bring, not only to oneself but also to others. Nonetheless, this often can be accomplished in surprisingly little time, given the extent of mindscape to be covered. David Sloan Wilson (2003, p. 27) explains this most fundamental and distinguishing human capacity that also is common among all normal individuals:

> [O]ur ability to function as groups may require sophisticated cognitive mechanisms that appear effortless only because they are automated. Decades were required to understand the neurobiology of vision, and a similar effort may be required to understand the neurobiology of moral systems. The concept of an innate psychology of functional groups is not just a radical conjecture of evolutionary biologists. It is supported by some of the most distinguished research programs in the social sciences.... A branch of social psychology known as social identity theory shows how easily people think of themselves as members of groups, especially in opposition to other groups...[P]eople spontaneously establish, enforce, and largely abide by social norms

in the absence of a formal legal system.... There is great opportunity for a synthesis on this subject between the established branches of the social sciences and evolutionary biology, upon which all functional explanations must ultimately rest.

As many of the references in preceding chapters strongly suggest, reports of dissatisfaction with the quality of Western life appear to be more frequent and intense as time rolls on, attenuated only by a growing sense of helplessness. Some of this negative perception may stem from the ambiguity experienced by those who have become aware that much of their own thought, as well as that of others, emanates from their deeper, more humanly meaningful emotions and feelings. David J. Hess (2007, p. 9) observes a specific symptom that crystalizes the West's current conditions: "One of the defining characteristics of recent history is the collapse of the optimism associated with scientific progress and technological innovation." We have invested our resources and ourselves in them quite heavily for several centuries, for a long time in the expectation of a greatly improved quality of life. Other critics similarly find that Western life has become at once frustratingly complicated yet depressingly vacant for many if not the majority, both those who are financially quite stable and those who evidently are less so.

Our expectations were only partially well-founded.

Our lives are over-crowded with a relatively insignificant busy-ness that streams by too rapidly for much meaning to be salvaged, leaving little time, space and energy for it to be assessed, and time passes too quickly for its experience to be internalized as the profile of one's own life, because we have made it so. Humanity is not a commodity extruded to fit one model; humanity is highly capable of shaping itself in ways more natural and appropriate to our species. An educated guess—supported by documents itemizing human rights and dignities—indicates that we human beings prefer to be treated as such and not as instruments in a vast economic and technological system over which we are becoming more and more convinced that we exercise less and less control.

The Significance of Perspective

The capacity to assume an objective perspective does unquestionably have its special value, which we invoke often and with little effort, and by applying a variety of perspectives it affords us the advantage of better understanding. But in its putative "pure" form—that is, unmodified by subjective information—the rigidly objective stance has caused us to stray from our nature simply by relinquishing beliefs, feelings and sensitivities, even if momentarily, in the purpose of more closely defining the technical issue solely in *its* own terms and on *its* own conditions. Yet, *it* has no conditions other than those we give *it*. Literary and cultural theorist Gerald Graff (1979, p. 24) makes a disquieting assessment of the strict objectivity that can be formed in the blanket adoption of a rigidly objective approach to judgment and decision about human situations, conditions and futures:

> The logic which associates objective thinking with social domination and exploitation is not difficult to reconstruct. To apprehend something objectively is to separate oneself from that something and thus to view it as an "object" or "thing" distinct from oneself. It follows—or it is made to follow—that the objective way of looking at the world is necessarily detached, uninvolved, "value-free," and from the point of view of human interests and needs, inhuman.

Subjectivity, on the other hand, creates the framework for every normal human's intellectual make-up and for the understanding found in introspection, any individual's most profound and carefully developed thought. To cast it aside for the "purity" of objectivity, meaning the disregard of our most human attributes *for the sake of efficiency and appearance* is highly irrational in any social context. And if the goal is to be effective, which of course it must be, toward what *ultimate* effect? By all accounts, objectivity is an admirable, pragmatic and extraordinarily human capacity, in many instances an unequivocally necessary stance, so this essay does not question the validity of objectivity's place in our biological and social survival: humans have evolved both subjective and objective capacities far beyond those of any other species (H. C. Barrett, 2015; L. Barrett, 2011; de Waal, 2009; Gazzaniga, 2008). But individual human reactions surely are not extraneous to the consideration of their ultimate social effects, for it is difficult even to imagine the value of a decision or plan that ignores the values pertinent to its human context. Yet this appears to be the increasingly dominant attitude in the West: it is an attitude singly designed for industrial purposes. There is no objectivity without the thinker first being subjective, primarily because normal human objectivity is adopted in the conscious effort to assess one's own thought. Thomas Nagel (1986, p. 221) acknowledges this in his conclusion about objectivity's value when he writes, "The objective self is a vital part of us, and to ignore its quasi-independent operation is to be cut off from oneself as much as if one were to abandon one's subjective individuality. There is no escape from alienation or conflict of one kind or another." As the two sides of a complete person, objectivity and subjectivity function together in a variable balance within our context of fluid conditions and states, circumstances and situations.

Even from the most objective point of view, however, it really is irrational to remove knowledge of human qualities from decisions related to human beings, for it is supremely natural for humans to sort through the significance of likely outcomes for self and others. We cannot truly understand others without first understanding ourselves. Requisite qualities for accomplishing this state of mind are present in the consciousness of all normal beings and therefore are active in the social mind. It is wholly unnatural that modern society has been made to feel unsophisticated or ashamed simply because emotion and feelings—some arising from moral and ethical concern but all from consideration of others—have attached themselves to each of us since earliest childhood as a human reminder of our responsibility for the common good. A sense both latent and learned throughout our culture's evolution, it is our nature. Opposition to this sense amounts to the willful exclusion of the human element.[6] Owen Barfield (1977, p. 188) declares this in his allegation: "The vaunted progress of 'knowledge,' which has been going on since the seventeenth century, has been progress in alienation. The alienation of nature from humanity, which the exclusive pursuit of objectivity in science entails, was the first stage; and was followed with the acceptance of man himself as part of a nature so alienated, by the alienation of man from himself." Much of our social change repeatedly labeled "impressive human progress" surely would not have eventuated without strategic objectivity. But in the current social environment it gradually has become the frame through which all the world is supposed to be viewed from the West, where the exclusion of subjectivity is becoming the political correctness of decision-making. One unfortunate consequence of this phenomenon is especially perceptible among the general population, which increasingly is assessed as too often unhappy, forever discontent, and usually feeling alone with the confounding and defeating question: why do we so often think individually in one way and act collectively in another?

Out of the mass of disparate and changing ideas and emotions that flow through the mind, and owing to our acute awareness of self, subjective thought is the sphere of consciousness that analyzes, constructs, and continuously reconstructs and synthesizes the human reality of worldview. The mind concentrates on and is keenly alert to the ongoing connectivity of knowledge as it generates new images in worldview, so sociologists Carolyn Ellis and Michael G. Flaherty (1992, p. 4) find, "Subjectivity is situated such that the voices in our heads and the feelings in our bodies are linked to political, cultural, and historical contexts." Because everyone is engaged in this recycling series of mental events, each individual and each culture also is engaged in an ongoing internal dialectic predisposed to the self, which is a thinking, feeling, knowing being, each well aware that all others are too. It is how we evolve as a culture in a society. This mixing process accounts for what may sometimes appear irrational within a culture as thoroughly conditioned and therefore prone to rigid rationality as the West's. Introduced in Chapter 6 and discussed earlier in this one, self-identity is to the greatest extent formed by social processes, so subjective thought, heavily dependent on reflexivity, is the ultimate source of social norms and situated at the center of decisions.

Objectivity and subjectivity are mental modes natural to humans. Humanity has experienced eons in evolving as it has because of a unique ability to manage these perspectives in favor of itself as a *reflection of the species*, their value having been tested by a vast multitude of individuals and cultures. Just as there is no objectivity without subjectivity, there is no subjectivity without objectivity because neither can be defined satisfactorily without the other. There is no purity about either, but together they do require balance, which fluctuates according to situation, condition and aspiration, and they account for other extraordinary human capacities such as language, cooperation, and the conjecture of another's thoughts. We cannot successfully find refuge from the dilemmas of judgment, either by pretending a situation or condition will automatically resolve itself and vanish, or by indiscriminately quantifying any issue that may, however remote or contrived, reveal select features amenable to calculation. Failure to find the appropriate balance of knowledge in judgment only creates further problems, often of a different nature. We tend to diminish or suppress our subjectivity for many reasons amounting only to a seriously misguided diversion from our evolved and arguably successful path through life, but subjectivity accounts for how normal people actually think. A healthy, normal mind works on a balance between these two frames of thought. It maintains a dual function, constituting a state entirely pertinent to Nagel's (1986, p. 214) view: "There is a recognizable human desire to find our existence significant no matter how cosmic a view we take, and a consequent discomfort with the partial disengagement that objectivity induces."

The thought of a world with little or no meaning because it takes so little account of humanity is, at very least, an unsettling possibility, for balancing subjectivity and objectivity is a natural way for both individual and society to proceed appropriately, and always has been, each instance wearing down the extreme rough edges of the other to accommodate the *ultimate human* purpose without causing undue disruption. Absolute subjectivity could lead only to fatal conflict among individuals and absolutely devastating war between societies, for our normal behavior, if driven solely by emotion, would soon be worse than that of any grouping of undomesticated animals but much worse because of our large, flexible and creative brain. Objectivity forces us to deal with the reality William James (1950, p. 22) was able to describe in but one simple phrase, writing, "The greatest enemy of any one of our truths may be the rest of our truths." On the other hand, the opposite and present course—that of eliminating subjectivity at every opportunity except commercial marketing—has been followed too often and now too far to be judged in healthy balance. From his scientific viewpoint, physicist Carlo Rovelli (2016, pp. 77–78) casts a more commanding thought:

> I believe that our species will not last long. It does not seem to be made of the stuff that has allowed the turtle, for example, to continue to exist more or less unchanged for hundreds of millions of years, for hundreds of times longer, that is, than we have

even been in existence. We belong to a short-lived genus of species. All of our cousins are already extinct. What's more, we do damage.

Throughout the past half millennium, industrial strategies, principles, and values have become so clear, simple, legendary and obviously successful for commercial enterprise that the citizenry has adopted them gladly, even for personal purposes when possible. Given the abundance of objective proof, people can easily perceive that objective reasoning is the safest, surest and most precise guide for any undertaking. But new cultural norms then evolve in the changing social environment to introduce newer perspectives, obscuring that picture.[7] This approach to change is badly misleading today, if efficiency and technical effectiveness are, indeed, the *ultimate* goals of our collective decisions, which is most doubtful. "No system can function effectively or in the long run survive, if parts cannot be related to one another in some degree of harmony and in which parts are individually subordinated to the whole," warns Leslie A. White (2008, p. 435). This common sense often has been ignored but more often suppressed, because so many believe our progress must be *objectively* demonstrable.

Time To Take Responsibility

It is well within the nature of normal humans to sense and respond to emotion and feelings about ourselves and others. We are careful not to harm each other physically or psychologically, so we adjust our interactions and may even utilize others' inferred feelings by responding to them in special ways, sometimes as a means of gaining their support for our own intentions. Psychologists and neuroscientists observe that normal people recognize in others the significance of their expressed emotion, feelings and morality, because these sources of cognition are part of the human self we review prior to adopting a stance or engaging in an action, as Antonio Damasio (2010, pp. 157–158) explains:

> An enriched material me is also capable of delivering knowledge to the mind. In other words, the self-as-object can also operate as knower.... Of necessity, conscious states of mind handle knowledge based on different sensory material—bodily, visual, auditory, and so forth—and manifest varied qualitative properties for the different sensory streams. Conscious states of mind are *felt*.[8]

Our every-day courtesies in all languages and all cultures have their place in the human social scheme, established since humanity first defined itself by framing our mutual acknowledgment. They constitute a most fundamental albeit simple symbol of our sociality, without which we would no longer meet the definition of human. When the symbols of this spirit begin to whither under what arguably is deliberate attack, more decline is likely to follow. Human quality of life depends on much more than the material dimension can even begin to provide, and several facts reveal sufficient reason for us to ensure their significant presence in our critical acts of decision.: all normal humans possess emotion, feelings and morality; these sensing monitors of our intentions and behavior have been with us since our species emerged and are among our initial learning experiences in life, contributing substantively to our uniquely flexible cognitive system, the lessons continuously refreshed through experience. Were emotion, feelings and morality not fundamental to human life, it is unimaginable that artistic expression or entertainment of any kind could have survived, not even the profession of advertising, which depends foremost on the emotive dynamics of self-interest and cultural competition. These sensitivities, in conjunction with our extraordinary capacity to manage their balance with objective knowledge, make us human in the most profound way because we identify with them, we recognize them in others, and know all normal individuals experience similar sensitivities and thought patterns. These significant human qualities are dismissed in the mistaken interest of efficiency's supposed effectiveness when, in the longer term, their suppression can prove harmful merely by gradually, quietly, surreptitiously lessening the quality of life for all, as it now seems to be doing.

Conclusion

Responsibility is perfectly within humanity's scope, which E.M. Adams (1997, p. 39) indicates in writing that "we are the only beings on this planet who live by rational knowledge and critical judgment under a self-concept within our worldview. Furthermore, only human beings live in a society organized by, and governed under, a moral constitution." Since our emergence as *Homo sapiens*, humanity has evolved a sense of responsibility from which all generations have greatly benefited in many aspects of life. But along the way, we created an agency that has been drawing us away from nature—our own nature—and now our resistance to its grand attraction morphs into passivity, as though we've lost all hope. It falls to each of us, as participants, to assume individual responsibility. In one way or another, these conflicts already occupy our individual mind but have been obscured and baffled by the rising mountain of less significant distractions we believe unalterable. It is most likely that the only way we can return to determining a less threatening, more stable evolutionary course, is first by understanding that, although we are natural creatures we have permitted our attention toward an artificial utility to absorb so much of our energies that we no longer are benefiting fully—as human beings—from our capacities. We can reverse the present course by invoking our longer-term subjective information, particularly when engaged in decisions. We can enhance our control over this set of circumstances only with tenacious participation in pertinent discussion within diverse social groups. Since we are endowed with the features needed to accomplish such change, we should use them to our individual advantage but protect them for all.

Chapter Notes

Chapter 1

1. Daniel Goleman (2006, p.152) provides a summary explanation of nature and nurture working together: "The human brain is designed to change itself in response to accumulated experience." He adds (p. 151), "It is biologically impossible for a gene to operate independently of its environment. Genes are *designed* to be regulated by signals from their immediate surround, including hormones from the endocrine system and neurotransmitters in the brain—some of which, in turn, are profoundly influenced by our social interactions. Just as our diet regulates certain genes, our social experiences also determine a distinct batch of such genomic on-off switches. Our genes, then, are not sufficient in themselves to produce an optimally operating nervous system." The nature vs. nurture debate is addressed in more depth by Richerson and Boyd (2005) and cognitive scientist and psychologist Steven Pinker (2013).

2. Sociologists Peter L. Berger and Thomas Luckmann (1966, pp. 62–64) place knowledge of any kind at the center of this linguistic phenomenon because, "What is taken for granted as knowledge in the society comes to be coextensive with the knowable, or at any rate provides the framework within which anything not yet known will come to be known in the future. This is the knowledge that is learned in the course of socialization and that mediates the internalization within individual consciousness of the objectivated structures of the social world. Knowledge, in this sense, is at the heart of the fundamental dialectic of society. It 'programs' the channels in which externalization produces an objective world. It objectifies this world through language and the cognitive apparatus base on language, that is, it orders it into objects to be apprehended as reality. It is internalized again *as* objectively valid truth in the course of socialization. Knowledge about society is thus a *realization* in the double sense of the word, in the sense of apprehending the objectivated social reality, and in the sense of ongoingly producing this reality."

3. Gazzaniga (2005, p. 168) explains the significance of sociality in human life: "Research long ago recognized that the essential function of the human brain is to make decisions; it is a decision-making device. On no dimension of human consciousness are more decisions made than on social issues, the second-by-second, minute-by-minute judgments we make all day long about our standing and situation in a social group."

4. Cognitive psychologist Elizabeth S. Spelke and developmental psychologist Katherine Kinzler (2007, p. 92) write "Research in evolutionary psychology suggests that people are predisposed to form and attend to coalitions. A rich and long-standing literature in social psychology confirms this predisposition to categorize oneself and other humans into groups." Richerson & Boyd (2005, p.196) summarize their theory about how gene-culture coevolution caused humans to cooperate in large, complex, symbolically marked groups: "First, cultural adaptation potentiates cultural evolution of cooperation and symbolic marking. Human culture allows rapid, cumulative evolution of complex adaptations and is particularly adaptive in variable environments. Such rapid adaptation has radically increased the amount of

heritable cultural variation between human groups, which means that intergroup competition (always present) gives rise to the cumulative evolution of cultural traits that enhanced the success of groups…. Second, culturally evolved social environments favor an innate psychology that is suited to such environments. Culturally evolved social environments in which prosocial norms are enforced by systems of sanction and reward, individual selection will favor psychological predispositions that make individuals more likely to gain social rewards and avoid social sanctions."

5. Zoltan Torey (2014, pp. 118–119) associates the emergence of speech with that of *Homo sapiens*. "In summary, the human chapter of evolution began with the neotenous regression to year one as the critical age for language. The motor-wiring of the speech areas followed, giving the brain access to itself. This led to language, to the brain's genesis of and control of saliences. This raised cognition to a higher plane and established the 'self' as an integral part of its own cognition. Finally, the mind's generation of mental options, in combination with the brainstem's decision-making role, gave us the selection mechanism, the key to our functional autonomy, the only kind of freedom that can be had in a deterministic world. It is an amazing trajectory on all counts. It is the key to the limitless horizons of the mind."

6. Michael S. Gazzaniga (2011, p. 133) explains, "The idea that we have an essence beyond our physical selves comes so easily to us that we would think it odd if you were to resort to a mere physical description to describe someone." We humans also understand that we are quite different from other animate beings, as Gazzaniga (2008, p. 255) notes, writing, "Children from the age of three already infer that something that falls into the animate category has some essence that makes it what it is and does not change."

7. Hicks (2011, p. 6–7) places dignity at the core of sociality, writing, "What seems to be of the utmost importance to humans is how we feel about who we are. We long to look good in the eyes of others, to feel good about ourselves, to be worthy of others' care and attention. We share a longing for dignity—the feeling of inherent value and worth. When we feel worthy, when our value is recognized, we are content. When a mutual sense of worth is recognized and honored in our relationships, we are connected. A mutual sense of worth also provides the safety necessary for both parties to extend themselves, making continued growth and development possible…. The human experience of worth and vulnerability is fundamentally emotional; it emanates from one of the oldest parts of our brains, from what neuroscientists call the limbic system…. This highly sensitive aspect of humanity—our vulnerability to being violated by others—serves a critical, though odd, function: it promotes our survival. It warns us when danger is imminent, when someone or something threatens us."

8. For example, Ron Bontekoe (2008, p. 39) finds, "The consumer culture undermines human dignity in two ways. On the one hand, in accustoming us to the idea of instant gratification of our desires, it renders us less capable of showing restraint in those situations where patience and forbearance are required. On the other hand, our dignity is directly assaulted when we are treated as a means, rather than an end, by someone hoping to manipulate us into purchasing something. Insofar as we become accustomed to this treatment, we come to expect to be manipulated, and to view manipulation itself as something less objectionable than it actually is." Political scientist James Q. Wilson (1993, p. xv) reminds us, "We are human, with all the frailties and inconsistencies that this implies; but we also wish, when we observe ourselves with any sort of detachment, to avoid becoming less than human." Other aspects of the erosion of human dignity are addressed in chapter 6.

9. Historian Lynn Avery Hunt (2007, p. 23, 27, 34) observes, "While English speakers continued to prefer 'natural rights' or just plain 'rights' throughout the eighteenth century, the French invented a new expression in the 1760s—'rights of man' (*droits de l'homme*)…. Human rights are not just a doctrine formulated in documents; they rest on a disposition toward other people, a set of convictions about what people are like and how they know right and wrong in the secular world…. To have human rights, people had to be perceived as separate individuals who were capable of exercising independent moral judgment…. In short, I am insisting that any account of historical change must in the end account for the alter-

ation of individual minds. For human rights to become self-evident, ordinary people had to have new understanding that came from new kinds of feelings."

10. Donnelly (2013, p. 108) also ties this level of importance to the central position they hold in human cultural life: "Denying that human rights derive from or are defined by culture implies neither the irrelevance of culture to human rights nor cultural homogenization. Quite the contrary, an overlapping consensus approach emphasizes the importance of people using their own local cultural resources on behalf of their own human rights. Not only is the universality of human rights fully compatible with a world of rich cultural diversity, a central purpose of human rights is to protect the rights of different individuals, groups, and peoples to make those choices of path." Neuroscientist and lawyer Oliver R. Goodenough (2001, p. 272) writes, "typically, legal scholars have used behavioral traits with an established evolutionary basis to help understand law."

11. In explaining how an individual's knowledge changes, Bronowski (2002, p. 37) also defines the concept of *worldview*: "No knowledge can be certain that continues to expand with us as we live inside the growing flesh of our experience. Our experiences do not merely link us to the outside world; they are us and they are the world for us; they make us part of the world. We get a false picture of the world if we regard it as a set of events that have their own absolute sequence and that we merely watch." Clifford Geertz (1973, p. 127) proffers another perspective on the concept of worldview: "A people's ethos is the tone, character, and quality of their life, its moral and aesthetic style and mood; it is the underlying attitude toward themselves and their world that life reflects. Their world view is their picture of the way things in sheer actuality are, their concept of nature, of self, of society. It contains their most comprehensive ideas of order."

Chapter 2

1. For example, anthropologist Daniel Miller (1987, p. 152) describes a particularly pertinent source of social tension arising from two kinds of capital vying for dominance in Western society: cultural capital and economic capital: "The relationship between the two kinds of capital—cultural and economic—is uneasy. On the one hand, education provides a means by which business capital may reproduce its social order.... There is, however, also an antagonism between the two orders, as the holders of cultural capital deride money capital as mere wealth and its conspicuous expressions as high vulgarity, while the holders of money capital regard the pretensions and esoteric forms of high cultural capital as parasitic and irrelevant.... Society, then, is not to be understood in terms of a simple hierarchy, but as a continual struggle over the hierarchy of hierarchies; that is, whether, in this case, that of wealth should prevail over that of knowledge."

2. Goleman elaborates (2006, p. 151), writing, "It is biologically impossible for a gene to operate independently of its environment. Genes are *designed* to be regulated by signals from their immediate surround, including hormones from the endocrine system and neurotransmitters in the brain—some of which, in turn, are profoundly influenced by our social interactions. Just as our diet regulates certain genes, our social experiences also determine a distinct batch of such genomic on-off switches. Our genes, then, are not sufficient in themselves to produce an optimally operating nervous system."

3. Cultural evolution reflects the pattern of biological evolution, according to Darwin's work, whose fundamental idea, writes Alex Mesoudi (2011, p. 26), is "that all biological change can be described in terms of just three basic preconditions: variation, competition, and inheritance. If any of these cannot be demonstrated, then evolution simply does not happen (indeed, this is an important and often underappreciated point: that the theory of evolution is falsifiable). Since *The Origin*, biologists have established without a shadow of a doubt that Darwin's theory is correct as applied to biological change."

4. And Wilson (2003, p. 36) explains, "[T]he basic genetic architecture of the human mind has probably not changed much since the advent of agriculture approximately ten thousand years ago. As we have seen, when evolution is interpreted too narrowly as genetic evolution, all of recorded history becomes a mystery from an evolutionary perspective, something that happened but cannot be explained." Wilson

(2003, p. 32) expands this idea: "[M]any of the mechanisms guiding cultural evolution take place beneath conscious awareness. We have a tendency to attribute too much importance to conscious rational thought. We imagine ourselves solving problems by explicitly thinking, talking, experimenting, imitating, and so on. These conscious processes are important agents of cultural change, but they are the tip of an iceberg of automated cognitive processes that take place beneath our conscious awareness, some of which are very sophisticated. This means that cultures can evolve to be smart in ways that are invisible to their own members."

5. In this regard, Michael S. Gazzaniga (2011, pp. 68–69) surveys the magnitude of human consciousness: "Our conscious awareness is the mere tip of the iceberg of nonconscious processing. Below our level of awareness is the very busy nonconscious brain hard at work. Not hard for us to imagine are the housekeeping jobs the brain constantly juggles to keep homeostatic mechanisms up and running, such as our heart beating, our lungs breathing, and our temperature just right. Less easy to imagine, but being discovered left and right over the past fifty years, are the myriads of nonconscious processes smoothly putt-putting along. Think about it. To begin with there are all the automatic visual and other sensory processing we have talked about…. What we always must keep in mind is that our brains, hence all these processes, have been sculpted by evolution to enable us to make better decisions that increase our reproductive success."

6. Berger & Luckmann (1966, pp. 60–61) indicate "Language provides the fundamental superimposition of logic on the objectivated social world. The edifice of legitimations is built upon language and uses language as its principal instrumentality. The 'logic' thus attributed to the institutional order is part of the socially available stock of knowledge and taken for granted as such." They (p. 141) describe this transforming experience further: "Generally speaking, the conversational apparatus maintains reality by 'talking through' various elements of experience and allocating them a definite place in the real world. This reality-generating potency of conversation is already given in the fact of linguistic objectification. We have seen how language objectifies the world."

7. Therefore, according to political scientist Frank Fischer (2009, p. 191), "Both science and liberal political theory have sought to root out all forms of knowing based on subjective modes of thought. However, he continues, "Rather than the impossible task of rooting out all subjectivity, it should be tamed and managed through deliberation." Fischer (2009, p. 273) also notes the larger ambience of this impulse to confine subjectivity: "Interpreters of modern social systems from Comte to Weber, Elias, and Habermas have identified the de-emotionalization of public behavior as an essential precondition for the technical and cultural rationalization that has defined essential aspects of modernity. Indeed, Elias (1997) has described the process of modern civilization as nothing less than the learning of emotional control. Civilization, he has argued, involves a dampening of the forms of pre-modern emotional expression, emphasizing in their place interests and the reservation of feeling and affection. Feeling and passion, as Hirschman (1997) has explained, were replaced in economic and political life by the concept of interest." Fischer (2009, p. 272) also quite significantly points out that people often feel guilty or inadequate when they act on emotion: "Electoral research, in fact, shows that most voters make emotional, intuitive responses in choosing which candidates to support; they then later offer post-hoc rationalizations to explain these decisions, at times below the level of conscious awareness."

8. Berger & Luckmann (1966, pp. 82–83) explain: "Reification is the apprehension of human phenomena as if they were things, that is, in non-human or possibly suprahuman terms. Another way of saying this is that reification is the apprehension of the products of human activity *as if* they were something else than human products—such as facts of nature, results of cosmic laws, or manifestations of divine will. Reification implies that man is capable of forgetting his own authorship of the human world, and further, that the dialectic between man, the producer, and his products is lost to consciousness. The reified world is, by definition, a dehumanized world. It is experienced by man as a strange facticity, an *opus alienum* over which he has not control rather than as the *opus proprium* of his own productive activity."

9. Johnson-Laird (2006, p. 88) finds, "A computer may be able to beat the world chess champion, they say, but it doesn't have feelings. In fact, the evidence implies that emotions antedate *Homo sapiens* by at least two hundred million years. All social mammals, including rats, have the brain organs for basic emotions, and all of them appear to experience these emotions. The function of emotions is to prepare us for various courses of action or inaction. They are faster than conscious reasoning in getting us to react. They make us smart in an emergency, but they can make us dumb when they swamp our conscious reasoning. They communicate our state of mind to others. We are usually aware of the cause of an emotion. We are never aware of the transition to the emotion. We are usually aware of the emotion, and it can influence our intentional actions. But, when our intellect pulls us one way, and our emotion pulls us another way, we are powerless to switch off the emotion. Sometimes we cannot even control our behavior."

10. Cultural theorist Michael Thompson (1979, p. 57) emphasizes the non-technical knowledge that might be expected of the decision and planning intended to involve or have an effect upon substantial segments of the society: "So we can say that, inside our heads, in our thoughts, and in our language, we carry a more or less coherent model of the world—a world view—a way of making sense of our environment, social and physical. We also have a more or less coherent set of moral injunctions: our idea, not of how the world is, but of how it should be. But, as well as believing, we also act. When we act we are part of the world and, indeed, are actually changing the world: so we have a world view with our minds whilst our bodies form a small part of that world. We can speak of world view and of action and we can enquire how, if at all, they relate one to the other."

11. Archeologist Steven Mithen (2007, p. 261) reviews the evolutionary background of the human capacity for reflection: "Once language appeared, it would have had profound consequences for human cognition. Language changed the way we think by 'collapsing' the domain-specific mentality that had provided the structure of the human mind since the time of *H. ergaster*. According to Carruthers, by using imagined sentences in our heads, the outputs of one type of cognitive domain could now be combined with those from others to create a new type of conscious thought. He terms this process 'inter-modular integration,' whereas I use the term 'cognitive fluidity.'"

12. Cognitive psychologist Steven Pinker (2011, p. 175) relates reflection to the common activity of reading: "Reading is a technology for perspective-taking. When someone else's thoughts are in your head, you are observing the world from that person's vantage point. Not only are you taking insights and sounds that you could not experience firsthand, but you have stepped inside that person's mind and are temporarily sharing his or her attitudes and reactions. As we shall see, 'empathy' in the sense of adopting someone's viewpoint is not the same as 'empathy' in the sense of feeling compassion toward the person, but the first can lead to the second by a natural route. Stepping into someone else's vantage point reminds you that the other fellow has a first-person, present-tense, ongoing stream of consciousness that is very much like your own but not the same as your own. It's not a big leap to suppose that the habit of reading other people's words could put one in the habit of entering other people's minds, including their pleasures and pains."

13. Archer (2007, pp. 317–318) continues: "Correspondingly, similarity, familiarity, solidarity and conviviality were progressively undermined. With them went the conditions propitious to sustaining communicative reflexivity—because the strength of 'contextual continuity' diminished as modernity advanced. In parallel, the concern promoted by the modernizing process amongst it 'beneficiaries' tended to the singly end of becoming 'better off,' whether this was described in terms of acquiring disproportionate and unmerited quantities of scarce resources, as the extraction of increased and increasing surplus value, or as the accumulation of external signs of inward grace. Human concerns thus underwent commodification, with external goods displacing internal ones, human relationships reducing to exchange relations, and the religious enchantment of the world giving way to its secularized disenchantment—registered first and foremost amongst those most proximately involved. The common denominator of these changes, in relation to human concerns, was the systematic promotion of

instrumental rationality over value rationality. The formation of value-commitments, as ends in themselves—expressive of one's personal identity—diminished accordingly, with nineteenth-century secularization being the most commonly cited index of this process."

14. Theory of Mind is the capacity of normal individual humans to surmise the intentions and related thought of others in a general way and, of course, use that information to gauge their own thought and subsequent related actions. Sociologist G. H. Mead (p. 244) credits English psychologist Charles Spearman (1863–1945) with first describing the attribute in 1904. Anthropologist H. Clark Barrett (2008, p. 184) observes, "there remains a vast gap between what we know of individual specialized cognitive mechanisms, or modules, and how they interact to produce observed behavior.... A theory of mind system, for example, would be of little use unless it interfaced with attentional systems for gathering information, motor systems for guiding behavior, and others." In that regard, developmental psychopathologist Simon Baron-Cohen (1995, p. 26) suggests, "What mindreading allows one to do is predict behavior even in situations where there are no behavioral cues" and "it allows us to make sense of communication." Tomasello & Rakoczy (2003, p. 121) identify the human uniqueness of ToM: "Human beings and only human beings cognize the world in ways leading to the creation and use of natural languages, complex tools and technologies, mathematical symbols, graphic symbols from maps to art, and complicated social institutions such as governments and religions. The puzzle is that other primates have created none of these things even though some—the great apes—are as closely related to humans as horses are to zebras, lions are to tigers, rats are to mice."

Chapter 3

1. The model epistemology is natural science. In other fields this process follows accepted disciplinary methodologies such as peer review and the subsequent communication intended to circulate new knowledge among others, including those who may have no more than a passing interest in knowledge validation. But such practice excludes the vast majority of the population that may ultimately be affected in some way by the implementation of this new knowledge. Sociologist Immanuel Wallerstein (2004, pp. 8–9) explains this acceptance: "How do we know that a new scientific claim is valid or even plausible? Amid the reality of an ever increasing degree of complex specialization of knowledge, for each specific scientific allegation, all but a very small number of persons are bereft of a capacity for individual rational judgment either about the quality of the evidence proffered or about the tightness of the theoretical reasoning applied to the analysis of the data.... We tend to use the criteria of cumulative attestation by reputed authority."

2. Stephen Jay Kline (1995, pp. 198–199) provides insight into a problem germane to this essay: "These processes of specialization and professionalization have been of overriding importance in the history of the human race. The work of these specialized communities underlies much, but not all, of what we saw about the acceleration of human powers.... At the same time, we have largely lost a unifying overview of any kind, a difficulty long lamented by many scholars, particularly by humanists. From the view of verifying knowledge and from the view of the social uses of the new knowledge, we have also lost nearly all of what the larger society and the larger community of scholars deem appropriate in various special research programs. To a great extent, each discipline has become an independent intellectual 'dukedom' unconstrained by larger social units. This has led a few specialists to the extreme belief that their discipline has the right to support for its work uncoupled from any responsibility to the social order or to the priorities of the society."

3. For purposes of this essay, information is the triggering device for thought, the element that connects information with knowledge extant in the human mind. Thought invokes introspection (discussed in chapter 2), which is an internal function related to self, and the acquisition of new knowledge most often is a conscious effort. When information or knowledge is a product rather than a process, it properly is a *source* of information or a *source* of knowledge but is not information or knowledge itself, which resides only in the mind, as the presence of knowledge requires an aware-

ness of it as such. Of the many definitions of the word information I have studied, anthropologist and cyberneticist Gregory Bateson's (2000, p. 459) definition fits my attempt most closely. He states, "In fact, what we mean by information—the elementary unit of information—is a *difference which makes a difference* [emphasis in the original], and it is able to make a difference because the neural pathways along which it travels and is continually transformed are themselves provided with energy. The pathways are ready to be triggered. We may even say that the question is already implicit in them." Owing to the readiness of extant knowledge the connection can be made and the information converted to knowledge. Knowledge is both process and product; information is only a product, but people can inform others. People exchange both information and knowledge, but machines exchange only information. This significant distinction lies in the fact that knowledge is subjective, the mind making the connections. When we inform someone of something, it is passing from within our knowledge connectedness to the other individual as information, but when that information is connected via the other's cognitive processes it is knowledge.

4. Bell (1973, p. 26) elaborates on this idea: "What is true of technology and economics is true, albeit differentially, of all modes of knowledge: the advances in a field become increasingly dependent on the primacy of theoretical work, which codifies what is known and points the way to empirical confirmation. In effect, theoretical knowledge increasingly becomes the strategic resource, the axial principle, of a society. And the university, research organizations, and intellectual institutions, where theoretical knowledge is codified and enriched, become the axial structures of the emergent society."

5. A decline in socialization can be seen from several perspectives: Economist and historian Robert L. Heilbroner (1962, p. 230) observes a "central weakness of the market system—its inability to formulate public needs above those of the market place. So long as the public need roughly coincides with the sum of the private interests to which the market automatically attends, this failing of the market system is a minor one. But in an advanced economic society, it tends to become ever more important. As primary wants [he doesn't say needs] become satisfied, the public aim turns toward stability and security, objectives not attainable without a degree of public control."

6. The free market also continues in globalization, but Alford & Friedland (1985, p. 442) admonish that "transnational capital and the forces at work in the world economy have reproduced in international form the system Marx envisaged in the nineteenth century—a 'placeless' capital able to exploit national state boundaries, either remaining with them for protection or moving between them for competitive advantage, bringing with it mass migrations of labor. The human and social costs of these developments are incalculable.... Political conflicts are increasingly moving beyond production-based issues of class and toward interests and identities deriving from age, gender, family, community, church and public policies themselves. Conflicts between the sexes, the generations, regions, as well as between public providers and their clients, increasingly dominate the political state."

7. Historian and philosopher Sidney Hook (1933, p. 209) contends, "Materialism as a philosophy arose out of an attempt to substitute for religious cosmogonies an account of the world drawn from principles and materials familiar to man in everyday activity." However, the ground for a true consumer society likely was established in the nineteenth century Europe, yielding the purchasing power necessary to the conversion of a new cultural worldview into social action, for, according to mechanical engineer and humanist Stephen Kline (1995, pp. 206–207), "Economic growth then was so rapid in Europe that there was a net monetary deflation over the entire nineteenth century, that is, a given amount of a particular currency would buy more goods in 1900 than it had in 1800 in the industrializing European nations. This is nearly unique in history; inflation has been rampant most of the time in money economies nearly everywhere else."

8. Robert Reich (2007, p. 7) explains how "supercapitalism" gained a grip on Western culture: "In this transformation, we in our capacities as consumers and investors have done significantly better. In our capacities as citizens seeking the common good, however, we have lost ground. The shift began when technologies developed by

government to fight the Cold War were incorporated into new products and services. This created possibilities for new competitors, beginning in transportation, communications, manufacturing, and finance. These cracked open the stable production system and, starting in the late 1970s and escalating thereafter, forced all companies to compete more intensively for customers and investors. Consumer power became aggregated and enlarged by mass retailers like Wal-Mart that used the collective bargaining clout of millions of consumers to get great deals from suppliers. Investor power became aggregated and enlarged by large pension funds and mutual funds, which pushed companies to generate higher returns. As a result, consumers and investors had access to more choices and better deals."

9. This has been a much debated issue for which cognitive psychologist Elizabeth S. Spelke and developmental psychologist Katherine D. Kinzler (2007, p. 89) provide a brief historiography: "Cognitive science has been dominated by two views of human nature. On one view, the human mind is a flexible and adaptable mechanism for discovering regularities in experience: a single learning system that copes with all the diversity of life. On the competing view, the human mind is a collection of special-purpose mechanisms, each shaped by evolution to perform a particular function. The first view traces back to Enlightenment thinkers such as Locke (1689) and Hume (1748) and has been invigorated more recently by cognitive psychologists and neural network theorists.... The second view was inspired by Darwin (1871) and gained prominence with the rise of evolutionary psychology."

10. Louise Barrett (2011, p. 92) also demonstrates that "an animal's brain is part of its body, and that bodies and brains work together to produce effective behavior; it is imperative that we don't lose sight of this fact and think that we can somehow consider brains in isolation from bodies. To be more precise, we should abandon talk of brains altogether and talk about the increasing size and complexity of the nervous system as a whole. It is a mistake to think of the brain as somehow being in charge of the body, with the rest of the nervous system reduced to a set of 'message cables' that merely ferry information to and from the brain, and the body reduced to the means by which the brain is ferried around the world.... It seems that, again, our focus on our own large brains has caused us to overlook the possibility that cognition is a property of whole organisms and not of brains alone."

11. About the process by which this stabilization functions, Antonio Damasio (2010, p. 259) finds, "It is often overlooked that information from the body's interior is conveyed directly to the brain by numerous chemical molecules that course in the bloodstream and bathes parts of the brain that are devoid of blood-brain barrier, namely, the area postrema in the brain stem and a variety of regions known collectively as the circumventricular organs." Among other findings, Damasio (p. 280) adds, "When the mind is informed of the actions taken by our organism, the feeling associated with the information signifies that the actions were engendered by our self. Both information and authentication of ongoing actions are essential to motivate the deliberation of future actions. Without that sort of felt, validated information, we would not be able to assume moral responsibility for the actions taken by our organism."

12. "Babies first enter the social world through imitation. They understand they are like other people and imitate human actions, but not those of objects," according to neuroscientist Michael S. Gazzaniga (2011, p. 143). Evolutionary and theoretical biologist Peter Hammerstein and evolutionary psychologist Jeffrey R. Stevens (2012, pp. 6–7) theorize that "learning from each other enables us to accumulate information across generations and acquire the tools, beliefs, and practices that single individuals could never have invented.... The crucial point here is that children learn to do what they are supposed to do without much cognitive interference. Human learning is biased toward conformism.... This has the advantage that we do not waste our time trying to figure out what may be difficult or impossible to understand."

Chapter 4

1. Since the Western secularization of thought, science has remained a mystery for the public and continues to be intellectually distanced. Historians Margaret C. Jacob and Larrry Stewart (2004, pp. 31–32)

describe the most noted examples: "Galileo, Descartes, and Newton each contributed mightily to the revolution that made matter mechanical, that is, atomic, unmoved unless acted upon by other matter, and best understood because capable of mathematical and experimental explication. In the new understanding of nature, much of what the scholastics taught was discarded—qualities, forms, tendencies, the incorporeality of the heavens, the stationary earth—and replaced forever by atoms and forces and the uniformity of terrestrial and celestial matter. By 1650 in England, France, The Netherlands, and Italy, clusters of natural philosophers had become convinced that the way forward lay in the new conceptual structure known as the mechanical philosophy, best described by Descartes.... By the 1670s it had become possible to think of light as a body with weight and hence with a finite speed."

2. Discussing the spread of science, Smith (1972, pp. 173–174) adds, "The attacks of Swift, Addison and others, thought they gave scientists a bad press, did, however show that scientific ideas and discoveries were, by the end of the [eighteenth] century, of interest to the educated classes in England, who read not only such satirical works but also the growing flood of books in which the scientists themselves expounded and sometimes even attempted to popularize their ideas. Indeed, this developing interest in scientific books was a European phenomenon, and between 1600 and 1700 the literate sections of European society, at least in the western half of the Continent, absorbed from such works the basic ideas of the scientific revolution. This in turn helped to produce the tremendous secularization of thought which characterized the last decades of the seventeenth century and the first decades of the eighteenth—the change in intellectual assumptions of a large part of the educated classes which the distinguished French historian Paul hazard aptly christened *la crise de la conscience européenne*."

3. Historian of science Robert Friedel (2007, p. 10) places the history of technology in a pertinent evolutionary context: "Another approach to the history of technology that has a long history as well as some current popularity is based on an analogy between technological development and Darwinian evolution. Technologies are seen as akin to species, and inventions are variations or mutations. This approach can have several virtues: it emphasizes the ubiquity of variations, both large and small; it calls attention to the importance of selection, by which societies determine which innovations are worthy of surviving and reproducing and which are not; and it can provide an escape from the teleology of most progressive accounts, the notion that technological change is inherently directed toward some final goal."

4. By the end of the nineteenth century, according to sociologist of science Dorothy Nelkin (1987, p. 94), "belief in science as the embodiment of neutrality and rationality was firmly entrenched. Thus, in the first decades of the twentieth century, scientific values were penetrating many social and political institutions: witness the increased emphasis on technical expertise in government, the growth of realism in literature and art, and the political reforms of the progressive movement. In this context a scientific—that is, neutral—presentation of the facts was defined as the enlightened basis of a responsible press. This spirit of objectivity converged with the idea that scientific knowledge prevailed over all other forms of knowledge to shape the conventions of the press." And the news media, as a mass influence on the framing of public thinking, perhaps often unwittingly, has subtly spread and maintained this perception.

5. Carolyn Merchant (1980, p. 193) observes a particular kind of loss that will be examined more closely in subsequent chapters: "As the unifying model for science and society, the machine has permeated and reconstructed human consciousness so totally that today we scarcely question its validity. Nature, society, and the human body are composed of interchangeable atomized parts that can be repaired or replaced from outside.... The removal of animistic, organic assumptions about the cosmos constituted the death of nature—the most far-reaching effect of the Scientific Revolution. Because nature was now viewed as a system of dead, inert particles moved by external, rather than inherent forces, the mechanical framework itself could legitimate the manipulation of nature. Moreover, as a conceptual framework, the mechanical order had associated with it a framework

of values based on power, fully compatible with the directions taken by commercial capitalism."

6. Kropotkin (1955, p. 58) complements this thought with his correction, "The fittest are thus the most sociable animals, and sociability appears as the chief factor of evolution, both directly, by securing the well-being of the species while diminishing the waste of energy, and indirectly, by favouring the growth of intelligence. Moreover, it is evident that life in societies would be utterly impossible without a corresponding development of social feelings, and, especially of a certain collective sense of justice growing to become a habit. If every individual were constantly abusing its personal advantages without the others interfering in favour of the wronged, no society-life would be possible." Kropotkin's interpretation and similar conclusions have been substantiated only within the past three decades by evolutionary biologists, sociobiologists, neuroscientists, psychologists and others, in a scholarly and scientific wave that supports the recurring theme in this essay.

7. Philosopher of science David Papineau (2000, p. 183) explains the evolutionary significance of means-end reasoning: "We 'calculate' the answers in accord with such principles, rather than relying on our intuitive sense of the right answer, precisely because we have learned that our intuitive judgments are an unreliable guide to the truth, and because we know that reasoning in line with the probability calculus and propositional logic is guaranteed to track the truth. I would be prepared to argue that this ability, to identify and deliberately adopt reliable methods of belief formation, has played a huge part in the development of human civilization. Of course, it is not the only factor that separates us from other apes, and indeed I shall argue below that this deliberate pursuit of reliability rests on a number of further abilities which may also be peculiar to humans."

8. Sociologist of science Bernard Barber (1998, pp. 39–40) presents a useful précis of the dynamism generated by human values: "[Values] are structures of preference in the choices that confront all actors. All action systems endlessly, sometimes explicitly, sometimes not, confront actors with the dilemma of choice between or among alternative structures of preference.... The structure of values in a social system influences action at all levels, from interaction in small groups to that in the total society.... While values and norms have their parts to play in the interaction that makes up social systems, so also do other cultural, social structural, and personality components. There is always a certain amount of incompatibility and resulting tension in even the most stable and harmonious of social systems."

9. Archeologist Steven Mithen (2000, pp. 216–217) describes the special significance of materiality in human cultural evolution: "The cultural and cognitive transformation that occurred between 60,000 and 30,000 years ago arose because humans learnt a clever trick. They learnt how to exploit material culture to extend their minds beyond the limits of their brains alone. By creating artefacts that represented ideas that could only have a transient existence within the mind, it became possible to regenerate those ideas, communicate those ideas, and allow for cross-fertilization of ideas between individuals in such a way that completely new constructs could be developed. Similarly, by using material culture to store knowledge, the bounds of biological memory could be transcended. Once material culture is used in this fashion, the cultural contexts within which children develop and mature are transformed. And hence their brains will be networked in new fashions, and this will facilitate the possibility of further extensions of mind into the material world. In this regard cultural and biological changes are intimately linked. By extending the mind into material culture a new evolutionary trajectory was initiated.... And hence in little more than 50,000 years, by having 'given up' their near-total reliance on the brain alone, humans have mentally evolved from having thoughts about no more than stone tools and acquiring food to having thoughts about subjects no less than the origins of the Universe and the nature of the human mind itself."

10. H. Clark Barrett (2015, p. 285) notes that this attention to the commonweal is also biological: "In biology, it's recognized that an important factor influencing the design of multicellular organisms is that the different parts of those organisms must, in a sense, cooperate for the greater good in order for

the whole body to survive. Similarly, the diverse processes of mind must cooperate in running the body.... In order to do this, each process must be designed to only take over the body when it's fitness-best to do so and step down when other processes should be given priority. Therefore, psychological processes should have design features—the equivalent of volume knobs on their outputs—that are calibrated to their role in the [neural] democracy (by natural selection, reaction norms, experience, interaction) and are adjusted according to immediate circumstance."

11. Fox (1967, p. 47) explains, "Ironically, the techniques for producing and marketing the greatest variety of goods at the lowest cost and for persuading men to expand their consumption—the techniques of industrial combination and advertising—could also be used to abuse consumers. If monopolies were allowed to maintain high prices, they would be forced to use advertising in order to persuade consumers that they needed goods they could not afford."

12. The idea that thought concentrated on money can detract from thought focused on other ideals is explained at least in part by Robert Reich's (2007, p. 7) account of the attraction found in 'supercapitalism': "In this transformation, we in our capacities as consumers and investors have done significantly better. In our capacities as citizens seeking the common good, however, we have lost ground. The shift began when technologies developed by government to fight the Cold War were incorporated into new products and services. This created possibilities for new competitors, beginning in transportation, communications, manufacturing, and finance. These cracked open the stable production system and, starting in the late 1970s and escalating thereafter, forced all companies to compete more intensively for customers and investors. Consumer power became aggregated and enlarged by mass retailers like Wal-Mart that used the collective bargaining clout of millions of consumers to get great deals from suppliers. Investor power became aggregated and enlarged by large pension funds and mutual funds, which pushed companies to generate higher returns. As a result, consumers and investors had access to more choices and better deals."

Chapter 5

1. Randolph M. Nesse (2001, p. 311) describes the evolutionary human context of my assertion: "The basic principle of sociobiology remains clear and incontrovertible: behavior regulation mechanisms for all species are shaped, inevitably and necessarily, to induce actions that tend (in the long run, on the average, in the natural environment) to increase the frequency of that individual's genes in future generations." Dennis Krebs (2004, p. 321) proffers the reminder, "The biological function of morality is to enable individuals to maximize their benefits from interactions with others by upholding fitness-enhancing systems of cooperation."

2. Sociologist Lewis Coser (1965, p. 252) finds an interesting and direct connection between the general culture and the workplace, where "A corollary of increasing industrialization and rationalization is the fact that the ratio of organized activities to unorganized, spontaneous ones increases and that the individual is deprived of autonomy.... Much cultural productivity that may once have been a matter of handicrafts, so to speak, becomes rationalized so that the production of ideas resembles in major respects the production of other commodities."

3. Sociologist Zygmunt Bauman (2000, p. vi) finds that a new kind of common sense has devolved from this unquestioning alignment with quantification: "The fault of 'common sense' ... is that it shares in the delusions of reason; it accepts reason's pretense to omniscience and omnipotence, its right to pronounce on every aspect of human acts and feelings and its right to dismiss, declare null and void or invalid, all verdicts which jar with its own or which simply claim and enjoy the support of another authority. Our common sense—the common sense of the modern era—denies sense to everything that cannot be measured, calculated and show credentials of utility. It looks down its nose at 'mere sentiments.' Indeed, sentiments—our feelings and affections—are by definition 'un-calculable,' as they spring apparently from nowhere without proper warning and seldom, if ever, can prove accreditation by a recognized authority; and so they stand for the very opposite of common sense and everything that needs to be

fought back, suppressed and 'cleansed out' of human thought and action for the thought and action 'to make sense.'"

4. Intellectual historian and philosopher Stephen Gaukroger (2012, p. 69) posits the historical background for quantification's introduction of objectivity into the general population: "[T]he move from specialist disinterested judgement to standardization.... In large part, this came with the move to global interaction and trade, where the kind of honesty and trust that had accompanied face-to-face transactions was no longer available. Where one did not know those with whom one was trading, a set of impersonal rules guiding the transaction, in accountancy practice for example, was a good substitute. These needed a common language beyond that of individual laws and customs, and arithmetic and statistics were a language that everyone engaged in these interactions could understand. They provided a universal means of communication, and they obviated the need for personal trust and judgement."

5. Anthropologist Pascal Boyer (2000, pp. 97–98) explains that this is because "cultural concepts are not 'downloaded' from one mind to another. They are built by inferences from cultural input. But this has important consequences. The processes in question do not reduce to 'decoding' other peoples' thoughts from their overt gestures or utterances. They create new representations.... The way this happens is massively constrained by prior assumptions in memory. That communication consists of inferences rather than decoding would suggest that any communicative act can create extremely different representations in different individuals, and this is indeed the case. Communication in a group creates many variants of people's representations."

6. Hurford (2007, p. 243) continues that, leading toward "the emergence of language were an enhancement of the capacity for learning arbitrary symbols, and of the disposition to combine symbols with deictic gestures.... I suggest, then, that a crucial precursor to the appearance of these proto-linguistic abilities was not in itself a specifically linguistic change, but rather a shift in the normal social relationships between individuals in a group." The interplay of sociality and language are addressed further in chapter five of this essay. DeSalle & Tattersall (2012, pp. 295–296) summarize the biological implications of speech: "It seems reasonable to conclude that the emergence of complex symbolic cognition was permitted by some kind of internal rewiring of the brain: a change that was most plausibly acquired in the evidently major developmental reorganization that took place at the origin of anatomically recognizable *Homo sapiens*."

7. An appropriate definition of meaning is difficult to find, although there are many books on the subject and innumerable journal articles, but philosopher, sociologist and psychologist G. H. Mead (1934, p. 76) has designed a provocative definition: "Meaning is thus a development of something objectively there as a relation between certain phases of the social act; it is not a psychical addition to that act and it is not an 'idea' as traditionally conceived … meaning is implicit—if not always explicit—in the relationship among the various phases of the social to which it refers, and out of which it develops. And its development takes place in terms of symbolization at the human evolutionary level."

8. Sociologist Orrin E. Klapp (1986, p. 115) relates this aspect of social epistemology to the current emphasis on and deference to information: "We expect meaning formation to be slow or insufficient compared with the speed and amount of information accumulating in modern society. So society suffers a growing gap between input of actual information and the construction of meanings, especially shared values, 'we' feeling, and a sense of togetherness—unable to construct meanings fast enough to give its members a sense of living in a common world in which they can believe.... So the vast mountain of information today in a strange way becomes a measure of our meaninglessness."

9. Langdon Winner (1986, p. 5) uses the term "technological somnambulism" for this mental state in his observation, "In the twentieth century it is usually taken for granted that the only reliable sources for improving the human condition stem from new machines, techniques, and chemicals." John Kenneth Galbraith (1978, p. 171) had generalized on this kind of explanation several years earlier, by presciently noting, "The process by which social goals become adapted to the goals of the corporation and ultimately the technostructure is not analyt-

ical or cerebral. Rather it reflects a triumph of unexamined but constantly reiterated assumption over thought."

10. But political philosopher Charles Taylor (1985, p. 92) also perceives the direct infusion of the natural science epistemology into the social sciences: "There is a constant temptation to take natural science theory as a model for social theory: that is, to see theory as offering an account of underlying processes and mechanisms of society, and as providing the basis of a more effective planning of social life. But for all the superficial analogies, social theory can never really occupy this role. It is part of a significantly different activity." Historian of science and technology Rosalind Williams (1990, p. 22), in accord with Lewis Mumford, Carolyn Merchant, and Max Weber, concludes, "Once nature is subjected to scientific rationalism it ceases to be a vital source of human meaning and becomes a matter of fact rather than a matter of value." Nature itself becomes only a fact.

11. Carla Bagnoli (2011, p. 62) contends that "the experience of Moral emotions is constitutive of the exercise of practical reason. The categorical authority of moral reasons does not depend upon, but constitutively implies, moral emotions." She introduces (p. 1) her book with a concise statement of the fundamental problem: "The place of emotions in morality is the subject of widespread and divisive philosophical controversies.... The basic worry is that emotions interfere with the deliverances of reason, and often provide motives that are in competition with morality. A more radical worry is that emotions undermine our status of rational agents insofar as we are not in control of them, but we are possessed by them. Emotions undermine autonomy, which is a requirement for rational agency." C. Daniel Batson (2011, p. 161) finds, "Altruism is a more pervasive and powerful force in human affairs than has been recognized. Failure to appreciate its importance has handicapped attempts to understand what motivates our action and what brings us satisfaction. It has also handicapped efforts to build better interpersonal relations and a more caring, humane society. Recognizing the scope and power of altruism is not all that is needed to overcome these handicaps. But it is a crucial first step."

12. Though specific genes may be 'selfish,' humans generally are not. Joseph Henrich, et al. (2004, p. 8) find, "Literally hundreds of experiments in dozens of countries using a variety of experimental protocols suggest that, in addition to their own material payoffs, people have social preferences: subjects care about fairness and reciprocity, are willing to change the distribution of material outcomes among others at a personal cost to themselves, and reward those who act in a pro-social manner while punishing those who do not, even when these actions are costly. Initial skepticism about the experimental evidence has waned as subsequent experiments with high stakes and with ample opportunity for learning failed to substantially modify the initial conclusions."

13. Archer (2003, p. 343) provides a particularly pertinent definition of this term which, though quite common, is of extraordinary significance in cultural change: "'Stances' are basic orientations of subjects to society. In other words, the 'stance' is ventured as a generative mechanism, at the personal level, with the tendential capacity to regulate relations between the person and her society. In short, they *constitute* the micro-macro link."

14. We know from personal experience that the negative feelings we automatically generate internally are warnings. Michael S. Brady (2013, p. 76) further observes, "The epistemic role and value of emotional experience thus depends upon the existence of reliable causal links between emotional experience and the occurrence of the 'core relational themes' of danger, insult, contamination, loss, shamefulness, wrongness, and the like. Emotions, when reliably correlated with such things, can be sources of information about the evaluative world, and when such emotional experiences generate the relevant evaluative beliefs, we have good reason to believe what we do about that world."

15. Hammerstein & Stevens (2012, pp. 15–16) indicate, "An evolutionary theory of decision mechanisms, therefore, strongly undermines the approach that dominated decision theory in economics for more than the last hundred years. Research combining evolution and cognition does indeed give us good reasons to knock economic decision theory off its pedestal.... From an evolutionary perspective there seems to be a logic behind decision making in humans and animals, but it is a logic

that makes individuals successful in real life without caring about axioms of rationality."

16. Anthropologist Robin Dunbar (2000, p. 251) refers to specific supportive research, concluding, "What these data suggest is that hominid group sizes did not rise substantially above those typical of living apes (typically around 50–80) until the appearance of *Homo erectus* (a little after two million years ago). Although there is a steady increase in projected group size with time, the increase is slow and of limited scale. Group size does not begin to show a sudden acceleration until the appearance of the earliest *Homo sapiens* specimens (about 500,000 years ago)," adding (p. 253), "If this is even roughly realistic, it implies that *Homo erectus* (the point at which the 100 group size mark was first breached) is marked by the development of the ability to engage in third-order intentionality, and anatomically modern *Homo sapiens* (dated to around 120,000 years bp) is marked by the appearance of fourth-order intentionality. This is, of course, a very rough calculation and we should not put too much faith in it until there has been time to evaluate more closely the relationship between neocortex volume and cognitive skills."

17. Moreover, this efficiency comes at a cost, according to Daniel Bell (1976, p. 116), who refers to the loss of psychic distance: "The loss of psychic distance means the suspension of time. Freud has said that in the unconscious there is no sense of time: one experiences the events of the past not *as if* they were of the present, but with the immediacy, the *actualité*, of the present. This is why the unconscious, with its storehouse of the past, and especially of childhood terrors, remains so threatening and has to be held down. The meaning of maturity, for Freud, was the ability to interpose the necessary distance, a sense of past and present, in order to make the necessary distinctions between what was past, as past, and what derived from the present. But the thrust of modernist culture is to disrupt or breakup that sense of past and present."

18. Daniel Boorstin (1980, p. 3) contends, "Whatever the motive, we see the knowledge industry being transformed, and even to some extent displaced, by an information industry. In the schoolroom, history tends to be displaced by current events." At the level of higher education, David J. Hess (2007, p. 46) finds, "[D]uring the last 30 years of the twentieth century demand for career-oriented undergraduate degrees in the United States increased between fivefold and tenfold, whereas demand declined or rose only marginally for the traditional liberal arts fields." Scholarship and science have lost interest in the synthesis of existing knowledge in favor of discovering or creating new knowledge through analysis, delving into a subject more deeply, which has had similar effect on research in virtually all fields particularly during the past century and a half of knowledge fragmentation. And while the current negative assessment of education is voluminous, it can be sifted down to a few particularly poignant thoughts as follow: Among the more prolific critics, Neil Postman (1995, p. 26) laments, "There was a time when educators became famous for providing reasons for learning; now they become famous for inventing a method," and further (1992, p. 174) that "education is an instrument of economic policy and of very little else." Daniel Bell (1973, p. 423) contends there is no "search for the relatedness of discordant knowledge," while Martha C. Nussbaum (1997, p. 19) similarly indicates from another perspective, "To unmask prejudice and to secure justice, we need argument, an essential tool of civic freedom," fearing (p. 14), "We may continue to produce narrow citizens who have difficulty understanding people different from themselves, whose imaginations rarely venture beyond their local setting. It is all too easy for the moral imagination to become narrow in this way."

19. Sociologist Manuel Castells (2009, p. 38) advances a relevant theory about the cultural influence of the internet, placing it in a larger sphere: "The common culture of the global network society is a culture of protocols of communication enabling communication between different cultures on the basis not of shared values but of the sharing of the value of communication. This is to say: the new culture is not made of content but of process as the constitutional democratic culture is based on procedure, not on substantive programs. Global culture is a culture of communication for the sake of communication. It is an open-ended network of cultural meanings that can not only coexist, but also interact and modify each other on the basis of this exchange. The

culture of the network society is a culture of protocols of communication between all cultures in the world, developed on the basis of the common belief in the power of networking and of the synergy obtained by giving to others and receiving from others."

Chapter 6

1. Torey (2014, p. 19) writes, "What we are conscious of is no longer just the sensory totalization of the brain, but an augmented product that features the additional output of a new, off-line response mechanism. This mechanism, with its expressive arm of language, generates images and thoughts." He explains (2014, pp. 125–126), "The conscious mind, able to monitor itself and foresee outcomes, is responsible for the mental options it presents to the brainstem ... although we are not free in the absolute or entelechy sense, we are responsible for our actions.... Although it is true that human records did not survive, the emergence of the 'self' is easy to trace. It first appeared and became an identifiable experience when the brain gained voluntary motor access to itself, first to name, and later to speak and generate, the proprioception that is the self's experiential core. All the aspects of brain process that were submerged before could now be labeled, thought, experienced, and handled by the language-wielding new subsystem, the mind." In sum, Torey (2014, p. 149) writes, "The off-line mechanism generates language; language creates the organism's sense of self or agency, which is an integral feature of reflective functioning. As a result of language, human experience is always double stranded. It is composed of what we experience and of the sensation that *we* are experiencing it."

2. Antonio Damasio (2010, pp. 286–288) places the emergence of the self in its evolutionary context: "Once self comes to mind, the game of life changes, albeit timidly at first. Images of the internal and external worlds can be organized in a cohesive way around the protoself and become oriented by the homeostatic requirements of the organism. Then the devices of reward and punishment and drives and motivations, which had been shaping the life process in earlier stages of evolution, help with the development of complex emotions. Then social intelligence begins to be flexible.... It is certain that the self matured, slowly and gradually but unevenly, and that the process was taking place in several parts of the world, not necessarily at the same time. Still, it is known that our most direct human ancestors were walking the earth about 200,000 years ago, and that around 30,000 years ago humans were producing cave paintings, sculptures, rock carvings, metal castings, and jewelry, and possibly making music.... A mind capable of symbolic processing was obviously at work there."

3. Miller (2010, pp. 293–294) explains further, writing, "It is one of the principal tasks of those who design and oversee the market system, including governments and—under the direction of governments—regulators, to ensure that the ultimate purposes of markets (and, therefore, market actors) are in fact achieved, that is, to contain and channel the pursuit of economic self-interest. Perhaps there is a lack of clarity in the collective minds of governments and regulators in relation to their role in this regard.... Moreover, if one looks, for example, at the objectives of many regulators, one typically finds only limited aims, such as to reduce crime and protect consumers, and procedural concerns, such as to promote competition and efficiency. There is little or no reference to what I have been referring to as the ultimate ends of markets, that is, the outcome the invisible hand is supposed to bring about."

4. Michael S. Gazzaniga (2011, p. 114) finds, "The belief that we have free will permeates our culture, and this belief is reinforced by the fact that people and societies behave better when they believe that is the way things work." Elsewhere, Gazzaniga (2005, p. 101) notes, "The brain is an evolved system, a decision-making device that interacts with its environment in a way that allows it to learn rules to govern how it responds." Valerie Tiberius (2008, p. 35) narrows the scope, writing, "To be self-directed is to live in accordance with your own values and standards. While this value may seem individualistic, it is not as individualistic as it sounds. Self-direction is relative to the individual in the sense that the goals a person must achieve to count as self-directed must be *her* goals, shaped by her values. But the content of these goals and values need not be self-regarding or self-interested."

5. Moral philosopher Richard Joyce

(2006, p. 227) generally finds, "No one denies that emotions affect motivations (one might even claim that they necessarily do so), and if one can have emotions without the usual associated beliefs, then one's motivations can be engaged without these beliefs. More generally, it should be borne in mind that there is plenty of evidence that our motivations can be influenced in subtle, surprising, and somewhat puzzling ways.... Smiling voluntarily really does affect one's emotions in a positive way," he states, citing research. And he supplies other examples: "Perhaps allowing moral thoughts and emotions a live role in one's psychological economy, *even while lacking the associated moral beliefs*, is one such unobvious means of engaging motivation. Such thoughts and emotions may become habitual, or even aspects of character." Joyce (p. 94) adds, "At least some of these emotions are cognitively rich, and among the concepts necessary for having certain emotions are evaluative concepts. It is for this reason that this is a prerequisite for moral judgment.... The emotions—at least, the 'basic' emotions—are widely acknowledged to be adaptive mechanisms, each designed by biological natural selection to perform a task that involves physiological, psychological, and behavioral elements of the organism in such a way as to encourage it to respond adaptively to recurrent types of fitness-relevant threats and opportunities in the environment."

6. Social philosopher and historian Joseph A. Bulbulia (2007, p. 622) finds that "religious commitment is rampant. It appears in all cultures, is nearly universal among foragers (whose life-ways resembles those of our distant ancestors), and even remains popular in scientifically advanced societies." He also observes (p. 624) that "*minimally adjusted* anthropomorphic thought is religiosity's universal mode." DeSalle and Tattersall (2012, p. 251) describe the place of spirituality in society, writing that "spirituality in the general sense is a more or less ubiquitous feature of human populations, and thus something it's even more important for us to understand. And the obvious starting question is why it exists in the first place.... Spiritual feelings are a product of the more generalized capacity to think in symbols, in which case religion, while seemingly a 'universal' human behavior, is probably best viewed as a complex set of behaviors sharing a substrate but independently derived in different cultures."

7. The historiography of scholarship pertaining to morality's evolution is as complex as the function itself, but Michael Ruse (1997, pp. 433–434) attempts to simplify it by describing its two basic approaches: "First, there is the evolutionary ethics which tries to deduce the foundations of ethics from the evolutionary process itself, having used the process to infer the courses of right action.... The position is commonly known as Social Darwinism and is generally thought to be—following Darwinism's struggle for existence—an extension to the cultural realm of an extreme laissez-faire philosophy. In fact, however there are many variations, and by no means all are philosophies of the extreme right wing. Huxley, for instance, always thought in group terms, reasoning that one ought to strive for the good of the whole of society.... The alternative position, again as in epistemology depending on a *literal* reading of the consequences of evolution, suggests that there are innate dispositions for sociality, and that when made manifest in the course of development some of these have a moral force. Ethics—the sense that we have of right and wrong—is therefore something which is purely an adaptation, like eyes and teeth and genitalia. As such, it has no foundation or meaning beyond the feelings that it conveys. This position, which owes much to modern human sociobiology (the study of human social behavior from an evolutionary perspective), is rooted in modern-day Darwinism. It is structured by the conviction that, despite or rather because of the struggle for existence, much animal behavior is social and cooperative. This is because one can better serve one's own biological ends by such behavior than by competing flat out and in a violent fashion. We may be at the mercy of 'selfish genes,' to use Richard Dawkins's powerful metaphor, but we are not necessarily selfish humans, certainly not all of the time."

8. Anthropologists Allen W. Johnson and Timothy Earle (2000, pp. 388–389) also indicate that this trait begins to be instilled in humans at the earliest stage in their lives: "The compromise between short-term and long-term self-interest recapitulates the dialectic between freedom and responsibility that is already basic at the family level. Indi-

viduals want the freedom to use resources as they see fit to meet the needs of their own families, but they recognize that fighting with others over resources is dangerous and that trying to stand completely alone would abandon one of human-kind's greatest tools of survival, cooperative group activity."

9. Stephen Gaukroger (2012, p. 91) provides a brief look into the historical background of the debate about the need for morality: "From the end of the 16th century, with the appearance of travel books describing non-European lands and peoples, the possibility began to be raised—slowly at first, but coming to a head by the last decades of the 17th century—that a number of fundamental beliefs that had been taken to be universal were in fact culturally variable. Religion and morality were at the centre of this questioning. It was generally assumed in the 17th century that religion provided the unique basis for morality, and that without religion, there could be no morality. It was also taken as given that not only had all cultures embraced religion of one kind or another, but also that no great thinker had ever espoused atheism. But there were growing doubts, and matters came to a head in the 1690s with the publication of Bayle's defence of the possibility of a virtuous atheist. Bayle denied that religion was in fact universal and that it was something that attracted unanimous agreement. More radically, he also pointed out that, even if it were, this would in itself not constitute irrefutable grounds for accepting its legitimacy. Religion, Bayle argued, is neither necessary nor sufficient for morality, and a society of atheists would still be governed by the desire for honour and reputations, as well as rewards and punishments."

10. Zygmunt Bauman (2005, p. 108) emphasizes the flexibility of sociality in cultural and psychological change: "In a liquid, fast-flowing and unpredictable setting we need firm and reliable ties of friendship and mutual trust more than ever before. Friends, after all, are people we can count on for understanding and a helping hand in case we stumble and fall, and in the world we inhabit even the fastest surfers and the most sprightly skaters are not insured against that eventuality. On the other hand, though, those self-same liquid and fast-flowing settings privilege those who can travel light; if changed circumstances require a fast move and starting anew from scratch, long-term commitments and any ties difficult to untie may prove to be a cumbersome burden—ballast that needs to be thrown overboard. There is no good choice, then. You cannot have your cake and eat it—but this is precisely what you are pressed to do by the setting which you try to compose your life. Whatever choice you make, you are storing up trouble."

11. Richard Joyce (2006, p. 136) finds, "Young children do not merely show improved reasoning when dealing with deontic matters; at a remarkably early age they are able to discriminate among different kinds of deontic rules. Most notably, their capacity to distinguish moral from conventional transgressions emerges as early as the third year." Michael S. Gazzaniga (2005, p. 152) notes, "All members of the human species tend to feel and to react in predictable ways to situations that create the background for a moral choice," adding (p. 167), "A series of studies suggesting that there *is* a brain-based account of moral reasoning have burst onto the scientific scene.... Arguments that have raged for centuries about the nature of moral decisions and their sameness or difference are now quickly and distinctly resolved with modern brain imaging. The short form of the new results suggests that when someone is willing to *act* on a moral belief, it is because the emotional part of his or her brain has become active when considering the moral question at hand."

12. Boehm (2012, p. 173) describes the conscience process, placing it in an evolutionary context: "Minimally, both the prefrontal cortex and the paralimbic system are involved in the emotional reactions that contribute to personal social strategizing and self-control. And when the effects of group punishment began to improve our capacities in these areas, it was individual differences in the relevant brain functions that punitive social selection was able to work on in terms of underlying genes. Of course, with this social type of selection, as with natural selection more generally, it was basically variation in the phenotype that selection processes acted upon directly. Ultimately, the social preferences of groups were able to affect gene pools profoundly, and once we began to blush with shame, this surely meant that the evolution of conscientious self-control was well under way. The

final result was a full-blown, sophisticated modern conscience, which helps us to make subtle decisions that involve balancing selfish interests in food, power, sex, or whatever against the need to maintain a decent personal moral reputation in society and to feel socially valuable as a person." Boehm (pp. 217–218) identifies the basic purpose of the conscience, "namely, the personal absorption of rules and values. And this leads to the conformist tendencies in humans."

13. Charles Crawford (2004, p. 8) indicates, "Evolutionary psychologists have found good evidence for the evolution of specialized psychological mechanisms for engaging in reciprocal exchanges. It includes evidence that people have evolved mechanisms for detecting cheaters on reciprocal exchanges. These psychological mechanisms enabled human ancestors to reap the benefits of gains in trade. In the modern world, they underpin people's sense of justice and make the international economy possible." Frans de Waal (1996, p. 136) explains the moral centrality of reciprocity: "The anticipation of gain is central to the human moral contract—not in each and every exchange, of course, but overall. This is why no one can withdraw from the contract without dire consequences, such as ostracism, imprisonment, or execution.... Reciprocity can exist without morality; there can be no morality without reciprocity."

14. Richard Joyce (2006, p. 90) offers a logical explanation of the evolution of symbolic communication in response to the human individual and societal pressure of need: "The conclusion is that in the course of human evolution an increasing pressure was developing in favor of there being some new and more efficient means for exchanging information about the behavior and relationships of one's interactants. The pressure was first upon *Homo habilis*, and subsequently became so acute that we can assume that some evolution must have been struck upon. Language, it is argued, is that solution. One way to find out about another individual's trustworthiness is to observe her interactions with others; but if you are simultaneously trying to observe dozens of prospective interactants, then you are in trouble. But if one can *talk* to others who have interacted with the individuals in question, then a lot of information can be gathered very easily."

15. Evolutionary psychologist Harmon Holcomb (2004, p. 93) writes, "Moral obligations have an objective ground in the sense that any agent who recognizes the authority of moral ideals is bound by that act of recognition. Moral ideals are objective in a further sense, namely, they are universally aimed at and applicable, where universality presupposes a domain of individuals to which they are applicable. Over evolutionary history this domain has been from people's in-group to the whole of humanity, as evident in the world religions, and now even to some nonhuman animals. When two moral agents interact, both expect there to be some ideals about behavior governing their interaction, and may differ in how far they expect themselves and others to live up to that ideal. Realizing that the particular norms they believe in might be less than ideal, then, due to the common goal of having a moral ideal, they have a basis for discussing ideals, arriving at shared ideals or even changing ideals."

16. Herbert Gintis, Samuel Bowles, Robert Boyd and Ernst Fehr (2008, p. 314) contribute the following thought: "So unshakable among many biologists is the belief that true altruism is biologically impossible that until recently (and in some evolutionary psychology circles, still) the mere mention of altruistic motivation provokes ridicule. Indeed, some biologists *define* altruism to mean sacrificing inclusive fitness, in which case of course altruism could not evolve. But, this is a serious error. Of course, a gene that promotes self-sacrifice will die out unless those helped carry the mutant gene, or its spread is otherwise promoted. But, altruistic behavior can be observed and documented in the laboratory and so it must have evolved. As such, altruistic behavior must be fitness enhancing."

17. Dilworth (2010, p. 110) further explains this in terms of the "vicious circle principle," also an ecological principle: *"Humankind's development consists in an accelerating movement from situations of scarcity, to technological innovation, to increased resource availability, to increased consumption, to population growth, to resource depletion, to scarcity once again, and so on."* Sociologist David J. Hess (2007, p. 71) summarizes the process whereby technology develops with ever-increasing rapidity and according to guidelines: "The

relationship between new and old technology is characterized as one of subsumption. In other words, the new technology must meet the same goals but with greater speed and/or enhanced capacity, or it may have the same speed and capacity, but it should reduce energy and/or labor expenditures."

18. James Q. Wilson (1993, pp. 10 & 23) offers his explanation for the apparent decline of personal responsibility, placing it in a larger context: "The moral relativism of the modern age has probably contributed to the increase in crime rates, especially the increases that occur during prosperous times. It has done so by replacing the belief in personal responsibility with the notion of social causation and by supplying to those marginal persons at risk for crime a justification for doing what they might have done anyway."

Chapter 7

1. Jeremy Black (2014, p. 116) finds, "The relationship between the Scientific Revolution and the relative capability of the West was to emerge in the long term, but already by the end of the seventeenth century there was a significant contrast with non-Western science and technology. This contrast has been linked to the challenge posed by the West to the metaphysical foundations of other civilisations." Black (2014, p. 195) applies this idea to more recent times in his conclusion: "Moreover, as an aspect of the (practical and ideological) support for the idea of change by Western governments and among influential Western groups, non-Western societies were increasingly to be presented, and thus criticized, as unchanging and reactionary, indeed as sclerotic. This view contributed to pejorative Western assumptions about race and religion."

2. Cultural historian Margaret C. Jacob (1997, p. 73) describes the intellectual atmosphere of this transformation, ultimately produced by the growth of science: "We can date the transformation in the role of science in Western culture from the 1680s to the 1720s. Within one generation, largely in northern and Western Europe, the transformation was complete. Mechanically based science left the hands of the learned societies, coffee house lectures, and church sermons. As a result, science altered the way urban merchants, progressive aristocrats, literate gentlemen, some gentlewomen as a well as artisans and tradesmen, understood the physical world around them. The assimilation of science was so rapid, and its impact so great, that historians since the 1930s have identified the period in European culture from the 1680s to the 1720s as one of profound crisis. Out of the crisis emerged a mentality discernibly modern, a new cultural moment called in retrospect the 'age of enlightenment.' At that moment, high culture armed with scientific acumen distinguished itself completely and irrevocably from the culture of the untutored or semiliterate people. Science became essential to educated discourse; nature mechanized provided analogies and metaphors for every aspect of human experience."

3. Economic and social historian Joan Thirsk (1978, pp. 1–2) comments on the historical disposition of concern for the well-being of others: "Towards the end of the sixteenth century, however, concern for this abstract ideal, the commonweal, switched to more material concerns, and in the seventeenth century two of the key words that characterized the new era were 'project' and projector.' Everyone with a scheme, whether to make money, to employ the poor, or to explore the far corners of the earth had a 'project.' The concrete noun is significant. A project was a practical scheme for exploiting material things; it was capable of being realized through industry and ingenuity. It was not an unattainable dream like the commonweal. Yet in effect it did much to promote the commonweal, by creating employment, and dispersing more cash through all classes of society. As the projects of the seventeenth century worked themselves into the economy, they transformed its structure. They effected a redistribution of wealth."

4. Dennis L. Krebs (2011, p. 246) explains, "Humans differ from other primates in the magnitude and effectiveness of the prosocial behaviors they emit because the deferential, altruistic, and cooperative dispositions that have evolved in the human species can be activated by a significantly broader array of stimuli than comparable dispositions in other primate species can—especially stimuli emanating from inside their minds—and because humans are better than other primates at understanding what others need and how best to help them.... Whatever the original source, as humans

evolved, changes in environments and the expansion and reorganization of the human brain increased significantly the range of stimuli equipped to activate prosocial dispositions, rendering humans increasingly altruistic and cooperative by nature."

5. Krebs (2011, p. 257) describes the evolutionary context for the mass and variety of human populations maintained under considerable yet almost invisible control, even as they pass through immense and highly visible cultural change: "Virtually all people develop moral principles and behave in accordance with them, as long as it is not too costly. However, people may differ greatly in the strength of their convictions. When viewed through an evolutionary lens, we would expect to find biologically and developmentally based individual differences in the qualities that endow people with moral intelligence, the motivation to behave in moral ways, and the determination, courage, and will power, or ego strength, to achieve their moral goals; and research indicates that the heritability of these qualities is high. Some people are wise, other people are kind-hearted, and still others are courageous. A few people may possess all these qualities, at least to a moderate degree.... The basic assumptions underlying a functional approach to evolutionary ethics are that morality evolved for a reason—to help people solve adaptive problems and to achieve adaptive goals—and the better a moral idea, judgment, emotion, principle, behavior, strategy, or disposition fulfills this function, the more morally adequate it is."

6. Social psychologist C. Daniel Batson (2011, p. 53) states the case concisely: "Thus, there is a range of evidence consistent with the idea that parental nurturance may provide a biological substrate for intrinsic valuing of another's welfare and for empathy-induced altruism in humans. Although not conclusive, the existing evidence supports the plausibility of the idea that four evolutionary developments may underlie the human capacity to care for the welfare of both progeny and non-progeny as an end in itself, not simply as an instrumental means of caring for one's own welfare. The first development is the evolution in mammals of parental nurturance. Second is the evolution in humans and possibly a few other species of the ability to see others as sentient, intentional agents and, thereby, to recognize other's needs, even subtle ones. Third is the evolution of tender, empathic emotions as an important component of parental nurturance. Fourth is the evolution of cognitive capacities that make it possible to generalize valuing of another's welfare and tender, empathic feelings beyond offspring.... If humans are able to value another's welfare intrinsically, then versions of rational choice that assume all human behavior is directed toward maximizing one's own welfare need radical revision."

7. Responsibility is a social construct, writes Michael S. Gazzaniga (2005, p. 90): "Just as traffic is what happens when physically determined cars interact, responsibility is what happens when people interact. Personal responsibility is a public concept. It exists in a group, not in an individual. If you were the only person on earth, there would be no concept of personal responsibility. Responsibility is a concept you have about other people's actions and they about yours. Brains are determined; people (more than one human being) follow rules when they live together, and out of that interaction arises the concept of freedom of action."

8. Recalling mathematician and philosopher Alfred North Whitehead, Josiah Stamp (1937, p. 58) pronounced this caution more than eight decades ago: "when an adequate routine, the aim of every social system, is established, intelligence vanishes and the system is maintained by a co-ordination of conditioned reflexes." I suggest that his general idea portrays the West's current situation whereby the desired condition ironically has become a continuous and rapidly changing status quo.

9. Philosopher and cognitive scientist Paul Thagard and philosopher Tracy Finn (2011, p. 165) provide a clarifying example of the significance of reflection to morality in the particularly difficult area of decisions during the particular intensity of recent decades: "In other words, once we have given sufficient attention and reflection to a particular moral principle, we come to accept it as self-evident. Thus, disagreement can occur, and continue to occur until we have sufficiently reflected on the self-evident principles. As noted earlier, an intuitionist need not hold that self-evident principles are easily grasped or obviously true."

10. Thompson (1995, p. 32) further describes the cultural significance of the

time/space sensation: "In earlier historical periods the experience of simultaneity—that is of events occurring 'at the same time'—presupposed a specific locale in which the simultaneous events could be experienced by the individual. Simultaneity presupposed locality; 'the same time' presupposed 'the same place.' But with the uncoupling of space and time brought about by telecommunication, the experience of simultaneity was detached from the spatial condition of common locality. It became possible to experience events as simultaneous despite the fact that they occurred in locales that were spatially remote. In contrast to the concreteness of the here and now, there emerged a sense of 'now' which was no longer bound to a particular locale. Simultaneity was extended in space and became ultimately global in scope."

11. For instance, Matthew D. Lieberman (2013, p. 264) writes, "It's hard to find meaning in what we do if at some level it doesn't help someone else or make someone happier." Not least among the problems drawing ever-greater attention to our quality of life is the quality of formal education where, again, the problem is the narrowing scope of human life. And Martha C. Nussbaum (1997, p. 14) describes the implications of this condition: "Our campuses educate our citizens. Becoming an educated citizen means learning a lot of facts and mastering techniques of reasoning. But it means something more. It means learning how to be a human being capable of love and imagination. We may continue to produce narrow citizens who have difficulty understanding people different from themselves, whose imaginations rarely venture beyond their local setting. It is all too easy for the moral imagination to become narrow in this way. Yet logic suggests that an institutionally established educational experience is the best situated to nurture the value of human practicality in such a way that all the disciplinary content of formal education will make sense."

Chapter 8

1. We often refer to the state of well-being as "happiness," "satisfaction" or "contentment" with the overall course of one's life. Introducing a clinical yet readily understandable explanation for this general sense of well-being, behavioral scientist Daniel Nettle (2005, p. 4) proceeds from this observation: "The feeling of well-being emerges from the interplay of neural circuits that are the products of millions of years of evolution. In men as in mice, positive and negative emotions rely on separate, dedicated neural circuits, which respond to status, to threats, and to rewards in the environment. The systems controlling pleasure are not identical to those controlling desire. This is an important lesson; the psychology of aspiration is not that of satisfaction. We do not always want what we like or like what we want.... We are designed not for happiness or unhappiness, but to strive for the goals that evolution has built into us. Happiness is a handmaiden to evolution's purposes here, functioning not so much as an actual reward but as an imaginary goal that gives us direction and purpose." Business and economics editor David Pilling (2018) makes the case that the annual publication of statistics on gross national product introduces a basis for its confusion with well-being that can lead those whose lives may not have improved commensurate with GNP growth to unhappiness and perhaps their sense of being victims of deception.

2. Antonio Damasio (2010, pp. 296–297) also refers to two profound dimensions of this capacity to adapt psychologically: "Ultimately, because the arts have deep roots in biology and the human body but can elevate humans to the greatest heights of thought and feeling, they became a way into the homeostatic refinement that humans eventually idealized and longed to achieve, the biological counterpart of a spiritual dimension in human affairs. In brief, the arts prevailed in evolution because they had survival value and contributed to the development of the notion of well-being.... The greatest of all gifts depends, once again, on the intersection of the self and memory. Memory, tempered by personal feeling, is what allows humans to imagine both individual well-being and the compounded well-being of a whole society, and to invent the ways and means of achieving and magnifying that well-being. Memory is responsible for ceaselessly placing the self in an evanescent here and now, between a thoroughly lived past and an anticipated future, perpetually buffeted between the spent yesterdays and the tomorrows that are nothing but possibilities."

3. Philip N. Johnson-Laird (2006, pp. 83–84) helps unravel the emotion/reason knot: "Our emotions often impel us to act. But, we can still reason, and sometimes our reasoning conflicts with our emotion.... The traffic between reasoning and emotions moves in both directions. Inferences evoke emotions: emotions evoke inferences. Even though the main link in the evocation of an emotion is an unconscious transition from an evaluation, the first event in the causal chain may be a conscious inference.... Hence, the full range of inferences from unconscious intuitions to conscious deductions can create emotions."

4. About the process by which this stabilizing apparatus functions, Antonio Damasio (2010, p. 259) finds, "It is often overlooked that information from the body's interior is conveyed directly to the brain by numerous chemical molecules that course in the bloodstream and bathes parts of the brain that are devoid of blood-brain barrier, namely, the area postrema in the brain stem and a variety of regions known collectively as the circumventricular organs." Among other findings, Damasio (p. 280) adds, "When the mind is informed of the actions taken by our organism, the feeling associated with the information signifies that the actions were engendered by our self. Both information and authentication of ongoing actions are essential to motivate the deliberation of future actions. Without that sort of felt, validated information, we would not be able to assume moral responsibility for the actions taken by our organism."

5. Randolph Nesse (2001, p. 311) reports that "hundreds of studies in behavioral economics find that nonrational decisions are ubiquitous." Richerson and Boyd (2001, p. 210) find, "Microevolutionary studies seem to conflict with the idea that social change occurs entirely by rational choice, unless rational choice is understood to be a weak process relative to cultural transmission in the construction of individual behavioral repertoires."

6. Service by representative groups to determine decisions and plans may not be a product of human instinct, but surely is a function of human sociality. Collective benefit in determination by a representative group is examined by economist Mancur Olson, Jr. (1965, p. 21), who concludes that "any group or organization [with an economic purpose], large or small, works for some collective benefit that by its very nature will benefit all of the members of the group in question. Though all of the members of the group therefore have a common interest in obtaining this collective benefit, they have no common interest in paying the cost of providing that collective good. Each would prefer that the others pay the entire cost, and ordinarily would get any benefit provided whether he had borne part of the cost or not." He adds (p. 39), "Whether a group behaves exclusively or inclusively, therefore, depends upon the nature of the objective the group seeks, not on any characteristics of the membership."

7. Batson (2011, pp. 232–233) elaborates on the evolutionary significance of altruism: "Empathy-induced altruism offers benefits in the form of more and more sensitive help for those in need, less aggression, increased cooperation in competitive situations, improved attitudes toward and more action on behalf of stigmatized groups, and more positive close relationships. It may also provide health benefits to the altruistic helper.... And once we make room for altruism, we face the possibility that intrinsic value can be extended to states other than one's own and another's welfare. There may be prosocial motives other than egoism and altruism. Two additional prosocial motives deserve consideration: collectivism and principlism. Collectivism—motivation with the ultimate goal of benefiting some group or collective as a whole—may be a powerful resource when facing the social dilemmas that plague us in modern life. Principlism—motivation with the ultimate goal of upholding some moral principle—has long been extolled by religious teachers and moral philosophers. Whether collectivism and principlism are independent of and irreducible to egoism is not yet clear."

As Dennis L. Krebs (2011, pp. 159–160) explains the evolutionary force of altruism, it is at the core of humanity's distinguishing features: "Primitive forms of prosocial conduct stem from mental mechanisms that humans share with other animals, even though these forms of conduct may be affected in significant ways by mental capacities unique to humans. People sometimes help others impulsively, without concern for their own welfare. Like other animals, people can be taught to behave in prosocial ways by rewarding and punishing them. A suite of emotions disposes people to respect authority, to resist temptation, to help others, to uphold systems of cooperation, and to repair damaged relationships. These emotions may give rise to genuinely altruistic motivational states. The mechanisms that produce them evolved because they increased people's willingness to suffer short-term material, psychological, and biological costs in order to promote their long-term material, psychological, biological, and genetic interests."

8. Sober & Wilson (1998, p. 337) summarize their research on this subject: "The human capacity for culture thus sets in motion an evolutionary process in which some of the anti-functionalist's principal claims emerge as results. Cultural transmission opens the way for an elaborate edifice of phenotypes that enhance group-level functional organization. But this mechanism also leads to the evolution of behaviors that make no sense outside the cultural system that promotes them. Nonfunctional and even dysfunctional behaviors can ride along with adaptive behaviors as hitchhikers. These and other sources of nonfunctional behaviors can be understood from an evolutionary perspective. Just as selection does not require genetic determinism, so an evolutionary model of cultural change does not require an exclusive focus on the process of selection." A dozen years' research later, Alex Mesoudi (2011, pp. 184–185) concludes that "no society ever studied exhibits purely self-interested behavior, as standard economic theory predicts they should."

9. Hubert J. M. Hermans (2013, p. 46) explains: "When society is globalizing, the self is too. When society is becoming more complex, the self, as an intrinsic part of society, is reflecting this complexity and is challenged to give an *answer*. Stronger, we conceive of the self as a 'society of mind,' which, at the same time, functions as part of the society at large and changes together with it. Society, from its side, is not 'surrounding' the self as an external 'determinant,' but is a society-of-selves, to which the self gives its original contribution, as Mead (1934) already argued in his classic work *Mind, Self and Society*. An important consequence of this view is that changes and developments in the self lead to changes and developments in society at large and reversed. In other words, self and society are not mutually exclusive but inclusive."

10. John Tooby, Leda Cosmides, and H. Clark Barrett (2005, pp. 316–317) find, "[C]ontent-specific value processing is done by mechanisms that ultimately were shaped according to whether their rankings and decisions were, on balance, reproduction-promoting under ancestral conditions. So value exists for animals solely because natural selection built neurocomputational circuitry into our minds to compute it as one of several kinds of representation necessary for regulating our behavior according to evolutionarily functional performance criteria.... In short, many evolved motivational mechanisms, by virtue of the nature of the functions they serve, are necessarily functionally specialized rather than general purpose, are content dependent rather than content independent, introduce content not derived from the senses into the operation of the architecture, and do so ubiquitously."

11. Boyd, Richerson, and behavioral psychologist and anthropologist Joseph Henrich (2005, p. 260) outline this unique biological and cultural evolution: "Understanding the evolution of contemporary human cooperation requires attention to two different timescales: first, a long period of evolution in the Pleistocene epoch shaped the innate 'social instincts' that underpin modern human behavior. During this period, much genetic change occurred as a result of humans living in groups with social institutions *heavily influenced by culture*, including cultural group selection. On this timescale, genes and culture *coevolve*, and cultural evolution is plausibly a leading rather than lagging partner in this process. We sometimes refer to the process as 'culture-gene coevolution.' Then, only about 10,000 years ago, the origins of agricultural subsistence systems laid the economic basis for revolutionary changes in the scale of social systems. Evidence suggests that genetic changes in the social instincts over the last 10,000 years are insignificant. Evolution of complex societies, however, has involved the relatively slow cultural accumulation of institutional 'work-arounds' that take advantage of a psychology evolved to cooperate with distantly related and unrelated individuals belonging to the same symbolically marked 'tribe' while coping more or less successfully

with the fact that these social systems are larger, more anonymous, and more hierarchical than the late Pleistocene tribal-scale systems."

12. Robin Dunbar (1999, p.195) reports two highly pertinent research findings: "First, freeriders who take the benefit but do not repay the gift are likely to be successful in any population where the coalition time (the time required to establish bona fides before an exchange of resources is made is short.... The second point is that a freerider's ability to prosper is directly related to the size and dispersion of the population. This is a simple consequence of the fact that freeriders are better able to keep one step ahead of discovery when they are in a large pool of naïve individuals whom they are unlikely to re-encounter once they have been exploited. In effect, the search time to find the next naïve individual is low because the pool of potential interactees is large relative to the rate at which exchanges are made."

13. Freud (1994, p. 26) perceived not only the need for general cooperation in optimizing human mental and physical energies but also the necessity of curbing the aggression of those less committed to morality: "Human life in communities only becomes possible when a number of men unite together in strength superior to any single individual and remain united against all single individuals. The strength of this united body is then opposed as *right* against the strength of any individual, which is condemned as *brute force*. This substitution of the power of a united number for the power of a single man is the decisive step towards civilization. The essence of it lies in the circumstance that the members of the community have restricted their possibilities of gratification, whereas the individual recognized no such restrictions. The first requisite of culture, therefore, is justice—that is, the assurance that a law once made will not be broken in favour of any individual."

14. Boyd, Richerson, and Henrich (2005, p. 265) further explain the rise of a moral code, finding that "Complex human societies have to supplement the moralistic solidarity of tribal societies with formal police institutions. Otherwise, the large-scale benefits of cooperation, coordination, and division of labor would cease to exist in the face of selfish temptations to expropriate them by individuals, nepotists, cabals of reciprocators, organized predatory bands, greedy capitalists, and classes or castes with special access to means of coercion. At the same time, the need for organized coercion as an ultimate sanction creates roles, classes, and subcultures with the power to turn coercion to narrow advantage. Social institutions of some sort must police the police so that they will act in the larger interest to a measurable degree."

15. Robert Boyd, Peter J. Richerson, economist and behavioral scientist Herbert Gintis, and economist Samuel Bowles (2005, pp. 241–242) find, "[G]roup selection can lead to the evolution of altruistic punishment in larger groups because the problem of deterring free-riders in the case of altruistic cooperation is fundamentally different from the problem of deterring free riders in the case of altruistic punishment. This asymmetry arises because the payoff disadvantage of altruistic cooperators relative to defectors is independent of the frequency of defectors in the population, whereas the cost disadvantage for those engaged in altruistic punishment declines as defectors become rare because acts of punishment become very infrequent. Thus, when altruistic punishers are common, individual-level selection operating against them is weak."

16. Richard Joyce (2006, pp. 141–142) describes some of the evolutionary aspects of reciprocity: "Evidence from primatology, experimental economics, neuroscience, developmental psychology, and anthropology suggests that the human mind bears the traces of a past in which reciprocity played a big role.... Reciprocal partners may enter into such exchanges for selfish motives, or for altruistic motives, or their exchanges may be mere conditions or hardwired reflexes properly described neither as selfish nor altruistic. Genes inhabiting selfishly motivated reciprocating organisms may be soundly outcompeted by genes inhabiting reciprocating organisms who are moved directly by the welfare of their chosen exchange partners. And genes inhabiting reciprocating organisms motivated additionally by thoughts of moral duty, who will feel guilty if they defect, may do better still."

17. Torey (2014, p. 112) places this function of human decision in the evolutionary process: "The result of this Darwinian selection process is that all the competing action impulses present at the time remain

inhibited, except the one that is 'felt' by the brainstem to be the most congruent with the organism's values. The conscious mind, unaware of the evaluating transaction of the brainstem that disinhibits one of the options, but aware of having thought of the option, rationalizes that *it* has done the deciding."

Chapter 9

1. Anthropologist Donald T. Campbell (1976) has devised a statement, to codify his observations about the quantification trend: "The more any quantitative social indicator (or even some qualitative indicator) is used for social decision-making, the more subject it will be to corruption pressures and the more apt it will be to distort and corrupt the social processes it is intended to monitor." "Campbell's Law," as it is known, very clearly applies to the formal education environment.

2. Mithen (1990, pp. 262–263) explains his conclusion: "The prehistoric world in these pages has been first and foremost one inhabited by individuals unconstrained by social convention and ideology. These individuals interact, and compose a society which is not just the sum of these individuals, though what is remains unclear in this work. But my conception of the individual is rather clearer. He (she) is not just the 'economic man' of optimal foraging studies. He has imperfect knowledge and often makes erroneous choices (in terms of adaptation). But what knowledge he possesses is used creatively and he engages in co-operation as well as competition with other individuals. Emotions, characterised in an evolutionary framework as decision criteria, are at the centre of his/her existence. The behavior of these prehistoric foragers results from a complex mix of conscious and unconscious choices, with intended and unintended, recognized and unrecognized consequences. They live in an uncertain world in which neither the physical nor the social environment is constant. And most of all, they themselves are not constant but ever changing."

3. Cognitive psychologists Howard Leventhal and Klaus Scherer (1987, p. 16) were early in referring to a combination of cognitive processes that could "steer the emotion-cognition controversy away from potentially sterile semantic arguments about what is a cognition, and lead to more concrete, operational questions about the substance and operation of specific evaluation checks at different processing levels." They conclude (p. 23) that "it will be extremely rare to find emotional reactions totally separated from perceptual or cognitive reactions in the human animal," and would only occur only in the earliest stages of human life.

4. Freud (1994, p. 40) emphasizes the long-term importance of defending human need: "Culture has to call up every possible reinforcement in order to erect barriers against the aggressive instincts of men and hold their manifestations in check by reaction-formations in men's minds." So instead of weakening by failing to acknowledge them, especially in the critical act of social choice, we need to protect and strengthen them when possible. Dennis L. Krebs (2011, p. 258) summarizes his thought about the evolution and place of morality in cognition: "I have argued that the mental mechanisms that endow people with a moral sense evolved to help them resist the temptation to foster their immediate adaptive interests at the expense of other people's adaptive interests and to induce them to foster their long-term interests in ways that foster the interests of other members of their groups, by doing their share and by taking their share, by maintaining mutually beneficial social relations, by resolving conflicts of interest in adaptive ways, and by upholding (and improving) the systems of cooperation and social orders of their groups."

5. Dilworth (2010, p. 330) adds another dimension to this cultural phenomenon: "According to (Max) Weber, a man does not 'by nature' wish to earn more and more money, but simply to live as he is accustomed to living, and to earn as much as is necessary for that purpose. Wherever modern capitalism has increased the productivity of human labour by increasing its intensity, it has encountered the immensely stubborn resistance of this leading trait of pre-capitalism … we therefore see through the course of human existence an ever-strengthening trend towards the development of technology in response to the non-vital and perhaps only imagined needs of the wealthy and powerful."

6. Sociologist Barry Barnes (1995, p. 37) depicts a panorama of this strange social situation: "Functionalist theories in the social

sciences seek to describe, to understand and in most cases to explain the orderliness and stability of entire social systems. In so far as they treat of individuals, the treatment comes after and emerges from analysis of the system as a whole. Functionalist theories move from an understanding of the whole to an understanding of the parts of that whole, whereas individualism proceeds in the opposite direction. The two kinds of theory conflict in the methodological implications and their epistemological rationales."

7. Economist and game theorist H. Peyton Young (2002, p. 390) provides a definition of "norm" to help explain the complex function of cultural evolution: "The fundamental idea is that norms coalesce from the decentralized, uncoordinated choices of many interacting individuals. Roughly speaking, individuals are the particles of the system, and norms are the organizational forms that bind them together. Unlike particles, however, individuals make intentional choices based on perceived constraints and opportunities."

8. Damasio (2010, pp. 267–268) further clarifies: "The self focuses the mind process, it imbues the adventure of encountering other objects and events with a motivation, it infuses the exploration of the world outside the brain with a *concern* for the first and foremost problem facing the organism: the successful regulation of life. That concern is naturally generated by the self process, whose foundation lies in bodily feelings, primordial and modified. The spontaneously, intrinsically feeling self signals directly, as a result of the valence and intensity of its affective states, the degree of concern and need that are present at every moment."

Bibliography

> At a university one finds himself, if he has any vigor of imagination, in one of the widest environments the world can afford. He has access to the suggestions of the richest minds of all times and countries, and has also, or should have, time and encouragement to explore, in his own way, this spacious society. It is his business to think, to aspire, and grow; and if he is at all capable of it he does so. Philosophy and art and science and the betterment of mankind are real and living interests to him, largely because he is in the great stream of higher thought that flows through libraries.
> —*Charles Horton Cooley, 1902*

Adams, E. M. (Elie Maynard). 1997. *A Society Fit for Human Beings*. State University of New York Press.

Adas, Michael. 1989. *Machines as the Measure of Men: Science, Technology and Ideologies of Western Dominance*. Ithaca: Cornell University Press.

Alford, Robert R., and Roger Friedland. 1985. *Powers of Theory: Capitalism, the State, and Democracy*. New York: Cambridge University Press.

Archer, Margaret S. 2003. *Structure, Agency and the Internal Conversation*. Cambridge: Cambridge University Press.

Archer, Margaret S. 2007. *Making our Way through the World: Human Reflexivity and Social Mobility*. Cambridge: Cambridge University Press.

Arendt, Hannah. 1958. *The Human Condition*. Chicago: University of Chicago Press.

Atran, Scott. 2005. "Religion's Innate Origins and Evolutionary Background." *The Innate Mind: Culture and Cognition*, edited by Peter Carruthers, Stephen Laurence, and Stephen Stich. New York: Oxford University Press, pp. 302–317.

Ayres, C. E. (Clarence Edwin). 1944. *The Theory of Economic Progress*. Chapel Hill: University of North Carolina Press.

Bagnoli, Carla. 2011. "Emotions and the Categorical Authority of Moral Reason." *Morality and the Emotions*, edited by Carla Bagnoli. Oxford: Oxford University Press, pp. 62–81.

Barber, Bernard. 1998. *Intellectual Pursuits. Toward an Understanding of Culture*. Lanham: Rowman & Littlefield.

Bard, Alexander, and Jan Soderqvist. 2002. *Netocracy: The New Power Elite and Life after Capitalism*. London: Reuters.

Barfield, Owen. 1977. *The Rediscovery of Meaning, and Other Essays*. Middletown: Wesleyan University Press.

Barilan, Yechiel Michael. 2012. *Human Dignity, Human Rights, and Responsibility: The New Language of Global Bioethics and Biolaw*. Cambridge: MIT Press.

Barnes, Barry. 1995. *The Elements of Social Theory*. Princeton: Princeton University Press.

Baron-Cohen, Simon. 1995. *Mindblindness: An Essay on Autism and Theory of Mind*. Cambridge: MIT Press.

Baron-Cohen, Simon. 1999. "The Evolution of a Theory of Mind." *The Descent of Mind: Psychological Perspectives on Hominid Evolution*, edited by Michael C. Corballis and Stephen E. G. Lea. Oxford: Oxford University Press, pp. 261–277.

Barrett, H. Clark. 2008. "Evolved Cognitive Mechanisms and Human Behavior." *Foundations of Evolutionary Psychology*, edited by Charles Crawford and Dennis Krebs. New York: Lawrence Erlbaum, pp. 173–189.

Barrett, H. Clark. 2015. *The Shape of Thought: How Mental Adaptations Evolve*. New York: Oxford University Press.

Barrett, Louise. 2011. *Beyond the Brain: How Body and Environment Shape Animal and Human Minds*. Princeton: Princeton University Press.

Basalla, George. 1988. *The Evolution of Technology*. New York: Cambridge University Press.

Bateson, Gregory. 2000 [1972]. *Steps to an Ecology of Mind*. Chicago: University of Chicago Press.

Bateson, Gregory. 2002 [1979]. *Mind and Nature: A Necessary Unity*. Cresskill, NJ: Hampton Press.

Batson, C. Daniel. 2011. *Altruism in Humans*. New York: Oxford University Press.

Baudrillard, Jean. 1998 [1970]. *The Consumer Society: Myths and Structures*. London: Sage.

Bauman, Zygmunt. 2000. "Foreword." *The Demoralization of Western Culture*, by R. W. Fevre. London: Continuum, pp. vi-x.

Bauman, Zygmunt. 2005. *Liquid Life*. Malden: Polity Press.

Baumeister, Roy F. 2010. "The Human Mind and the Evolution of Cultural Animals." *Evolution, Culture, and the Human Mind*, edited by Mark Schaller, Ara Norenzayan, Steven J. Heine, Toshio Yamagishi, Tatsuya Kameda. New York: Psychology Press, pp. 23–38.

Becker, Carl L. 1936. *Progress and Power*. Stanford: Stanford University Press.

Bell, Daniel. 1973. *The Coming of Post-Industrial Society: a Venture in Social Forecasting*. New York: Basic Books.

Bell, Daniel. 1975 [1973]. "Technology, Nature, and Society." *Technology and the Frontiers of Knowledge*. Garden City: Doubleday, pp. 23–71.

Bell, Daniel. 1976. *The Cultural Contradictions of Capitalism*. New York: Basic Books.

Berger, Peter L., and Thomas Luckmann. 1966. *The Social Construction of Reality: A Treatise in the Sociology of Knowledge*. Garden City: Doubleday.

Berle, Adolf A., and Gardiner C. Means. 1931.

"Corporation." *Encyclopaedia of the Social Sciences*. New York: Macmillan, vol. 4, pp. 414–423.

Berman, Marshall. 1999. *Adventures in Marxism*. London: Verso.

Bjorklund, David F., and Anthony D. Pellegrini. 2002. *The Origins of Human Nature: Evolutionary Developmental Psychology*. Washington, D.C.: American Psychological Association.

Black, Jeremy. 2014. *The Power of Knowledge: How Information and Technology Made the Modern World*. New Haven: Yale University Press.

Blum, Lawrence A. 1994. *Moral Perception and Particularity*. Cambridge: Cambridge University Press.

Boehm, Christopher. 2012. *Moral Origins: The Evolution of Virtue, Altruism, and Shame*. New York: Basic Books.

Boeme, Gernot, and Nico Stehr. 1986. "The Growing Impact of Scientific Knowledge on Social Relations." *The Knowledge Society*, edited by Gernot Bohme and Nico Stehr. Dordrecht: Reidel, pp. 7–29.

Bogucki, Peter I. 1999. *The Origins of Human Society*. Malden: Blackwell

Boivin, Nicole. 2008. *Material Cultures, Material Minds. The Impact of Things on Human Thought, Society, and Evolution*. Cambridge: Cambridge University Press.

Bok, Sissela. 2010. *Exploring Happiness: From Aristotle to Brain Science*. New Haven: Yale University Press.

Bontekoe, Ron. 2008. *The Nature of Dignity*. Lanham: Rowman & Littlefield.

Boorstin, Daniel J. 1973. *The Americans: The Democratic Experience*. New York: Random House.

Boorstin, Daniel J. 1980. *Gresham's Law: Knowledge or Information?* Dallas: Somesuch Press.

Boulding, Kenneth E. 1985. *Human Betterment*. Beverly Hills: Sage Publications.

Bourdieu, Pierre. 1977. *Outline of a Theory of Practice*. Cambridge: Cambridge University Press.

Bowles, Samuel, and Herbert Gintis. 2002 "The Origins of Human Cooperation." *The Genetic and Cultural Evolution of Cooperation*, edited by Peter Hammerstein. Cambridge: MIT Press, 429–444.

Boyd, Robert, and Richerson, Peter J. 2005. *The Origin and Evolution of Cultures*. New York: Oxford University Press.

Boyd, Robert, Peter J. Richerson, and Joseph

Henrich. 2005. "Cultural Evolution of Human Cooperation." *The Origin and Evolution of Cultures*, edited by Robert Boyd and Peter L. Richerson. New York: Oxford University Press, pp. 251–281.

Boyd, Robert, Peter J. Richerson, Herbert Gintis, and Samuel Bowles. 2005. "The Evolution of Altruistic Punishment." *The Origin and Evolution of Cultures*, edited by Robert Boyd and Peter L. Richerson. New York: Oxford University Press, pp. 241–250.

Boyer, Pascal. 2000. "Evolution of the Modern Mind and the Origins of Culture: Religious Concepts as a Limiting-Case." *Evolution and the Human Mind: Modularity, Language and Meta-Cognition*, edited by Peter Carruthers and Andrew Chamberlain. Cambridge: Cambridge University Press, pp. 93–112.

Brady, Michael S. 2013. *Emotional Insight: The Epistemic Role of Emotional Experience*. Oxford: Oxford University Press.

Brewer, Talbot. 2011. "On Alienated Emotions." *Morality and the Emotions*, edited by Carla Bagnoli. Oxford: Oxford University Press, pp. 275–298

Bronowski, Jacob. 2002 [1965]. *The Identity of Man*. Amherst, N.Y.: Prometheus Books.

Bulbulia, Joseph A. 2007. "The Evolution of Religion." *Oxford Handbook of Evolutionary Psychology*, edited by R. I. M. Dunbar and Louise Barrett. Oxford: Oxford University Press, pp. 621–635.

Burke, Kenneth. 1954. *Permanence & Change. An Anatomy of Purpose*. Los Altos: Hermes.

Burnham, James. 1941. *The Managerial Revolution: What Is Happening in the World*. New York: John Day.

Buss, David M. 2014. *Evolutionary Psychology: The New Science of the Mind*. Second Edition. Boston: Pearson Education.

Butterfield, Herbert. 1957. *The Origins of Modern Science, 1300–1800*. Revised Edition. New York: Free Press.

Campbell, Colin. 1987. *The Romantic Ethic and the Spirit of Modern Consumerism*. Oxford: Blackwell.

Campbell, Donald T. 1974. "Evolutionary Epistemology." *The Philosophy of Karl Popper*, edited by Paul Schilpp. La Salle: Open Court.

Castells, Manuel. 2009. *Communication Power*. Oxford: Oxford University Press.

Chandler, Alfred D., Jr., and James W. Cortada. 2000. "The Information Age: Continuities and Differences." *A Nation Transformed by Information: How Information Has Shaped the United States from Colonial Times to the Present*. New York: Oxford University Press, pp. 281–299.

Clark, Gregory. 2007. *A Farewell to Alms: A Brief Economic History of the World*. Princeton: Princeton University Press.

Clark, Mary E. 2002. *In Search of Human Nature*. London: Routledge.

Cooley, Charles Horton. 1964 [1922; 1st ed. 1902]. *Human Nature and the Social Order*. Revised Edition. New York: Schocken Books.

Corballis, Michael C. 2011. *The Recursive Mind: The Origins of Human Language, Thought, and Civilization*. Princeton: Princeton University Press.

Coser, Lewis A. 1973. "Social Conflict and the Theory of Social Change." *Social Change. Sources, Patterns, and Consequences*. Second Edition, edited by Eva Etzioni-Halevy and Amitai Etzioni. New York: Basic Books, pp. 114–122.

Crawford, Charles. 2004. "Public Policy and Personal Decisions: The Evolutionary Context." *Evolutionary Psychology, Public Policy and Personal Decisions*, edited by Charles Crawford and Catherine Salmon. Mahwah: Lawrence Erlbaum, pp. 3–22.

Daele, Wolfgang van den. 2004. "Traditional Knowledge in Modern Society." *The Governance of Knowledge*, edited by Nico Stehr. New Brunswick: Transaction, pp. 27–39.

Damasio, Antonio. 2010. *Self Comes to Mind: Constructing the Conscious Brain*. New York: Pantheon Books.

Daniels, George H. 1971. *Science in American Society: A Social History*. New York: Knopf.

Darwin, Charles. 1859. *On the Origin of Species by Natural Selection*. London: John Murray.

DeSalle, Rob, and Ian Tattersall. 2012. *The Brain: Big Bangs, Behaviors, and Beliefs*. New Haven: Yale University Press.

Dessalles, Jean-Louis. 2007. *Why We Talk: The Evolutionary Origins of Language*. Oxford: Oxford University Press.

De Waal, Frans. 1996. *Good Natured: The Origins of Right and Wrong in Humans and Other Animals*. Cambridge: Harvard University Press.

De Waal, Frans. 2009. *The Age of Empathy: Nature's Lessons for a Kinder Society.* New York: Three Rivers Press.

Dicke, Klaus. 2002. "The Founding Function of Human Dignity in the Universal Declaration of Human Rights." *The Concept of Human Dignity in Human Rights Discourse*, edited by David Kretzmer and Eckart Klein. Kluwer, pp. 111–120.

Dilworth, Craig. 2010. *Too Smart for Our Own Good: The Ecological Predicament of Humankind.* Cambridge: Cambridge University Press.

Distin, Kate. 2011. *Cultural Evolution.* Cambridge: Cambridge University Press.

Donnelly, Jack. 2013. *Universal Human Rights in Theory and Practice.* Third Edition. Ithaca: Cornell University Press.

Dunbar, Robin. 2000. "On the Origin of the Human Mind." *Evolution and the Human Mind: Modularity, Language and Meta-Cognition*, edited by Peter Carruthers and Andrew Chamberlain. Cambridge: Cambridge University Press, pp. 238–253.

Durant, Will, and Ariel Durant. 1968. *The Lessons of History.* New York: Simon & Schuster.

Ellis, Carolyn, and Michael G. Flaherty. 1992. "An Agenda for the Interpretation of Lived Experience." *Investigating Subjectivity: Research on Lived Experience*, edited by Carolyn Ellis and Michael G. Flaherty. Newbury Park: Sage, pp. 1–13.

Ellul, Jacques. 1980 [1977]. *The Technological System.* New York: Continuum.

Eriksen, Thomas Hylland. 2001. *Tyranny of the Moment: Fast and Slow Time in the Information Age.* London: Pluto.

Ewen, Stuart. 1976. *Captains of Consciousness: Advertising and the Social Roots of the Consumer Culture.* New York: McGraw-Hill.

Fiddick, Laurence. 2004. "Natural Law and Natural Selection: Deontic Reasoning as Part of Evolved Human Nature." *Evolutionary Psychology, Public Policy and Personal Decisions*, edited by Charles Crawford and Catherine Salmon. Mahwah: Lawrence Erlbaum, pp. 169–196.

Fischer, Frank. 1990. *Technocracy and the Politics of Expertise.* Newbury Park: Sage.

Fischer, Frank. 2009. *Democracy & Expertise: Reorienting Policy Inquiry.* New York: Oxford University Press.

Ford, Dennis. 2007. *The Search for Meaning: A Short History.* Berkeley: University of California Press.

Foskett, D. J. (Douglas John). 1984. *Pathways for Communication: Books and Libraries in the Information Age.* London: Bingley.

Fox, Daniel M. 1967. *The Discovery of Abundance: Simon N. Patten and the Transformation of Social Theory.* Ithaca: Cornell University Press.

Frank, Robert H. 2008. "On the Evolution of Moral Sentiments." *Foundations of Evolutionary Psychology*, edited by Charles Crawford and Dennis Krebs. New York: Lawrence Erlbaum, pp. 371–379.

Fraser, J. T. (Julius Thomas). 1999. *Time, Conflict, and Human Values.* Urbana: University of Illinois Press.

Freud, Sigmund. 1994 [1930]. *Civilization and Its Discontents.* New York: Dover.

Friedel, Robert. 2007. *A Culture of Improvement. Technology and the Western Millennium.* Cambridge: MIT Press.

Frow, John. 1997. *Time and Commodity Culture: Essays in Cultural Theory and Postmodernity.* Oxford: Clarendon Press.

Fulcher, James. 2004. *Capitalism: A Very Short Introduction.* Oxford: Oxford University Press.

Gagnon, John H. 1992. "The Self, Its Voices, and Their Discord." *Investigating Subjectivity: Research on Lived Experience*, edited by Carolyn Ellis and Michael G. Flaherty. Newbury Park: Sage, pp. 221–243.

Galantiere, Lewis. 1950. "America Today: A Freehand Sketch." *Foreign Affairs* 28 (July): 525–547

Galbraith, John Kenneth. 1978. *The New Industrial State.* Third Edition. Boston: Houghton Mifflin.

Gärdenfors, Peter. 2003. *How Homo Became Sapiens: On the Evolution of Thinking.* Oxford: Oxford University Press.

Gaukroger, Stephen. 2012. *Objectivity: A Very Short Introduction.* Oxford: Oxford University Press.

Gazzaniga, Michael S. 2005. *The Ethical Brain.* New York: Dana Press.

Gazzaniga, Michael S. 2008. *Human: The Science Behind What Makes Us Unique.* New York: Ecco.

Gazzaniga, Michael S. 2011. *Who's in Charge? Free Will and the Science of the Brain.* New York: HarperCollins.

Geertz, Clifford. 1973. *The Interpretation of*

Cultures: Selected Essays. New York: Basic Books.

Gelernter, David. 2016. *The Tides of Mind: Uncovering the Spectrum of Consciousness.* New York: Norton.

Gilboy, Elizabeth Waterman. 1967 [1932]. "Demand as a Factor in the Industrial Revolution." *The Causes of the Industrial Revolution in England,* edited by R. M. Hartwell. London: Methuen, pp. 121–138.

Gintis, Herbert, and Samuel Bowles, Robert Boyd, Ernst Fehr. 2008. "Gene-Culture Coevolution and the Emergence of Altruistic Behavior in Humans." *Foundations of Evolutionary Psychology,* edited by Charles Crawford and Dennis Krebs. New York: Lawrence Erlbaum, pp. 313–329.

Glass, Bentley. 1985. *Progress or Catastrophe. The Nature of Biological Science and Its Impact on Human Society.* New York: Praeger.

Goleman, Daniel. 2006. *Social Intelligence: The New Science of Human Relationships.* New York: Bantam Books.

Goodenough, Oliver R. 2001. "Law and the Biology of Commitment." *Evolution and the Capacity for Commitment,* edited by Randolph M. Nesse. New York: Russell Sage Foundation, pp. 262–291.

Graff, Gerald. 1979. *Literature Against Itself: Literary Ideas in Modern Society.* Chicago: University of Chicago Press.

Habermas, Jürgen. 1971. *Knowledge and Human Interests.* Boston: Beacon Press.

Hammerstein, Peter. 2002. "Understanding Cooperation: An Interdisciplinary Challenge." *Genetic and Cultural Evolution of Cooperation,* edited by Peter Hammerstein. Cambridge: MIT Press, pp. 1–7.

Hammerstein, Peter, and Jeffrey R. Stevens. 2012. "Six Reasons for Invoking Evolution in Decision Theory." *Evolution and the Mechanisms of Decision Making,* edited by Peter Hammerstein and Jeffery R. Stevens. Cambridge: MIT Press, pp. 1–17.

Hammerstein, Peter, and Robert Boyd. 2012. "Learning, Cognitive Limitations, and the Modeling of Social Behavior." *Evolution and the Mechanisms of Decision Making,* edited by Peter Hammerstein and Jeffery R. Stevens. Cambridge: MIT Press, pp. 319–343.

Hartwell, R. M. 1967. "Introduction." *The Causes of the Industrial Revolution in England,* edited by R. M. Hartwell, London: Methuen, pp. 1–30.

Hayek, Friedrich A. von. 1979. *Law, Legislation and Liberty. Volume 3: The Political Order of a Free People.* Chicago: University of Chicago Press.

Heilbroner, Robert L. 1962. *The Making of Economic Society.* Englewood Cliffs: Prentice-Hall.

Heilbroner, Robert L. 1972 [1967]. "Do Machines Make History?" *Technology and Culture. An Anthology,* edited by Melvin Kranzberg and William H. Davenport. New York: Schocken Books, pp. 28–40. First published in the journal *Technology and Culture* (8 July 1967): 335–345.

Henrich, Joseph, and Robert Boyd, Samuel Bowles, Colin F. Camerer, Ernst Fehr, Herbert Gintis. 2004. "Overview and Synthesis." *Foundations of Human Sociality: Economic Experiments and Ethnographic Evidence from Fifteen Small-Scale Societies,* edited by Joseph Henrich, et al. New York: Oxford University Press, pp. 8–54.

Henrich, Joseph, et al. 2002. "The Cultural and Genetic Evolution of Human Cooperation." *Genetic and Cultural Evolution of Cooperation,* edited by Peter Hammerstein. Cambridge: MIT Press, pp. 445–468.

Hermans, Hubert J. M. 2013. "A Multivoiced and Dialogical Self and the Challenge of Social Power in a Globalizing World." *Subjectivity in the Twenty-First Century: Psychological, Sociological, and Political Perspectives,* edited by Romin W. Tafarodi. New York: Cambridge University Press, pp. 41–65.

Hess, David J. 2007. *Alternative Pathways in Science and Industry: Activism, Innovation,* and *the Environment in an Era of Globalization.* Cambridge: MIT Press.

Hicks, Donna. 2011. *Dignity: The Essential Role It Plays in Resolving Conflict.* New Haven: Yale University Press.

Hidaka, Brandon H. 2012. "Depression as a Disease of Modernity." *Journal of Affective Disorders* 140 (no. 3 November): 205–214.

Hochschild, Arlie Russell. 2003. *The Commercialization of Intimate Life: Notes from Home and Work.* Berkeley: University of California Press.

Høgh-Olesen, Henrik. 2010. "Homo Sapiens-Home Socious: A Comparative Analysis of Human Mind and Kind." *Human Morality & Sociality: Evolutionary & Comparative Perspectives,* edited by Henrik Høgh-Olesen. Hound Mills: Palgrave/Macmillan, pp. 235–271.

Holcomb, Harmon. 2004. "Darwin and Evolutionary Moral Psychology." *Evolutionary Psychology, Public Policy and Personal Decisions*, edited by Charles Crawford and Catherine Salmon. Mahwah: Lawrence Erlbaum, pp. 73–98.

Hook, Sidney. 1933. "Materialism." *Encyclopaedia of the Social Sciences*, edited by E. R. A. Seligman and Alvin Johnson. New York: Macmillan, vol. 10, pp. 209–220.

Horkheimer, Max. 1947. *Eclipse of Reason*. New York: Oxford University Press.

Hughes, Thomas P. 1994. "Technological Momentum." *Does Technology Drive History? The Dilemma of Technological Determinism*, edited by Merritt Roe Smith and Leo Marx. Cambridge: MIT Press, pp. 101–113.

Hunt, Lynn Avery. 2007. *Inventing Human Rights: A History*. New York: Norton.

Hurford, James R. 2007. *The Origins of Meaning*. Oxford: Oxford University Press.

Jacob, Margaret C. 1997. *Scientific Culture and the Making of the Industrial West*. New York: Oxford University Press.

Jacob, Margaret C., and Larry Stewart. 2004. *Practical Matter: Newton's Science in the Service of Industry and Empire, 1687–1851*. Cambridge: Harvard University Press.

James, William. 1950 [1907]. "What Pragmatism Means." *Pragmatism and American Culture*, edited by Gail Kennedy. Boston: Heath, pp. 1–23.

Janicki, Maria G. 2004. *Evolutionary Psychology, Public Policy and Personal Decisions*, edited by Charles Crawford and Catherine Salmon. Mahwah: Lawrence Erlbaum, pp.51–72.

Jenson, Keith. 2012. "Who Cares? Other-Regarding Concerns—Decisions with Feeling." *Evolution and the Mechanisms of Decision Making*, edited by Peter Hammerstein and Jeffery R. Stevens. Cambridge: MIT Press, pp. 299–317.

Johnson, Allen W., and Timothy Earle. 2000. *The Evolution of Human Societies: From Foraging Group to Agrarian State*. Second Edition. Stanford: Stanford University Press.

Johnson-Laird, Philip N. 2006. *How We Reason*. New York: Oxford University Press.

Joyce, Patrick. 1987. "The Historical Meanings of Work: An Introduction." *The Historical Meanings of Work*, edited by Patrick Joyce. Cambridge: Cambridge University Press, pp. 1–30.

Joyce, Richard. 2006. *The Evolution of Morality*. Cambridge: MIT Press.

Kasser, Tim. (2002). *The High Price of Materialism*. Cambridge: MIT Press.

Katz, Jack. 2012. "Emotion's Crucible." *Emotions Matter: A Relational Approach to Emotions*, edited by Dale Spencer, Kevin Walby, and Alan Hunt. Toronto: University of Toronto Press, pp. 15–39.

Kenrick, Douglas T., and Vladas Griskevicius. 2013. *The Rational Animal: How Evolution Made Us Smarter than We Think*. New York: Basic Books.

Kirby, Simon. 2007. "The Evolution of Language." *Oxford Handbook of Evolutionary Psychology*, edited by R. I. M. Dunbar and Louise Barrett. Oxford: Oxford University Press, pp. 669–681.

Kirkpatrick, Lee A. 2010. "From Genes to Memes: Psychology at the Nexus." *Evolution, Culture, and the Human Mind*, edited by Mark Schaller, Ara Norenzayan, Steven J. Heine, Toshio Yamagishi, Tatsuya Kameda. New York: Psychology Press, pp. 71–82.

Klapp, Orrin E. 1986. *Overload and Boredom: Essays on the Quality of Life in the Information Society*. New York: Greenwood Press.

Kline, Stephen Jay. 1995. *Conceptual Foundations for Multidisciplinary Thinking*. Stanford: Stanford University Press.

Kluckhohn, Clyde. 1961. "The Study of Values." *Values in America*, edited by Donald N. Barrett. Notre Dame: University of Notre Dame Press, pp. 17–45.

Knappett, Carl. 2005. *Thinking through Material Culture. An Interdisciplinary Perspective*. Philadelphia: University of Pennsylvania Press.

Knight, Chris, Robin Dunbar, and Camilla Power. 1999. "An Evolutionary Approach to Human Culture." *The Evolution of Culture: An Interdisciplinary View*, edited by Robin Dunbar, Chris Knight, and Camilla Power. New Brunswick: Rutgers University Press, pp. 1–14.

Konner, Melvin. 1991. "Human Nature and Culture: Biology and the Residue of Uniqueness." *The Boundaries of Humanity: Humans, Animals, Machines*, edited by James J. Sheehan and Morton Sosna.

Berkley: University of California Press, pp. 103–124.

Krebs, Dennis L. 2011. *The Origins of Morality: An Evolutionary Account.* New York: Oxford University Press.

Kropotkin, Petr. 1955 [1890–1896]. *Mutual Aid: A Factor of Evolution.* Boston: Extending Horizons Books. (first published serially)

Kuper, Adam. 1994. *The Chosen Primate: Human Nature and Cultural Diversity.* Cambridge: Harvard University Press.

Kupperman, Joel J. 1983. *The Foundations of Morality.* London: George Allen & Unwin.

Lash, Scott, and Celia Lury. 2007. *Global Culture Industry: The Mediation of Things.* Cambridge: Polity Press.

Leiss, William. 1976. *The Limits to Satisfaction: An Essay on the Problem of Needs and Commodities.* Toronto: University of Toronto Press.

Leiss, William, Stephen Kline, Sut Jhally, and Jacqueline Botterill. 2005. *Social Comunication in Advertising: Consumption in the Mediated Marketplace.* Third Edition. New York: Routledge.

Lerner, Max. 1968. "Big Technology and Neutral Technicians." *The American Culture. Approaches to the Study of the United States,* edited by Hennig Cohen. Boston: Houghton Mifflin, pp. 180–190.

Leventhal, Howard, and Klaus Scherer. 1987. "The Relationship of Emotion to Cognition: A Functional Approach to a Semantic Controversy." *Cognition and Emotion* 1: 3–28.

Lieberman, Matthew D. 2013. *Social: Why Our Brains are Wired to Connect.* New York: Crown Publishers.

Lieberman, Philip. 2013. *The Unpredictable Species: What Makes Humans Unique.* Princeton: Princeton University Press.

Lilley, Samuel. 1966. *Men, Machines and History: The Story of Tools and Machines in Relation to Social Progress.* Revised Edition. New York: International Publishers.

Lipovetsky, Gilles. 2005. *Hypermodern Times.* Cambridge: Polity Press.

Lury, Celia. 2011. *Consumer Culture.* 2d edition. New Brunswick: Rutgers University Press.

MacIver, Robert M. 1937. *Society: A Textbook of Sociology.* New York: Farrar & Rinehart.

Malinowski, Bronislaw. 1931. "Culture." *Encyclopedia of the Social Sciences,* edited by Edwin R. A. Seligman and Alvin Johnson. New York: Macmillan, vol. 4, pp. 621–646.

Margolis, Howard. 1982. *Selfishness, Altruism, and Rationality: A Theory of Social Choice.* New York: Cambridge University Press.

Marshall, Edward. M. 1995. *Transforming the Way We Work. The Power of the Collaborative Workplace.* New York: American Management Association.

Maryanski, Alexandra, and Jonathan H. Turner. 1992. *The Social Cage: Human Nature and the Evolution of Society.* Stanford: Stanford University Press.

Mazlish, Bruce. 2009. *The Idea of Humanity in a Global Era.* New York: Palgrave Macmillan.

Mead, G. H. (George Herbert). 1934. *Mind, Self & Society: From the Standpoint of a Social Behaviorist.* Chicago: University of Chicago Press.

Mead, Walter Russell. 2007. *God and Gold: Britain, America, and the Making of the Modern World.* New York: Knopf.

Menand, Louis. 2010. *The Marketplace of Ideas.* New York: Norton.

Menzies, Heather. 2005. *No Time: Stress and the Crisis of Modern Life.* Vancouver: Douglas & McIntyre.

Merchant, Carolyn. 1980. *The Death of Nature. Women, Ecology, and the Scientific Revolution.* San Francisco: Harper & Row.

Mesoudi, Alex. 2011. *Cultural Evolution: How Darwinian Theory Can Explain Human Culture & Synthesize the Social Sciences.* Chicago: University of Chicago Press.

Midgley, Mary. 1978. *Beast and Man: The Roots of Human Nature.* Ithaca: Cornell University Press.

Miller, Daniel. 1987. *Material Culture and Mass Consumption.* London: Blackwell.

Miller, Seumas. 2010. *The Moral Foundations of Social Institutions: A Philosophical Study.* Cambridge: Cambridge University Press.

Mithen, Steven. 2007 [2005]. *Singing Neanderthals: The Origins of Music, Language, Mind, and Body.* Cambridge: Harvard University Press.

Mithen, Steven. 2000. "Mind, Brain and Material Culture: An Archeological Perspective." *Evolution and the Human Mind: Modularity, Language and Meta-Cognition,* edited by Peter Carruthers and Andrew Chamberlain. Cambridge: Cambridge University Press.

Mithen, Steven. 1990. *Thoughtful Foragers: A Study of Prehistoric Decision Making*. Cambridge: Cambridge University Press.

Mukerji, Chandra. 1983. *From Graven Images. Patterns of Modern Materialism*. New York: Columbia University Press.

Mumford, Lewis. 1934. *Technics and Civilization*. New York: Harcourt-Brace.

Mumford, Lewis. 1950 [1926]. "The Pragmatic Acquiescence." *Pragmatism and American Culture*. Edited by Gail Kennedy. Boston: Heath, pp. 36–49.

Mumford, Lewis. 1966. *The Myth of the Machine: Technics and Human Development*. New York: Harcourt, Brace & World.

Mumford, Lewis. 1972 [1963]. "Technics and the Nature of Man." *Technology and Culture: An Anthology*, edited by Melvin Kranzberg and William H. Davenport. New York: Schocken, pp. 200–215.

Nagel, Thomas. 1986. *The View from Nowhere*. New York: Oxford University Press.

Nef, John U. 1964. *The Conquest of the Material World*. Chicago: University of Chicago Press.

Nelkin, Dorothy. 1987. *Selling Science: How the Press Covers Science and Technology*. New York: Freeman.

Nelson, Richard R., and Sidney G. Winter. 1982. *An Evolutionary Theory of Economic Change*. Cambridge: Harvard University Press.

Nesse, Randolph M. 2001. "Natural Selection and the Capacity for Subjective Commitment." *Evolution and the Capacity for Commitment*, edited by Randolph M. Nesse. New York: Russell Sage Foundation, pp. 1–44.

Nesse, Randolph M. 2010. "Social Selection and the Origins of Culture." *Evolution, Culture, and the Human Mind*, edited by Mark Schaller, Ara Norenzayan, Steven J. Heine, Toshio Yamagishi, Tatsuya Kameda. New York: Psychology Press, pp. 137–150.

Nettle, Daniel. 2005. *Happiness: The Science behind Your Smile*. Oxford: Oxford University Press.

Nichols, Shaun. 2004. *Sentimental Rules: On the Natural Foundation of Moral Judgment*. Oxford: Oxford University Press.

Norenzayan, Ara. 2010. "Why We Believe: Religion as a Human Universal." *Human Morality & Sociality: Evolutionary & Comparative Perspectives*, edited by Henrik Høgh-Olesen. Hound Mills: Palgrave/Macmillan, pp. 58–71.

Norenzayan, Ara. 2013. *Big Gods: How Religion Transformed Cooperation and Conflict*. Princeton: Princeton University Press.

Nussbaum, Martha C. 1997. *Cultivating Humanity: A Classical Defense of Reform in Liberal Education*. Cambridge: Harvard University Press.

Olson, Mancur. 1965. *The Logic of Collective Action: Public Goods and the Theory of Groups*. Cambridge: Harvard University Press.

Osburn, Charles B. 2014. *The Western Devaluation of Knowledge*. Lanham: Rowman & Littlefield.

Papineau, David. 2000. "The Evolution of Knowledge." *Evolution and the Human Mind: Modularity, Language and Meta-Cognition*, edited by Peter Carruthers and Andrew Chamberlain. Cambridge: Cambridge University Press, pp. 170–206.

Parsons, Talcott. 1935. "Society." *Encyclopedia of the Social Sciences*, edited by Edwin R. A. Seligman and Alvin Johnson. New York: Macmillan, vol. 14, pp. 225–232.

Peccei, Aurelio. 1977. *The Human Quality*. Oxford: Pergamon Press.

Perkin, Harold. 1996. *The Third Revolution: Professional Elites in the Modern World*. London: Routledge.

Pilling, David. 2018. *The Growth Delusion: Wealth, Poverty, and the Well-Being of Nations*. New York: Crown Publishing.

Pinker, Steven. 2011. *The Better Angels of Our Nature: Why Violence Has Declined*. New York: Viking.

Pinker, Steven. 2013. *Language, Cognition, and Human Nature: Selected Articles*. New York: Oxford University Press.

Platt, Charles. 1998. "What's It Mean to be Human, Anyway?" *Composing Cyberspace: Identity, Community, and Knowledge in the Electronic Age*, edited by Richard Holeton. New York: McGraw-Hill.

Plotkin, Henry. 2007. "The Power of Culture." *Oxford Handbook of Evolutionary Psychology*, edited by R. I. M. Dunbar and Louise Barrett. Oxford: Oxford University Press, pp. 11–19.

Plumb, J. H. (John Harold). 1982. "The Acceptance of Modernity." *The Birth of a Consumer Society. The Commercialization* of *Eighteenth-Century England*, edited by Neil McKendrick, John Brewer and J. H. Plumb. London: Europa Publications, pp. 316–334.

Polanyi, Karl. 1944. *The Great Transformation*. New York: Rinehart.

Pool, Robert. 1997. *Beyond Engineering: How Society Shapes Technology*. New York: Oxford University Press.

Postman, Neil. 1992. *Technopoly: The Surrender of Culture to Technology*. New York: Vintage Books.

Postman, Neil. 1995. *The End of Education: Redefining the Value of School*. New York: Knopf.

Potter, David M. 1954. *People of Plenty: Economic Abundance and the American Character*. Chicago: University of Chicago Press.

Quinn, Warren. 1993. "Putting Rationality in Its Place." *Value, Welfare, and Morality*, edited by R. G. Fey and Christopher W. Morris. Cambridge: Cambridge University Press, pp. 26–50.

Rawls, John. 1957. "Justice as Fairness." *Journal of Philosophy* 54 (No. 22, October 24): 653–662.

Reich, Robert B. 2007. *Supercapitalism: The Transformation of Business, Democracy, and Everyday Life*. New York: Knopf.

Richardson, Frank C., and Robert L. Woolfolk. 2013. "Subjectivity and Strong Relationality." *Subjectivity in the Twenty-First Century: Psychological, Sociological, and Political Perspectives*, edited by Romin W. Tafarodi. New York: Cambridge University Press, pp. 11–40.

Richerson, Peter J., and Robert Boyd. 2001. "The Evolution of Subjective Commitment to Groups: A Tribal Instincts Hypothesis." *Evolution and the Capacity for Commitment*, edited by Randolph M. Nesse. New York: Russell Sage Foundation, pp. 186–220.

Richerson, Peter J., and Robert Boyd. 2005. *Not by Genes Alone: How Culture Transformed Human Evolution*. Chicago: University of Chicago Press.

Richerson, Peter J., Robert T. Boyd, and Joseph Henrich. 2002. *Genetic and Cultural Evolution of Cooperation*, edited by Peter Hammerstein. Cambridge: MIT Press, pp. 357–388.

Rojek, Chris. 2000. *Leisure and Culture*. New York.

Rovelli, Carlo. 2016 [2014]. *Seven Brief Lessons on Physics*. New York: Riverhead Books.

Rozin, Paul. 2010. "Towards a Cultural/Evolutionary Psychology: Cooperation and Complementarity." *Evolution, Culture, and the Human Mind*, edited by Mark Schaller, Ara Norenzayan, Steven J. Heine, Toshio Yamagishi, Tatsuya Kameda. New York: Psychology Press, pp. 9–22.

Ruse, Michael. 1997. "Philosophy and Paleoanthropology: Some Shared Interests?" *Conceptual Issues in Modern Human Origins Research*, edited by G. A. Clark and C. M. Willermet. New York: Aldine de Gruyter, pp. 423–435.

Ruse, Michael. 2001. Morality and Commitment." *Evolution and the Capacity for Commitment*, edited by Randolph M. Nesse. New York: Russell Sage Foundation, pp. 221–236.

Ruse, Michael. 2012. *The Philosophy of Human Evolution*. New York: Cambridge University Press.

Ruse, Michael, and Edward O. Wilson. 2009 [1986]. "Moral Philosophy as Applied Science." *Philosophy after Darwin: Classic and Contemporary Readings*, edited by Michael Ruse. Princeton: Princeton University Press, pp. 365–379.

Sassatelli, Roberta. 2006. "Virtue, Responsibility and Consumer Choice: Framing Critical Consumerism." *Consuming Cultures, Global Perspectives: Historical Trajectories, Transnational Exchanges*, edited by John Brewer and Frank Trentmann. Oxford: Berg, pp. 219–250.

Schor, Juliet B. 1998. *The Overspent American. Upscaling, Downshifting, and the New Consumer*. New York: Basic Books.

Schwartz, Barry. 1986. *The Battle for Human Nature: Science, Morality and Modern Life*. New York: Norton.

Schwartz, Jeffrey M. and Sharon Begley. 2002. *The Mind and the Brain: Neuroplasticity and the Power of Mental Force*. New York: HarperCollins.

Searle, John R. 2010. *Making the Social World: The Structure of Human Civilization*. New York: Oxford University Press.

Sennett, Richard. 2006. *The Culture of the New Capitalism*. New Haven: Yale University Press.

Shammas, Carole. 1990. *The Pre-industrial Consumer in England and America*. Oxford: Clarendon Press.

Sharot, Tali. 2011. *The Optimism Bias*. New

York: Pantheon. (Tali summarizes the book in an article bearing the same title in *Time* June 6, 2011, pp. 41–46).

Shils, Edward. 1981. *Tradition*. Chicago: University of Chicago Press.

Simmel, Georg. 2004 [1907]. *The Philosophy of Money*. Third Enlarged Edition. London: Routledge.

Sklair, Leslie. 1991. *Sociology of the Global System*. Baltimore: Johns Hopkins University Press.

Skyrms, Brian. 2014. *Evolution of the Social Contract*, 2nd edition. New York: Cambridge University Press.

Smit, Harry. 2014. *The Social Evolution of Human Nature: From Biology to Language*. Cambridge: Cambridge University Press.

Smith, Alan G. R. 1972. *Science and Society in the Sixteenth and Seventeenth Centuries*. London: Thames and Hudson.

Smith, Roger. 2007. *Being Human: Historical Knowledge and the Creation of Human Nature*. New York: Columbia University Press.

Sober, Elliott, and David Sloan Wilson. 1998. *Unto Others: The Evolution and Psychology of Unselfish Behavior*. Cambridge: Harvard University Press.

Solomon, Ty. 2015. *The Politics of Subjectivity in American Foreign Policy Discourses*. Ann Arbor.

Soros, George. 2000. *Open Society: Reforming Global Capitalism*. London: Little, Brown.

Spelke, Elizabeth S. and Katherine D. Kinzler. 2007. "Core Knowledge." *Developmental Science* 10 (No. 1): pp. 89–96.

Spengler, Joseph J. 1961. "Theory, Ideology, Non-Economic Values, and Politico-Economic Development." *Tradition, Values, and Socio-Economic Development*, edited by Ralph Braibanti and Joseph J. Spengler. Durham: Duke University Press, pp. 3–56

Stamp, Josiah. 1937. *The Science of Social Adjustment*. London: Macmillan.

Stanley, Manfred. 1978. *The Technological Conscience: Survival and Dignity in an Age of Expertise*. New York: Free Press.

Stanovich, Keith E. 2010. *Decision Making and Rationality in the Modern World*. New York: Oxford University Press.

Suddendorf, Thomas. 1999. "The Rise of the Metamind." *The Descent of Mind: Psychological Perspectives on Hominid Evolution*, edited by Michael C. Corballis and Stephen E. G. Lea. Oxford: Oxford University Press, pp. 218–260.

Tattersall, Ian. 1998. *Becoming Human: Evolution and Human Uniqueness*. New York: Harcourt Brace.

Taylor, Charles. 1985. *Philosophy and the Human Sciences*. Cambridge: Cambridge University Press.

Taylor, Jacqueline. 2011. "Moral Sentiment and the Sources of Moral Identity." *Morality and the Emotions*, edited by Carla Bagnoli. Oxford: Oxford University Press, pp. 257–274.

Teilhard de Chardin, Pierre. 1959 [1955]. *The Phenomenon of Man*. New York: Harper & Row.

Thagard, Paul. 2010. *The Brain and the Meaning of Life*. Princeton: Princeton University Press.

Thagard, Paul, and Tracy Finn. 2011. "Conscience: What Is Moral Intuition?" *Morality and the Emotions*, edited by Carla Bagnoli. Oxford: Oxford University Press, pp. 150–169

Thirsk, Joan. 1978. *Economic Policy and Projects. The Development of a Consumer Society in Early Modern England*. Oxford: Clarendon Press.

Thompson, Edward P. 1963. *The Making of the English Working Class*. New York: Random House.

Thompson, John B. 1984. *Studies in the Theory of Ideology*. Cambridge: Polity Press.

Thompson, Michael. 1979. *Rubbish Theory: The Creation and Destruction of Value*. Oxford: Oxford University Press.

Tiberius, Valerie. 2008. *The Reflective Life: Living Wisely with our Limits*. Oxford: Oxford University Press.

Tomasello, Michael. 1999. *The Cultural Origins of Human Cognition*. Cambridge: Harvard University Press.

Tomasello, Michael. 2008. *Origins of Human Communication*. Cambridge: MIT Press.

Tomasello, Michael. 2009. *Why We Cooperate*. Cambridge: MIT Press.

Tomasello, Michael, and Hannes Rakoczy. 2003. "What Makes Human Cognition Unique? From Individual to Shared to Collective Intentionality." *Mind & Language* 18 (No. 2, April): 121–147.

Tooby, John, Leda Cosmides, and H. Clark Barrett. 2005. "Resolving the Debate on Innate Ideas: Learnability Constraints and the Evolved Interpenetration of Motivational and Conceptual Functions." *The

Innate Mind: Structure and Contents, edited by Peter Carruthers, Stephen Laurence, and Stephen Stich. New York: Oxford University Press, pp. 305–337.

Torey, Zoltan. 2014. *The Conscious Mind*. Cambridge: MIT Press.

Trentmann, Frank. 2006. "Knowing Consumers—Histories, Identities, Practices: An Introduction." *The Making of the Consumer: Knowledge, Power and Identity in the Modern World*. Oxford: Berg, pp. 1–30.

Turkle, Sherry. 2011. *Alone Together: Why We Expect More from Technology and Less from Each Other*. New York: Basic Books.

Turner, Jonathan H. 1997. *The Institutional Order: Economy, Kinship, Religion, Polity, Law, and Education in Evolutionary and Comparative Perspective*. New York: Peason Longman.

Vanderburg, Willem H. 2005. *Living in the Labyrinth of Technology*. Buffalo: University of Toronto Press.

Veblen, Thorstein. 1914. *The Instinct of Workmanship, and the State of the Industrial Arts*. New York: Macmillan.

Vigotsky, Lev Semenovich. 1962. *Thought and Language*. Cambridge: MIT Press.

Wallerstein, Immanuel. 2004. *The Uncertainties of Knowledge*. Philadelphia: Temple University Press.

Weber, Max. 1930. *The Protestant Ethic and the Spirit of Capitalism*. London: Allen & Unwin.

Weinert, Matthew S. 2015. *Making Human: World Order and the Global Governance of Human Dignity*. Ann Arbor: University of Michigan Press.

White, Leslie. 2008. *Modern Capitalist Culture*, edited by Burton J. Brown, Benjamin Urish and Robert L. Carneiro. Walnut Creek: Left Coast Press.

White, Lynn, Jr. 1968. *Machina Ex Deo: Essays in the Dynamism of Western Culture*. Cambridge: MIT Press.

Whiten, Andrew. 1999. "The Evolution of Deep Social Mind in Humans." *The Descent of Mind: Psychological Perspectives on Hominid Evolution*, edited by Michael C. Corballis and Stephen E. G. Lea. Oxford: Oxford University Press, pp. 173–193.

Williams, Bernard. 1991. "Prologue: Making Sense of Humanity." *The Boundaries of Humanity: Humans, Animals, Machines*, edited by James J. Sheehan and Morton Sosna. Berkley: University of California Press, pp. 13–23.

Williams, Raymond. 2009 [1980]. "Advertising: The Magic System." *The Advertising and Consumer Culture Reader*, edited by Joseph Turow and Matthew P. McAllister. London: Routledge, pp. 13–24.

Williams, Robin M., Jr. 1979. "Change and Stability in Values and Value Systems: A Sociological Perspective." *Understanding Human Values, Individual and Societal*, edited by Milton Rokeach. New York: Free Press, pp. 15–46.

Williams, Rosalind. 1990. *Notes on the Underground. An Essay on Technology, Society, and the Imagination*. Cambridge: MIT Press.

Williams, Rosalind. 2002. *Retooling: A Historian Confronts Technological Change*. Cambridge: MIT Press.

Wilson, David Sloan. 2003. *Darwin's Cathedral: Evolution. Religion. And the Nature of Society*. New York: Oxford University Press.

Wilson, David Sloan. 2007. "The Role of Group Selection in Human Psychological Evolution." *The Evolution of Mind: Fundamental Questions and Controversies*, edited by Steven W. Gangestad and Jeffry A. Simpson. New York: Guilford Press, pp. 213–220.

Wilson, Edward O. 1975. *Sociobiology: The New Synthesis*. Cambridge: Harvard University Press.

Wilson, James Q. 1993. *Moral Sense*. New York: Free Press.

Winner, Langdon. 1986. *The Whale and the Reactor: A Search for Limits in the Age of High Technology*. Chicago: University of Chicago Press.

Wood, Ellen Meiksins. 2003. *Empire of Capital*. London: Verso.

Wyman, Emily, and Michael Tomasello. 2007. *Oxford Handbook of Evolutionary Psychology*, edited by R. I. M. Dunbar and Louise Barrett. Oxford: Oxford University Press, pp. 227–236.

Young, H. Peyton. 2002. "The Power of Norms." *Genetic and Cultural Evolution of Cooperation*, edited by Peter Hammerstein. Cambridge: MIT Press, pp. 389–399.

Zukin, Sharon. 2004. *Point of Purchase. How Shopping Changed American Culture*. New York: Routledge.

Index

abstract thought 52, 129
abundance and scarcity 52, 89, 182
Adams, E.M. 51, 59, 112, 183
adaptation 185*ch*1*n*4, 205*ch*8*n*2; social goals 196*ch*5*n*9
Adas, Michael 58, 137, 138
Addison, Joseph 193*ch*4*n*2
advertising 97–98, 195*ch*4*n*11
aggression 208*ch*8*n*13, 209*ch*9*n*4
agriculture emerges 207*ch*8*n*11
Alford, Robert R. 60, 104, 191*ch*3*n*6
altruism 127–128, 164, 197*ch*5*n*11, 202*ch*6*n*16, 206*ch*8*n*7, 206*ch*8*n*7; *see also* morality
altruistic punishment 208*ch*8*n*15
Archer, Margaret S. 37, 38, 39, 189*ch*2*n*13, 197*ch*5*n*13
Arendt, Hannah 80
arts 205*ch*8*n*2
arts and homeostatic refinement 205*ch*8*n*2
artworks 199*ch*6*n*2
Atran, Scott 115, 169
Ayres, C.E. 74

Bagnoli, Carla 112, 197*ch*5*n*11
balance *see* homeostasis
Barber, Bernard 194*ch*4*n*8
Barfield, Owen 28, 180
Barilan, Yechiel Michael 22
Barnes, Barry 209*ch*9*n*6
Baron-Cohen, Simon 190*ch*2*n*14
Barrett, H. Clark 7, 8, 26, 85, 119, 134, 144, 162, 163, 179, 190*ch*2*n*14, 194*ch*4*n*10, 207*ch*8*n*10
Barrett, Louise 7, 8, 9, 18, 119, 136, 172, 179, 192*ch*3*n*10
Basalla, George 99
Bateson, Gregory 33, 162, 191*ch*3*n*3
Batson C. Daniel 164, 167, 197*ch*5*n*11, 204*ch*7*n*6, 206*ch*8*n*7
Baudrillard, Jean 130
Bauman, Zygmunt 195*ch*5*n*3, 201*ch*6*n*10
Baumeister, Roy F. 29, 110
Bayle, Pierre 201*ch*6*n*9
Becker, Carl L. 48
Begley, Sharon 26, 150

belief formation 194*ch*4*n*7
Bell, Daniel 19, 31, 48, 50, 56, 79, 88, 97, 191*ch*3*n*4, 198*ch*5*n*17, 198*ch*5*n*18
Berger, Peter L. 30, 44, 45, 185*ch*1*n*2, 188*ch*2*n*6, 188*ch*2*n*8
Berle, Adolf A. 132
Berman, Marshall 54
bias 30
biological and cultural evolution 187*ch*2*n*4
Bjorkland, David F. 128, 129
Black, Jeremy 7, 43, 45, 50, 55, 56, 203*ch*7*n*1
Blum, Lawrence 113, 121
Boehm, Christopher 14, 103, 117, 121, 122, 123, 124, 127, 163, 201*ch*6*n*12
Bogucki, Peter I. 118
Boivin, Nicole 134
Bok, Sissela 159
Bontekoe, Ron 145, 186ch1*n*8
Boorstin, Daniel 142, 198*ch*5*n*18
Boulding, Kenneth E. 172
Bourdieu, Pierre 168
Bowles, Samuel 103, 202*ch*6*n*16, 208*ch*8*n*15
Boyd, Robert 11, 15, 16, 50, 57, 71, 94, 99, 102, 127, 160, 168, 185*ch*1*n*1, 185*ch*1*n*4, 202*ch*6*n*16, 206*ch*8*n*5, 207*ch*8*n*1, 208*ch*8*n*14, 208*ch*8*n*15
Boyer, Pascal 196*ch*5*n*5
Brady, Michael 35, 144, 197*ch*5*n*14
brain 26–29, 65, 171, 174, 181, 194*ch*4*n*9, 199*ch*6*n*1, 199*ch*6*n*4, 205*ch*8*n*1, 208*ch*8*n*17; and body 192*ch*3*n*10; and emotion 189*ch*2*n*9; rewiring 196*ch*5*n*6; *see also* mind
Brewer, Talbot 171
Bronowski, Jacob 23
Bulbulia, Joseph A. 200*ch*6*n*6
Burke, Kenneth 85
Burnham, James 56
Buss, David M. 7, 8, 95, 127
Butterfield, Herbert 70, 91

Campbell, Colin 149
Campbell, Donald T. 209*ch*9*n*1
Campbell's Law, anthropology 209*ch*9*n*1
capitalism 58–61, 76–79, 193*ch*4*n*5, 209*ch*9*n*5
Castells, Manuel 198*ch*5*n*19

Index

Chandler, Alfred D., Jr. 58
change 151, 209*ch9n*2; by choice 206*ch8n*5; *see also* cultural evolution; deception; free riders; judgment; morality
choice 22–23, 52, 53, 55, 57, 95, 102–103, 106, 130, 151, 165, 176–178, 194*ch4n*8, 195*ch4n*12, 197*ch5n*15, 201*ch6n*10, 206*ch8n*5, 208*ch8n*17, 209*ch9n*2, 209*ch9n*4, 210*ch9n*7; and context 106–108
circumventricular organs 206*ch8n*4
citizens' voice 55, 104, 132–133, 142, 148, 156, 178
civilization 188*ch2n*7, 194*ch4n*7, 208*ch8n*13
Clark, Gregory 137
Clark, Mary E. 13
coalitions 185*ch1n*4
cognition *see* mind
cognitive evolution 194*ch4n*9
cognitive fluidity 189*ch2n*11
cognitive inheritance cognitive science 192*ch3n*9
cognitive skills and neocortex volume 197*ch5n*16
Cold War 191*ch3n*8, 197*ch5n*12
collaboration *see* cooperation
collective benefit 206*ch8n*6
collective choice 206*ch8n*6
collectivism 206*ch8n*7
commerce and industry 42–44, 47–56, 81–82, 83–84, 139
commodification 189*ch2n*13
commodities 52, 54, 60, 115; *see also* materialism
common sense 182, 195*ch5n*3
commonweal 109, 163, 194*ch4n*10
communication, linguistic 196*ch5n*5; *see also* language
competition 49–50, 93, 195*ch4n*12, 209*ch9n*2
complex societies 207*ch8n*11
complex/tribal societies 208*ch8n*14
conflict resolution 209*ch9n*4
conformity 192*ch3n*12, 201*ch6n*12; *see also* culture
conscience 123–125; *see also* morality
conscience in evolution 201*ch6n*12
consciousness 28–29, 188*ch2n*5, 199*ch6n*1, 208*ch8n*17; *see also* mind
consumer power 192*ch3n*8, 195*ch4n*12; *see also* citizen's voice
consumer society 23, 100, 161, 186*ch1n*8
consumption 129; *see also* mass consumption; mass production; mass retailers
cooperation 15–18, 116–120, 144–145, 167–170, 194*ch4n*10, 207*ch8n*11, 208*ch8n*13, 209*ch9n*4; and survival 200*ch6n*8
Copernicus 139
Corballis, Michael C. 16
corporations *see* industry; Industrial Revolution
Cortada, James W. 58

Coser, Lewis 195*ch5n*2
Cosmides, Leda 26, 85, 163, 207*ch8n*10
courtesies 6, 19, 182
Crawford, Charles 202*ch6n*13
creativity 209*ch9n*2
cultural adaptation 187*ch2n*4
cultural and biological evolution 187*ch2n*2
cultural and economic capital 187*ch2n*1
cultural diversity 187*ch1n*10
cultural evolution 8–9, 42–44, 58, 94–97, 102–103, 185*ch1n*4, 187*ch2n*3, 206*ch8n*5
cultural traits 185*ch1n*4
culture and industry 83–89; *see also* consumer society; cultural evolution
culture of communication 198*ch5n*19

Daele, Wolfgang van den 32, 101
Damasio, Antonio 7, 32, 93, 101, 102, 103, 110, 119, 147, 158, 160, 163, 174, 182, 192*ch3n*11, 199*ch6n*2, 205*ch8n*2, 206*ch8n*4, 210*ch9n*8
Daniels, George H. 77
Darwin, Charles 15, 77, 102, 109, 129, 164, 187*ch2n*3, 192*ch3n*9, 193*ch4n*3, 194*ch4n*9, 200*ch6n*7
Dawkins, Richard 200*ch6n*7; *see also* selfish genes
deception 162; *see also* free riders decision *see* choice
decline in sociality 182–183, 191*ch3n*5
deontic rules *ch6n*11
DeSalle, Rob 33, 71, 80, 200*ch6n*6
Descartes, Rene 140, 192*ch4n*1
Dessalles, Jean-Louis 14
de Waal, Frans 45, 113, 116 144, 161, 175, 179, 202*ch6n*13
Dicke, Klaus 21
dignity and respect 6, 18–22, 120, 186*ch1n*7, 186*ch1n*8
Dilworth, Craig 58, 132, 146, 177, 202*ch6n*17, 209*ch9n*5
Distin, Kate 18
diversity of moral populations 15, 204*ch7n*5
diversity of population 173
Donnelly, Jack 22, 187*ch1n*10
Dunbar, Robin 103, 167, 169, 197*ch5n*16, 208*ch8n*12
Durant, Ariel 76
Durant, Will 76

Earle, Timothy 200*ch6n*8
economic decision theory 197*ch5n*15, 207*ch8n*8
economic growth 191*ch3n*7
economic man 160
Economic Man 209*ch9n*2
economy 51–55; and culture fused 86–87
education 205*ch7n*11, 209*ch9n*1; *see also* higher learning
efficiency 84; *see also* reason
Ellis, Carolyn 180
Ellul, Jacques 148

Index

emotion 199*ch*6*n*5; and feelings 113, 160, 168, 170, 189*ch*2*n*9, 208*ch*8*n*17, 210*ch*9*n*8; and morality 197*ch*5*n*1, 201*ch*6*n*11; and reason 205*ch*8*n*3, 209*ch*9*n*3
emotional control 188*ch*2*n*7
empathy 113, 189*ch*2*n*12, 204*ch*7*n*6, 206*ch*8*n*7
Encyclopedie 140
Encyclopoedia Britannica 140
Enlightenment, social environment 203*ch*7*n*2
epistemology 68–70, 72, 190*ch*3*n*1, 190*ch*3*n*2, 197*ch*5*n*14, 209*ch*9*n*6
Eriksen, Thomas Hylland 46
ethics 87; *see also* morality; reason
evolution and technology 72
evolution of language 202*ch*6*n*14
Ewen, Stuart 82, 156
experience 46, 83, 96, 169, 195*ch*4*n*10, 199*ch*6*n*1, 205*ch*7*n*11
expressions of thought 187*ch*2*n*4

fairness 162–163
feelings *see* emotion and feelings
Fehr, Ernst 202*ch*6*n*16
Fiddick, Laurence 147
Finn, Tracy 204*ch*7*n*9
Fischer, Frank 48, 78, 101, 106, 153, 171, 188*ch*2*n*7
fitness 194*ch*4*n*6, 195*ch*5*n*1; and altruism 202*ch*6*n*16
Flaherty, Michael G. 180
Ford, Dennis 89, 106, 157
Foskett, D.J. 95
Fox, Daniel M. 34, 85, 195*ch*4*n*11
Fraser, J.T. 12
free market 52, 191*ch*3*n*6, 199*ch*6*n*3
free riders and cheaters 167, 263, 208*ch*8*n*12
free will 199*ch*6*n*4
freedom/responsibility 111–112, 200*ch*6*n*8
Freud, Sigmund 125, 198*ch*5*n*17, 208*ch*8*n*13, 209*ch*9*n*4
Friedel, Robert 193*ch*4*n*3
Friedland, Roger 60, 104, 191*ch*3*n*6
friendship 54, 129, 201*ch*6*n*10
Frow, John 64
Fulcher, James 77
functionalist social theory 209*ch*9*n*6

Gagnon, John H. 38
Galantiere, Lewis 153
Galbraith, John Kenneth 42, 152, 196*ch*5*n*9
Galileo 139
Gardenfors, Peter 129, 130, 147, 298
Gaukroger, Stephen 30, 31, 35, 196*ch*5*n*4, 201*ch*6*n*9
Gazzaniga, Michael S. 7, 10, 40, 45, 59, 93, 97, 114, 119, 144, 162, 174, 179, 185*ch*1*n*3, 186*ch*1*n*6, 188*ch*2*n*5, 192*ch*3*n*12, 199*ch*6*n*4, 201*ch*6*n*11, 204*ch*7*n*7
Geertz, Clifford 23, 187*ch*1*n*11
Gelemter, David 34, 41, 175

genetic architecture 187*ch*2*n*4
genetic environment 185*ch*1*n*1, 187*ch*2*n*2
genetic inheritance 170, 185*ch*1*n*1, 187*ch*2*n*2, 195*ch*5*n*1
Gilboy, Elizabeth Waterman 43, 60
Gintis, Herbert 103, 202*ch*6*n*16, 208*ch*8*n*15
Glass, Bentley 1
globalization 52, 57, 59, 61, 86, 146, 191*ch*3*n*6, 198*ch*5*n*19, 207*ch*8*n*9
GNP (gross national product) 205*ch*8*n*1; golden rule prevalence 127
goals 87, 177, 179, 182, 193*ch*4*n*3, 196*ch*5*n*9
Goleman, Daniel 9, 11, 19, 26, 47, 122, 185*ch*1*n*1, 187*ch*2*n*2
Goodenough, Oliver R. 187*ch*1*n*10
gossip 14
Graff, Gerald 179
Griskevicius, Vladas 9, 59, 119
Grosses verstandiges Universal-Lexikon aller Wissenschaften und Kilnste 140
group level-functional organization 207*ch*8*n*8
group selection 208*ch*8*n*15
guilt 208*ch*8*n*16

Habermas, Jiirgen 74
habitus 168–169
Hammerstein, Peter 160, 162, 192*ch*3*n*12, 197*ch*5*n*15
happiness 125, 152, 205*ch*8*n*1
Hartwell, R.M. 59
Hayek, Friedrich von 49
hegemony *see* industrial hegemony health 47, 181
Heilbroner, Robert L. 74, 191*ch*3*n*5
Henrich, Joseph 57, 71, 168, 197*ch*5*n*12, 207*ch*8*n*11, 208*ch*8*n*14
Hermans, Hubert J.M. 27, 100, 207*ch*8*n*9
Hess, David J. 178, 198*ch*5*n*18, 202*ch*6*n*17
Hicks, Donna 19, 186*ch*1*n*7
Hidaka, Brandon 47, 129
higher learning 205*ch*7*n*11; *see also* education
Hochschild, Arlie Russell 59
Hogh-Olesen, Henrik 10, 113
Holcomb, Harmon 202*ch*6*n*15
homeostasis 108, 192*ch*3*n*11, 205*ch*8*n*2, 206*ch*8*n*4, 209*ch*9*n*6, 210*ch*9*n*8
Hook, Sidney 191*ch*3*n*7
Horkheimer, Max 98
human group size 197*ch*5*n*16
human mass and diversity 204*ch*7*n*5
human maturation 119, 128–129, 164–165, 180, 186*ch*6*n*6, 192*ch*3*n*12, 198*ch*5*n*17, 201*ch*6*n*11, 204*ch*7*n*6
human nature 192*ch*3*n*9
human predictability 40
human rights 18–22, 186*ch*1*n*9, 187*ch*1*n*10
human traits 125
humanity distanced from nature 174–176
Hume, David 194*ch*4*n*9
Hunt, Lynn Avery 80, 186*ch*1*n*9

Index

Hurford, James R. 10, 14, 15, 19, 37, 40, 95, 109, 118, 145, 146, 162, 170, 196*ch*5*n*6

ideas as commodities 195*ch*5*n*2
identity 109–111, 177, 183
ideology 53, 72–76, 209*ch*9*n*2
imagination 177, 198*ch*5*n*18, 205*ch*7*n*11
imitation 192*ch*3*n*12
individual/collective minds 180
industrial ethos 182, 187*ch*1*n*11
industrial hegemony 131–133
Industrial Revolution 59, 60
influence *see* industrial hegemony
information 46, 154, 196*ch*5*n*8, 197*ch*5*n*14; defined 191*ch*3*n*3; gathering 190*ch*2*n*14
intelligence 29
internet 198*ch*5*n*19
introspection 37–39, 188*ch*2*n*7
investor power 191*ch*3*n*8

Jacob, Margaret C. 36, 139, 140, 192*ch*4*n*1, 203*ch*7*n*2
James, William 182
Janicki, Maria G. 162
Jensen, Keith 35, 40, 101, 127
Johnson, Allen W. 200*ch*6*n*8
Johnson-Laird, Philip N. 7, 35, 59, 93, 125, 144, 162, 189*ch*2*n*9, 205*ch*8*n*3
Joyce, Patrick 141
Joyce, Richard 112, 122, 124, 199*ch*6*n*5, 201*ch*6*n*11, 202*ch*6*n*14, 208*ch*8*n*16
judgment 29–30, 107–108, 166, 181; suppression of 30–32; vs. standardization 196*ch*5*n*4; *see also* morality
justice 114, 162–163, 202*ch*6*n*13, 208*ch*8*n*13

Kasser, Tim 88, 152
Katz, Jack 66
Kenrick, Douglas T. 9, 59, 119
Kinzler, Katherine D. 147, 185*ch*1*n*4, 192*ch*3*n*9
Kirby, Simon 13, 95
Klapp, Orrin E. 196*ch*5*n*8
Kline, Stephen Jay 190*ch*3*n*2, 191*ch*3*n*7
Kluckhohn, Clyde 80
Knight, Chris 169
knowledge 22, 44–46, 48–51, 90, 108, 189*ch*2*n*10, 198*ch*5*n*18; and information 66, 191*ch*3*n*3; 198*ch*5*n*18; and language 185*ch*1*n*2; and learning 11, 13, 185*ch*1*n*2; and reality 185*ch*1*n*2; society 49; synthesis 198*ch*5*n*18
Konner, Melvin 8
Krebs, Dennis L. 28, 116, 117, 119, 122, 126, 144, 147, 195*ch*5*n*1, 203*ch*7*n*4, 204*ch*7*n*5, 206*ch*8*n*7, 209*ch*9*n*4
Kropotkin, Petr 77, 194*ch*4*n*6
Kuper, Adam 8, 18

language 12–14, 16, 26–27, 95–97, 186*ch*1*n*5, 188*ch*2*n*6, 189*ch*2*n*11, 199*ch*6*n*1; emergence 196*ch*5*n*6, 202*ch*6*n*14; and logic 188*ch*2*n*6

Lash, Scott 86
Leiss, William 54
Lerner, Max 151
Leventhal, Howard 209*ch*9*n*3
Lieberman, Matthew D. 7, 18, 45, 93, 103, 109, 144, 164, 205*ch*7*n*11
Lieberman, Philip 57, 94
lifestyle 63
Lilley, Samuel 137
Lipovetsky, Gilles 55, 83–84, 105
Locke, John 194*ch*4*n*9
Luckmann, Thomas 30, 44, 45, 185*ch*1*n*2, 188*ch*2*n*6, 188*ch*2*n*8
Lury, Celia 86, 111

machine model 193*ch*4*n*5
Maciver, Robert 72, 141, 158
Malinowsky, Bronislaw 128
Marshall, Edward M. 167
mass communication 96–97, 103
mass consumption 60–67, 139, 151–154; *see also* consumer society
mass media 193*ch*4*n*4
mass production 52, 61–67; *see also* industry
mass retailers 191*ch*3*n*8, 195*ch*4*n*12
materialism 81–83, 191*ch*3*n*7, 194*ch*4*n*9
Mazlish, Bruce 19
Mead, G.H. 110, 190*ch*2*n*14, 196*ch*5*n*7, 207*ch*8*n*9
Mead, Walter Russell 138
meaning 97–99, 178, 181, 196*ch*5*n*7, 196*ch*5*n*8, 197*ch*5*n*10, 205*ch*7*n*11
Means, Gardiner C. 132
means-end reasoning 194*ch*4*n*7
mechanical cognition 87, 136, 171
memory 177, 194*ch*4*n*9, 196*ch*5*n*5, 205*ch*8*n*2
Menand, Louis 42, 46
Menzies, Heather 107
Merchant, Carolyn 85, 193*ch*4*n*5, 197*ch*5*n*10
Mesoudi, Alex 187*ch*2*n*3, 207*ch*8*n*8
metarepresentation 169–170
Midgley, Mary 10, 111, 125, 166
Miller, Daniel 187*ch*2*n*1
Miller, Seamus 111, 199*ch*6*n*3
mind 25–28, 33, 87–88, 180–181, 185*ch*1*n*1, 186*ch*1*n*5, 194*ch*4*n*10, 208*ch*8*n*16, 210*ch*9*n*8; and body 206*ch*8*n*4; and culture 67; and decision 185*ch*1*n*3; and evolution 180–181; *see also* metarepresentation; objectivity; subjectivity
mindreading *see* Theory of Mind
Mithen, Steven 17, 174, 189*ch*2*n*11, 194*ch*4*n*9, 209*ch*9*n*2
modernity 54, 57, 87, 110, 189*ch*2*n*13, 198*ch*5*n*11
money 49, 51, 77, 81, 105–106, 132, 151, 191*ch*3*n*7, 195*ch*4*n*12
moral ideals 202*ch*6*n*15
moral obligations 202*ch*6*n*15
morality 87, 115, 120, 161–165, 204*ch*7*n*5,

209*ch*9*n*4; biological function 195*ch*5*n*1; evolution 200*ch*6*n*7; history 201*ch*6*n*9; *see also* motivation
motivation 83, 110, 112–133, 152, 199*ch*6*n*2, 199*ch*6*n*5, 200*ch*6*n*5, 204*ch*7*n*5, 206*ch*8*n*4, 210*ch*9*n*8; *see also* morality
Mukerji, Chandra 73
multicellular organisms 194*ch*4*n*10
Mumford, Lewis 62, 197*ch*5*n*10

Nagel, Thomas 179, 181
natural science 69–70; epistemology 72, 78, 90–91, 176, 197*ch*5*n*10
natural selection 126, 173, 194*ch*4*n*10, 195*ch*4*n*10, 207*ch*8*n*8, 208*ch*8*n*15
nature distanced from humanity 73, 88, 174–176, 180, 197*ch*5*n*10
nature/nurture 185*ch*1*n*1
Nef, John 36
Nelkin, Dorothy 91, 103, 193*ch*4*n*4
nervous system 185*ch*1*n*1, 192*ch*3*n*10; *see also* brain
Nesse, Randolph M. 118, 122, 162, 195*ch*5*n*1, 206*ch*8*n*5
Nettle, Daniel 205*ch*8*n*1
network society 198*ch*5*n*19
new ideas 33, 98
Newton, Isaac 192*ch*4*n*1
Nichols, Shaun 120
Norenzayan, Ara 114, 124
norms 42, 109, 110, 116, 202*ch*6*n*15, 210*ch*9*n*7
Nussbaum, Margaret C. 198*ch*5*n*18, 205*ch*7*n*11

objective knowledge 6–7
objective/subjective knowledge 154
objectivity 30–32, 35–36, 179; *see also* mind
Olson, Mancur 206*ch*8*n*6
organic stability 6, 192*ch*3*n*11; *see also* homeostasis
Osburn, Charles B. 93, 94
outcomes of decision and choice 179

Papineau, David 194*ch*4*n*7
Parsons, Talcott 86
Peccei, Aurelio 76, 151
Pellegrini, Anthony D. 128, 129
Perkin, Harold 131
perspective 178–182
Pilling, David 205*ch*8*n*1
Pinker, Steven 8, 185*ch*1*n*1, 189*ch*2*n*12
planning, personal 44
pleasure/desire 205*ch*8*n*1
Pleistocene 71, 207*ch*8*n*11
Plumb, J.H. 70
Polanyi, Karl 78
political conflict 191*ch*3*n*6
Pool, Robert 75
population diversity 15–16, 184
Postman, Neil 71, 166, 198*ch*5*n*18
Potter, David 166

Power, Camila 169
prehistoric foragers 209*ch*9*n*2
presentism 105–106,
principlism 206*ch*8*n*7
professionalization 190*ch*3*n*2
progress 6, 77, 180, 182
public knowledge of science 192*ch*4*n*1
public opinion *see* citizens' voice

quality of life 136–138, 155, 156, 178, 183, 205*ch*7*n*10
quantification 93–94, 196*ch*5*n*4, 209*ch*9*n*1; vs. judgment and personal trust 196*ch*5*n*4
Quinn, Warren 162

Radoczy, Hannes 9, 190*ch*2*n*14
rationality *see* reason
Rawls, John 162
reading 189*ch*2*n*12
reason 79–80, 84–89, 99–101, 165–167, 170–171, 189*ch*2*n*13
reciprocity 126–127, 170, 202*ch*6*n*13, 208*ch*8*n*16
reflection 189*ch*2*n*11, 204*ch*7*n*9
Reich, Robert 47, 104, 132, 133, 148, 156, 191*ch*3*n*8, 195*ch*4*n*12
reification 188*ch*2*n*8
religion 54, 113–115, 200*ch*6*n*6, 201*ch*6*n*9, 201*ch*6*n*11; and morality 201*ch*6*n*9
responsibility 128–131, 182–184, 203*ch*6*n*18, 204*ch*7*n*7, 206*ch*8*n*4; and feelings 206*ch*8*n*4; *see also* commonweal
reward and punishment 199*ch*6*n*2
Ricardo, David 51
Richardson, Frank C. 39
Richerson, Peter J. 11, 15, 16, 50, 57, 71, 94, 99, 102, 127, 168, 185*ch*1*n*4, 206*ch*8*n*5, 207*ch*8*n*11, 208*ch*8*n*14, 208*ch*8*n*15
right vs. brute force 208*ch*8*n*13
Rojek, Chris 142
routine 204*ch*7*n*8
Rovelli, Carlo 170, 181
Ruse, Michael 115, 200*ch*6*n*7

salutations and courtesies 6, 118
Sassatelli, Roberta 148
Scherer, Klaus 209*ch*9*n*3
Schor, Juliet B. 155
Schwartz, Barry 8, 33, 64, 147, 150
Schwartz, Jeffrey M. 26, 150
science 50, 173–174; growth 193*ch*4*n*2, 203*ch*1*n*2; and industry 68–70; *see also* technology
Scientific Revolution 193*ch*4*n*5, 203*ch*1*n*1
Searle, John R. 20, 22, 95, 102
secularization 192*ch*4*n*1
security 125
self 33, 109–112, 118, 121, 179, 181, 182, 186*ch*1*n*6, 86*ch*1*n*7, 199*ch*6*n*1, 199*ch*6*n*2, 205*ch*8*n*2, 207*ch*8*n*9, 209*ch*9*n*2, 210*ch*9*n*8

self-consciousness 149
self-direction 199*ch*6*n*4
self-interest 199*ch*6*n*4, 200*ch*6*n*8
selfish genes 197*ch*5*n*12, 200*ch*6*n*7, 208*ch*8*n*16; *see also* Dawkins, Richard
Sennett, Richard 53, 104, 106, 141
shame 201*ch*6*n*12
Shammas, Carole 48, 52
Sharot, Tali 159
Shils, Edward 62, 87
Simmel, Georg 99
simultaneity, space and time 204*ch*7*n*10
skepticism 69–70
Sklair, Leslie 63, 96, 100
Smit, Harry 35, 95, 120
Smith, Adam 51, 58, 133, 149
Smith, Alan G.R. 69, 141, 193*ch*4*n*2
Smith, Roger 143
Sober, Elliott 25, 102, 144, 162, 164, 175, 207*ch*8*n*8
social change *see* cultural evolution
social conflict 15, 177, 209*ch*9*n*4
social Darwinism 77, 139, 200*ch*6*n*7
social dialectic 185*ch*1*n*1, 185*ch*1*n*2
social discourse 7; *see also* salutations and courtesies
social environment 172–174, 186*ch*1*n*4
social instincts 207*ch*8*n*11
social institutions 208*ch*8*n*14
social knowledge 185*ch*1*n*2, 185*ch*1*n*3
social learning 192*ch*3*n*12; *see also* human maturation
social mind 40, 180, 193*ch*4*n*4
social organization 18; *see also* population
social priorities and choices 154–157; *see also* choice
social recognition of science 203*ch*7*n*3
social relationships 128; *see also* friendship
social trust in science 193*ch*4*n*4; *see also* science; technology
sociality 5, 10–12, 14, 54, 153–154, 67, 159, 161, 191*ch*3*n*5, 206*ch*8*n*7; and language 196*ch*5*n*6; of other primates 203*ch*7*n*4
sociobiology 195*ch*5*n*1
Solomon, Ty 34, 109
Sonderqvist, Jan 107
Soros, George 105, 151
speech *see* language
Spelke, Elizabeth S. 147, 185*ch*1*n*4
Spencer, Herbert 77
Spengler, Joseph J. 67
spiritual feelings 200*ch*6*n*6
spread of scientific knowledge 193*ch*4*n*2
stability *see* homeostasis
Stamp, Joseph 204*ch*1*n*8
stance 197*ch*5*n*13
Stanley, Manfred 21, 53
Stanovich, Keith E. 81
Stevens, Jeffrey 162, 192*ch*3*n*12, 197*ch*5*n*15

Stewart, Larry 192*ch*4*n*1
strategic planning 152–153
subjective thought *see* introspection; subjectivity
subjective/objective thought 166; *see also* mind; objectivity/subjectivity
subjectivity 6–7, 32–36, 143–144, 156–157, 170, 179–182
Suddendorf, Thomas 17, 39, 117, 175
supercapitalism 191*ch*3*n*8, 195*ch*4*n*12
survival of the fittest 194*ch*4*n*6; *see also* fitness
Swift, Jonathan 193*ch*4*n*2
systems theory 78–79

Tattersall, Ian 26, 28, 33, 71, 80, 100, 102, 200*ch*6*n*6
Taylor, Charles 197*ch*5*n*10
Taylor, Jacqueline 112, 120
technological development 209*ch*9*n*5
technological somnambulism 196*ch*5*n*9
technological subsumption 202*ch*6*n*17
technology 51, 55–58, 91–94, 134–139, 193*ch*4*n*3; and industry 70–76; rationality 31; *see also* industry; science technology
Teilhard de Chardin, Pierre 37, 39
Thagard, Paul 93, 160, 162, 204*ch*7*n*9
theoretical knowledge 191*ch*3*n*4
Theory of Mind 39–41, 190*ch*2*n*14
Thirsk, Joan 203*ch*7*n*3
Thompson, E.P. 76
Thompson, John B. 73, 150, 204*ch*7*n*10
Thompson, Michael 81, 189*ch*2*n*10
thought *see* mind
Tiberius, Valerie 122, 159, 199*ch*6*n*4
time consciousness 130–131, 150–151
time's rapid passage 57, 105–106
Tomasello, Michael 9, 12, 13, 14, 16, 17. 18, 66, 163, 190*ch*2*n*14
Tooby, John 26, 85, 163, 207*ch*8*n*10
Torey, Zoltan 12, 25, 28, 92, 109, 171, 186*ch*1*n*5, 199*ch*6*n*1, 208*ch*8*n*17
Tracy, Destutt de 73
Trentmann, Frank 62
tribal-scale systems 207*ch*8*n*11
trustworthiness 40, 202*ch*6*n*14
truth 181
Turkle, Sherry 32, 90, 135
Turner, Jonathan 32

understanding 25, 179, 203*ch*7*n*4
utility 52

values 51, 80–81, 101–102, 158–159, 163, 170, 186*ch*1*n*7, 194*ch*4*n*8, 207*ch*8*n*10, 208*ch*8*n*17
Vanderburg, Willem H. 51
Veblen, Thorstein 140
Vigotsky, Lev S. 46, 96
vision 177
vulnerability 186*ch*1*n*7

Index

Wallerstein, Immanuel 190*ch3n*1
Weal redistribution 203*ch7n*3
Weber, Max 79, 97*ch5n*10, 209*ch9n*5
well-being 158–161, 166–167, 203*ch7n*3, 205*ch8n*2, 205*ch8n*1; of progeny and non-progeny 204*ch7n*6; *see also* brain; mind
Western prejudice toward less-technically inclined peoples 203*ch7n*1
White, Leslie 74, 182
Whitehead, Alfred North 204*ch7n*8
Whiten, Andrew 11
Williams, Raymond 152
Williams, Robin M. 135
Williams, Rosalind 68, 74, 197*ch5n*10

Wilson, David Sloan 25, 27, 102, 120, 122, 144, 161, 162, 164, 177, 187*ch2n*4, 207*ch8n*8
Wilson, Edward O. 43
Wilson, James Q. 186*ch1n*8, 203*ch6n*18
Winner, Langdon 76, 153, 165, 196*ch5n*9
Wood, Ellen Meiksins 54, 59
Woolfolk, Robert L. 39
workplace influence 195*ch5n*2
World War II 46, 72, 74, 78, 86, 90, 153
worldview 22, 26, 79, 97–99, 136, 187*ch1n*11, 189*ch2n*10
Wyman, Emily 66

Young, H. Peyton 210*ch9n*7

www.ingramcontent.com/pod-product-compliance
Ingram Content Group UK Ltd.
Pitfield, Milton Keynes, MK11 3LW, UK
UKHW041946140426